*THE AMBIVALENCE OF
BERNARD MANDEVILLE*

THE AMBIVALENCE OF BERNARD MANDEVILLE

by
HECTOR MONRO

CLARENDON PRESS · OXFORD
1975

Oxford University Press, Ely House, London W. 1

GLASGOW NEW YORK TORONTO MELBOURNE WELLINGTON
CAPE TOWN IBADAN NAIROBI DAR ES SALAAM LUSAKA ADDIS ABABA
DELHI BOMBAY CALCUTTA MADRAS KARACHI LAHORE DACCA
KUALA LUMPUR SINGAPORE HONG KONG TOKYO

ISBN 0 19 812061 3

© *Oxford University Press 1975*

All rights reserved. No part of this publication may be reproduced, stored in a retrieval system, or transmitted, in any form or by any means, electronic, mechanical, photocopying, recording or otherwise, without the prior permission of Oxford University Press

*Printed in Great Britain by
Butler & Tanner Ltd
Frome and London*

A selfish gesture, now that you are dead
This isn't, anyway, your cup of tea
But, just because there's nothing to be said,
Let's say it: *In memoriam D. B. P.*

ACKNOWLEDGEMENTS

THIS book was written at the University of Victoria, British Columbia, during a year's sabbatical leave. I am grateful to Monash University for giving me leave, to the Association of Universities and Colleges of Canada for the award of a Canadian Commonwealth Fellowship, to a large number of Canadian philosophers for making my visit enjoyable, and especially to Professor Kenneth Rankin and his (and my) colleagues of the Philosophy Department at Victoria for their unfailing kindness and stimulating companionship.

D.H.M.

CONTENTS

1. THE TWO MANDEVILLES — 1
2. THE WIT — 25
3. THE DOCTOR — 48
4. THE SOCIAL REFORMER — 75
5. THE PSYCHOLOGIST — 104
6. THE THEOLOGIAN — 148
7. THE MORALIST — 178
8. THE REAL MANDEVILLE? — 249

APPENDIX Private Vices, Public Benefits in the 1970s — 268

SELECT BIBLIOGRAPHY — 270

INDEX — 279

I
THE TWO MANDEVILLES

MANDEVILLE is not an obscure writer, but it has nevertheless been found possible to interpret him in two diametrically opposed ways. On one view, he is a pious Christian, an ascetic, and an unusually austere moralist, who finds corruption even in apparently laudable or at least innocent activities. On the other, he is at best an easy-going man of the world, at worst a profligate, a cynic, a scoffer at all virtue and religion, and even (in the words of William Law, the author of *A Serious Call to a Devout and Holy Life*) a man who 'comes a missioner from the kingdom of darkness to do us harm'.[1]

In Mandeville's day, and even perhaps in ours, the second view is the commoner. The Grand Jury of the County of Middlesex, noting that the Almighty had, understandably, visited France with the plague but spared England, was afraid that the circulation of *The Fable of the Bees* might cause a change in the divine policy.[2]

John Wesley thought Mandeville even wickeder, at least in his writings, than Machiavelli or Voltaire, and as wicked as Mr. Sandeman.[3] Mandeville would have found it easy to explain why Wesley thought the opinions of a rival preacher more wicked than those of an unbeliever. In fairness, however, it should be said that the Sandemanians were commonly believed to be antinomians. But the coupling of Mandeville with Sandeman as well as Voltaire does leave some slight doubt as to which of the two Mandevilles roused Wesley's horror.

There is no such doubt about Fielding. Miss Matthews, in *Amelia*, says that Mandeville had taught her to regard the words 'virtue' and 'religion' as 'only cloaks under which hypocrisy

---

[1] W. Law, *Remarks upon a late Book entitled* The Fable of The Bees, 1724, ed. F. D. Maurice, Cambridge, 1845, p. 67.
[2] B. Mandeville, *A Vindication of the Book, from the Aspersions Contain'd in a Presentment of the Grand Jury of Middlesex, and an Abusive Letter to Lord C.* In *The Fable of the Bees*, ed. F. B. Kaye, 1924, vol. 1, p. 384.
[3] J. Wesley, *Journal of the Rev. John Wesley*, ed. Nehemiah Curnock, London, Epworth Press, 8 vols., 1909–16. Entry for 14 April 1756, vol. 4, p. 157.

may be the better enabled to cheat the world'. She is shaken a little when told that Mandeville also denied the existence of 'the best passion which the mind can possess', love: a charge also made against Mandeville by Fielding, speaking in his own person, in one of the introductory chapters in *Tom Jones*.[4]

Adam Smith has a chapter in the *Theory of Moral Sentiments* called 'Of Licentious Systems' [of Moral Philosophy]. The entire chapter is devoted to Mandeville. In the first edition, it is true, La Rochefoucauld is included as well, but Smith deleted this passage in the later editions at the request of the Duke's grandson. Only the plural remains in the chapter heading as a vestigial reminder, a kind of literary coccyx.[5]

With no titled descendants to intercede for him, Mandeville continued to be abused. Gibbon said that 'Morality as well as Religion must joyn' in applauding William Law for 'drawing his pen against the licentious doctrine' of *The Fable of the Bees*.[6] An anonymous writer in the *Gentleman's Magazine* of 1846 remarked that 'nobody would be the better for reading Mandeville' and that he tended 'to lower the standard of virtue, and to set life on a narrow expediency footing'.[7] Sir James Mackintosh, writing on the 'Progress of Ethical Philosophy' in the *Encyclopaedia Britannica*, dismissed him with the phrase: 'not to mention Mandeville, the buffoon and sophister of the alehouse'.[8] Even Leslie Stephen said that Mandeville 'represents scepticism in its coarsest and most unlovely stage'.[9] And it would be very easy to go on quoting similar remarks: a book published in 1959 calls him 'Mandeville, a tavern character whose malice sharpened his wit'.[10]

The main exponent of the other view is probably Mandeville himself: a somewhat suspicious fact that is not inconsistent with,

---

[4] *Amelia*, Book 3, Chapter 5; *Tom Jones*, Book 6, Chapter 1.

[5] Adam Smith, *Theory of Moral Sentiments*, 1759, Part VII, Section II, Chapter 4. For the La Rochefoucauld story, see 'Short Account of the Life and Writings of Adam Smith' in *Wealth of Nations*, London, Nelson, 1864, pp. vii–viii.

[6] Edward Gibbon, *Memoirs of My Life*, 1789, Chapter 1.

[7] *Gentleman's Magazine*, N.S. 25 (June 1846), 484, in one of a series of articles called 'Extracts from the Portfolio of a Man of the World'.

[8] Quoted by J. M. Robertson in his essay 'The Fable of the Bees', in *Essays toward a Critical Method*, London, 1889, p. 227. James Mill defended Mandeville in his *Fragment on Mackintosh*, 1835.

[9] L. Stephen, 'Mandeville's *Fable of the Bees*', in *Essays on Freethinking and Plain-speaking*, London, 1907, p. 315.

[10] Louis I. Bredwold, 'The gloom of the Tory Satirists', in J. Clifford, ed., *Eighteenth-Century English Literature*, New York, Oxford University Press, 1959, p. 16.

and might even tend to confirm, Law's opinion that he was an emissary of the Devil. But Mandeville is not alone in his presentation of himself. Francis Hutcheson conjectured: 'He has probably been struck with some old *Fanatick* Sermon upon *self-denial* in his youth, and can never get it out of his head since.'[11] Selby-Bigge thought his asceticism genuine, and his themes, when properly understood, 'the perpetual topics of the pulpit'.[12] Robert Browning put Mandeville firmly on the side of the angels, and called upon him to help refute the scepticism of Carlyle.[13] Browning, it is true, did not see Mandeville as a stern moralist, but as a kind of Pippa who sunnily insisted on seeing the Good that came unnoticed out of Evil. This was hardly Mandeville's own picture of himself; he would no doubt have preferred the writer in the *Monthly Mirror* for 1803, who said that he 'supports one of the tenets of our religion, the natural corruption of human nature, unless assisted by divine grace'.[14]

For the first of the two Mandevilles, the pious one, is a man who looks round him at a professedly Christian society, and is scandalized at what he sees. In his reply to Mandeville, Hutcheson is at pains to point out that Christianity 'no where condemns the Rich or Powerful for being so, or for desiring high Stations'.[15] True though this may be, it is the kind of remark that makes twentieth-century Christians squirm a little. Neither now nor in Mandeville's time would a visitor from another planet, observing the people among whom he found himself, suspect that they were committed to loving their enemies, turning the other cheek, renouncing the things of this world.

When Ministers of *Christ* assure their Hearers, that to indulge themselves in all earthly Pleasures and Sensualities, that are not clashing with the Laws of the Country, or the Fashion of the Age they live in, will be no bar to their future Happiness, if they enjoy them with Moderation; that nothing ought to be deem'd Luxury, that is suitable to a Person's Rank or Quality, and which he can purchase without hurting his Estate, or injuring his Neighbour; that no Buildings or

---

[11] F. Hutcheson, *Reflections upon Laughter and Remarks upon The Fable of the Bees*, in *Collected Works*, Georg Olms, Hildesheim, 1971, vol. 7, p. 407.
[12] L. A. Selby-Bigge, ed. *British Moralists*, Oxford, Clarendon Press, 1897, vol. 1, pp. xvi and xv.
[13] R. Browning, *Parleyings with Certain People of Importance in their Day*, 1887.
[14] Quoted in Kaye's edition of *The Fable of the Bees*, vol. 2, p. 438.
[15] F. Hutcheson, op. cit., p. 148.

Gardens can be so profusely sumptuous, no Furniture so curious or magnificent, no Inventions for Ease so extravagant, no Cookery so operose, no Diet so delicious, no Entertainments or Way of Living so expensive as to be Sinful in the Sight of God, if a Man can afford them, and they are the same as others of the same Birth or Quality either do or would make use of, if they could: That a Man may study and be sollicitous about Modes and Fashions, assist at courts, hunt after Worldly Honour, and partake of all the Diversions of the *beau monde*, and at the same time be a very good Christian; when Ministers of *Christ* I say, assure their Hearers of this, they certainly teach what they have no Warrant for from his Doctrine. For it is in Effect the same as to assert that the strictest Attachment to the World is not inconsistent with a Man's Promise of renouncing the Pomp and Vanity of it.[16]

This is Mandeville's first charge: worldliness, self-indulgence, complacency. England (Europe, for that matter) is only nominally Christian. Its real God is Mammon. Materialistic, money-grubbing, pleasure-seeking: the indictment is familiar, and has been repeated thousands of times, both before and since. The theme of *The Fable of the Bees* is that society is built entirely upon these worldly foundations: a genuine attempt by its members to lead a life of Christian devotion would bring it crashing down at once. The bees in Mandeville's fable, it will be remembered, were hypocritical or self-deceiving enough

> Always to rail at what they loved.

That is to say, they complained of dishonesty and self-seeking in others, while practising them themselves:

> One, that had got a Princely score,
> By cheating Master, King and Poor,
> Dar'd cry aloud, *The Land must sink
> For all its Fraud*; And whom d'ye think
> The Sermonizing Rascal chid?
> A Glover that sold Lamb for Kid.

Jove, indignant at this duplicity, and noticing that

> ... all the Rogues cry'd brazenly,
> *Good Gods, Had we but Honesty!*

---

[16] B. Mandeville, *An Enquiry into the Origin of Honour and the Usefulness of Christianity in War*, 1732, pp. 104–5 (Second Dialogue).

decides to teach them a lesson by granting them their prayer. The bees become honest and virtuous: with startling results. Lawyers, turnkeys, milliners, footmen, courtiers lose their livelihoods:

> All Places manag'd first by Three
> Who watched each other's Knavery,
> And often for a Fellow-feeling
> Promoted one another's stealing,
> Are happily supply'd by One,
> By which some thousands more are gone.

With luxurious living and conspicuous consumption abandoned, trade and commerce languish:

> The Price of Land and Houses falls
> Mirac'lous Palaces, whose Walls
> Like those of *Thebes*, were rais'd by Play,
> Are to be let ...
> . . . .
> The building Trade is quite destroy'd,
> Artificers are not employ'd;
> No Limner for his Art is fam'd,
> Stone-cutters, Carvers are not nam'd.
> Those that remain'd, grown temp'rate, strive
> Not how to spend, but how to live,
> And when they paid their Tavern Score,
> Resolv'd to enter it no more:
> No Vintner's Jilt in all the Hive
> Could wear now Cloth of Gold, and thrive.
> . . . .
>   The haughty *Chloe*, to live Great,
> Had made her Husband rob the State:
> But now she sells her Furniture,
> Which th' *Indies* had been ransack'd for;
> Contracts th' expensive Bill of Fare,
> And wears her strong Suit a whole Year:
> The slight and fickle Age is past,
> And Clothes, as well as Fashions, last.

Finally, the once large and prosperous community, the 'Spacious Hive well stockt with Bees', thronged with

> Millions endeavouring to supply
> Each other's Lust and Vanity

dwindles to a handful of hardy simple-lifers:

> Hard'ned with Toils and Exercise,
> They counted Ease itself a Vice;
> Which so improv'd their Temperance
> That, to avoid Extravagance,
> They flew into a hollow Tree,
> Blest with Content and Honesty.

So far, then, it is mainly luxury, self-indulgence, and self-deception that Mandeville is denouncing: the delusion (to update the clichés a little) that the affluent society, obsessed with material values, could also be a community of Christians. The real values of the fashionable world are described in the Preface to Part 2 of the *Fable*.

Virtue . . . is a very fashionable word, and some of the most luxurious are extremely fond of the amiable sound; tho' they mean nothing by it, but a great Veneration for whatever is courtly or sublime, and an equal Aversion to every thing, that is vulgar or unbecoming. They seem to imagine that it chiefly consists in a strict Compliance to the Rules of Politeness, and all the Laws of Honour, that have any regard to the Respect that is due to themselves. It is the Existence of this Virtue, that is often maintain'd with so much Pomp of Words, and for the Eternity of which so many Champions are ready to take up Arms. Whilst the Votaries of it deny themselves no Pleasure, they can enjoy either fashionably or in Secret; and instead of sacrificing the Heart to the Love of real Virtue, can only condescend to abandon the outward Deformity of Vice, for the Satisfaction they receive from appearing to be well-bred. It is counted ridiculous for Men to commit Violence upon themselves, or to maintain, that Virtue requires Self-denial; all Court-philosophers are agreed, that nothing can be lovely or desirable that is mortifying or uneasy. A civil Behaviour among the Fair in Publick and a Deportment, inoffensive both in Words and Actions, is all the Chastity, the polite World requires in Men. What Liberties soever a Man gives himself in private, his Reputation shall never suffer whilst he conceals his Amours from all those that are not unmannerly inquisitive, and takes care that nothing criminal can ever be proved upon him. *Si non castè saltem cautè*, is a Precept that sufficiently shews, what every Body expects; and tho' Incontinence is own'd to be a Sin, yet never to have been guilty of it is a Character, which most single men under thirty would not be fond of, even amongst modest Women.[17]

---

[17] *Fable of the Bees*, ed. F. B. Kaye, vol. 2, pp. 12–13 (Preface).

There were other ways, too, in which men's actual beliefs differed from their professions. The real ideal of the English gentleman was not the Christian saint, but the Man of Honour.

For ever since the Notion of Honour has been receiv'd among Christians, there have always been, in the same Number of People, Twenty Men of real Honour to one of real Virtue. The Reason is obvious. The Persuasions to Virtue make no Allowances, nor have any Allurements that are clashing with the Principle of it; whereas the Men of Pleasure, the Passionate and the Malicious, may all in their Turns meet with Opportunities of indulging their darling Appetites without trespassing against the Principle of Honour. A virtuous Man thinks himself obliged to obey the Laws of his Country; but a Man of Honour acts from a Principle which he is bound to think Superior to all Laws. . . A virtuous Man expects no Acknowledgments from others; and if they won't believe him to be virtuous, his Business is not to force them to it; but a Man of Honour has the Liberty openly to proclaim himself to be such, and to call to an Account Every body who dares to doubt of it; Nay, such is the inestimable Value he sets upon himself, that he often endeavours to punish with Death the most insignificant Trespass that's committed against him, the least Word, Look, or Motion, if he can find but any far-fetch'd Reason to suspect a Design in it to undervalue him, and of this No body is allowed to be a Judge but himself.[18]

There was of course a better side to the ideal of Honour, as Mandeville admitted. In one of the 'Remarks' added to the *Fable* he tells us that the Man of Honour 'is oblig'd always to be faithful to his Trust, to prefer the publick interest to his own, not to tell lies nor defraud or wrong any Body, and from others to suffer no Affront, which is a Term of Art for every Action designedly done to undervalue him'. He adds, however, that whereas all of these rules were faithfully observed by 'the Men of ancient Honour, of which I reckon *Don Quixote* to have been the last upon Record', their modern counterparts paid little attention to any but the last of them. 'In great Families', Mandeville tells us, Honour 'is like the Gout, generally counted Hereditary, and all Lord's Children are born with it . . . there is nothing that encourages the Growth of it more than a Sword, and upon the first wearing of one, some People have felt considerable Shoots of it in four and twenty Hours.'[19]

---

[18] B. Mandeville, *An Enquiry into the Origin of Honour and the Usefulness of Christianity in War*, 1732, pp. 43-4 (First Dialogue).
[19] *Fable of the Bees*, ed. Kaye, vol. 1, p. 199 (Remark R).

The real point, however, is that the ideal of Honour is inconsistent with Christianity. To see this one only needs to consider duelling or war.

The only thing of weight that can be said against modern Honour is, that it is directly opposite to Religion. The one bids you bear Injuries with Patience, the other tells you if you don't resent them, you are not fit to live. Religion commands you to leave all Revenge to God, Honour bids you trust your Revenge to nobody but your self, even where the Law would do it for you; Religion plainly forbids Murther, Honour openly justifies it: Religion bids you not shed Blood upon any account whatever: Honour bids you fight for the least Trifle: Religion is built on Humility, and Honour upon Pride . . .[20]

Mandeville denounces duelling in several places: in both parts of the *Fable* as well as in the *Origin of Honour*. That book, like Part 2 of the *Fable*, takes the form of dialogues in which Mandeville's spokesman and defender, Cleomenes, expounds Mandeville's ideas to a sceptical friend, Horatio. Horatio is 'a Man of strict Honour', who has himself fought a duel. In the *Origin of Honour*, Cleomenes' comments on duelling are given in a style worthy of Wesley or Sandeman themselves. A 'sincere follower of the Apostles, a downright Christian', he says, would first give all the obvious arguments against duelling.

But if all these could not divert the Dueller from his Purpose, he would attack his stubborn Heart in its inmost Recesses, and forget Nothing of what I told you on the Subject in our Second and Third Conversation. He would recommend to him the Fable of the *Bees*, and, like that, he'd direct and lay open to him the Principle of Honour, and shew him, how diametrically opposite the Worship of that Idol was to the Christian Religion: the First consisting in openly cherishing and feeding that very Frailty in our Nature, which the latter strictly commands us with all our Might to conquer and destroy. Having convinced him of the substantial Difference and Contrariety of the Two Principles, he would display to him, on the one Hand, the Vanity of Earthly Glory, and the Folly of Coveting the Applause of a Sinful World; and, on the other, the Certainty of a Future State and the Transcendency of everlasting Happiness over every Thing that is perishable. From such Remonstrances as these the good, pious Man would take an Opportunity of exhorting him to a Christian Self-denial, and the Practice of

---

[20] *Fable of the Bees*, ed. Kaye, vol. I, pp. 221–2 (Remark R).

real Virtue, and he would earnestly endeavour to make him sensible of the Peace of Conscience and solid Comforts that are to be found in Meekness and Humility, Patience and an entire Resignation to the Will of God.

Hor.: How long, pray, do you intend to go on with this Cant?

Cleo.: If I am to personate a Christian Divine, who is a sincere Believer, you must give me Leave to speak his Language.

Hor.: But if a Man had really such an Affair upon his Hands, and he knew the Person, he had to do with, to be a resolute Man that understood the Sword, do you think he would have Patience or be at leisure to hearken to all this puritanical Stuff, which you have been heaping together? Do you think (for that is the Point) it would have any Influence over his Actions?

Cleo.: If he believ'd the Gospel, and consequently future Rewards and Punishments, and he likewise acted consistently with what he believ'd, it would put an entire Stop to all and it would certainly hinder him from sending or accepting of Challenges, or ever engaging in anything relating to a Duel.

Hor.: Pray now, among all the Gentlemen of your Acquaintance, and such as you your Self should care to converse with, how many are there, do you think, on whom the Thoughts of Religion would have that Effect?

Cleo.: A great many, I hope.

Hor.: You can hardly forbear laughing, I see, when you say it; and I am sure, you your Self would have no Value for a Man whom you should see tamely put up a gross Affront: Nay I have seen and heard Parsons and Bishops themselves laugh at, and speak with Contempt of pretended Gentlemen, that had suffer'd of themselves to be ill treated without resenting it.[21]

Duelling is a test case which brings out clearly the contrast between Christian morality and the prevailing *mores*. Mandeville was not, of course, the only one to point this out. Richard Steele, for example, attacked duelling obliquely in *The Christian Hero* (1701), more forthrightly in *The Lying Lover* (1703), and quite explicitly in the *Tatler*[22] (which certainly influenced Mandeville, the contributor to the *Female Tatler*) and other periodicals. But Captain Steele, as he then was, wrote *The Christian Hero* as a soldier commending the Christian way of life to his fellow soldiers: it was left to Mandeville to suggest that war itself was also

[21] *Origin of Honour*, pp. 77–9 (Second Dialogue).
[22] See e.g. nos. 25, 29, and 31 of the *Tatler*.

incompatible with Christianity. The bees in the *Fable*, after they had been afflicted with virtue,

> ... have no Forces kept Abroad;
> Laugh at th' Esteem of Foreigners,
> And empty Glory got by Wars;
> They fight but for their Country's sake,
> When Right or Liberty's at Stake.[23]

In the *Origin of Honour*, however, Cleomenes (and so presumably Mandeville) goes further still: he is emphatic that 'there is Nothing contain'd in the Gospel, that can have the least Tendency to promote or justify War or Discord, Foreign or Domestick, Publick or Private; nor is there any the least Expression to be found in it, from which it is possible to excite or set People on to quarrel with, do Hurt to, or any Ways offend one another, on any Account whatever.'[24]

For all the lip-service paid to religion, the army chaplains, and the official prayers, the soldier cannot be permitted to be a genuine Christian.

If he has but Courage, and knows how to please his Officers, he may get drunk Two or Three Times a Week, have a fresh Whore every Day, and swear an Oath at every Word he speaks, little or no Notice shall be taken of him to his Dishonour; and if he be good humour'd, and forbears stealing among his Comrades, he'll be counted a very honest Fellow. But if, what *Christ* and his Apostles would have justify'd him in and exhorted him to do, he takes a Slap in the Face, or any other gross Affront before Company without resenting it, tho' from his intimate Friend, it cannot be endured; and tho' he was the soberest and the most chaste, the most discreet, tractable and best temper'd Man in the World, his Business is done ... and the Officers are forc'd to turn him out of the Regiment.[25]

Yet the full title of the *Origin of Honour* is *An Enquiry into the Origin of Honour and the Usefulness of Christianity in War*. It is generally believed, Horatio points out and Cleomenes concedes, that Christians make the best soldiers. This is possible, however, only through the perversion and distortion of Christianity. Morality, and 'even the Gospel', may be preached to soldiers

---

[23] *Fable of the Bees*, ed. Kaye, vol. 1, p. 32.
[24] *Origin of Honour*, pp. 156-7 (Third Dialogue).
[25] Ibid., pp. 150-1 (Third Dialogue).

at seasonable Times when they are in Winter Quarters, or in an idle Summer when there is no Enemy near, and the Troops perhaps are encamped in a Country, where no Hostilities should be committed. But when they are to enter upon Action, to besiege a large Town, or ravage a rich Country, it would be very impertinent to talk to them of Christian Virtues; doing as they would be done by; loving their Enemies, and extending their Charity to all Mankind . . . Then the Mask is flung off; not a Word of the Gospel, or of Meekness or Humility, and all Thoughts of Christianity are laid aside entirely.[26]

What is useful in war, then, is not genuine Christianity, but simply the belief that God is on one's side. Men are ready enough to believe this, especially if the outward acts of devotion are performed: frequent prayers, long and pathetic sermons, the singing of psalms, keeping the Sabbath. Mandeville demonstrates how the religious beliefs of the soldiers may be made serviceable by giving us the sermon of 'a crafty Divine':

Provisions had been scarce for some Time; the Enemy was just a Hand; and Abundance of the Men seem'd to have little Mind to fight when a Preacher, much esteem'd among the Soldiers, took the following Method: First, he set faithfully before them their Sins and Wickedness, the many Warnings they had received to repent, and God's long Forbearance, as well as great Mercy, in not having totally destroy'd them long ago. He represented their Wants, and Scarcity of Provision, as a certain Token of the Divine Wrath, and shew'd them plainly, that labouring already under the Weight of his Displeasure, they had no Reason to think, that God would connive longer at their manifold Neglects and Transgressions. Having convinc'd them, that Heaven was angry with them, he enumerated many Calamities, which, he said, would befal them; and several of them being such, as they had actually to fear, he was hearken'd to as a Prophet. He then told them, that what they could suffer in this World, was of no great Moment, if they could but escape Eternal Punishment; but that of this (as they had lived) he saw not the least Probability, they should. Having shewn an extraordinary concern for their deplorable Condition, and seeing many of them touch'd with Remorse, and overwhelm'd with Sorrow, he changed his Note on a Sudden, and with an Air of Certainty told them, that there was still one Way left, and but that one, to retrieve all, and avert the Miseries they were threaten'd with; which, in short, was to Fight well, and beat their Enemies; and that they had nothing else for it. Having thus disclosed his Mind to them, with all the Appearances

---

[26] Ibid., pp. 160–1 (Third Dialogue).

of Sincerity, he assumed a chearful Countenance, shew'd them the many Advantages, that would attend the Victory; assured them of it, if they would but exert themselves; named the Times and Places in which they had behaved well, not without Exaggeration, and work'd upon their Pride so powerfully, that they took Courage, fought like Lions, and got the Day.[27]

The distortion of Christianity to serve the worldly ambitions of priests and politicians is a favourite theme of Mandeville's. He devotes a whole book to it: his *Free Thoughts on Religion, the Church, and National Happiness*. The thesis here is really the same as in the *Fable*; Christian virtue is quite incompatible with worldly prosperity and greatness. It follows that if the Christian Church had become great and prosperous (as it undoubtedly had) it could only be by abandoning Christian virtue.

That the Church should have attained so much power and greatness was, Mandeville remarks, a very considerable achievement, considering the intractable material its priests had to work with:

The *Pagans*, whose religion was built upon poetry and fiction, had a wretched theology, that might be turn'd to any purpose, and the priests in their contrivances had no morals to cope with. In Mahometism there is more morality, and the notions of the Deity are better . . . but then the whole religion seems contriv'd to engage the sensual and voluptuous: in the alcoran it self many things are ludicrous and silly, and not a few that are soothing human passion. But in the Christian religion all is grave and solid; every part of it worthy of the most serious contemplation of a man, that can and dares think freely and thoroughly. The idea it furnishes us with of the Godhead is sublime, and as incomprehensible as it should be: in the doctrine of Christ there are no worldly allurements to draw the vicious, and all his followers are ty'd down to the strictest morality: the whole aim of the gospel is divine, nothing in it can possibly be construed so as to encourage priestcraft, or be serviceable to sooth any human passion, without doing the utmost violence to truth and good sense; and yet behold, what has been made of it![28]

So far Mandeville appears as a familiar figure: the prophet denouncing the wickedness of the times and the backsliding of

[27] *Origin of Honour*, pp. 215–17 (Fourth Dialogue).
[28] B. Mandeville, *Free Thoughts on Religion, the Church, and National Happiness*, 2nd ed., 1729, pp. 149–50 (Chapter 6).

his contemporaries. They worship false gods while blandly pretending to themselves that they are still good Christians; they pervert the most sacred things to serve worldly ends; the very clergy are bulwarks of hypocrisy and worldliness. They mistake the outward trappings of religion for true devotion and they cry peace where there is no peace, and there is no health in them.

But he goes still further. It is not merely that men are weak and sinful, and find it hard to live by what they know to be right. The truth is that the nature of man makes virtue impossible for him. Man is motivated by his passions, by self-love and by pride, the desire to think well of himself and have others think well of him. But no action is virtuous unless there is self-denial. No human actions, then, except those rare ones inspired by divine grace, are virtuous. What men mistake for virtue is something quite different: pride or self-righteousness or fear of public opinion. This is quite central to Mandeville's thought. It provides him with a theme on which he plays many variations. He is fairly light-hearted about it in *The Virgin Unmask'd*:

Lucinda: . . . All is not gold that glisters; many things are done daily for which People are extoll'd to the Skies that at the same time, tho' the Actions are Good, would be blamed as highly, if the Principle from which they acted, and the Motive that first edg'd them on, were thoroughly known. When People are too Lazy, or fearful to undertake any thing, they are praised for being Contented; and the Effects of Avarice are often called Temperance and Sobriety. I know two Married People that seem to be very Loving, and never displeased with one another, and indeed they Live so well, that they are thought a very happy couple: But you would hardly guess at the Reason of all this.
Antonia: Without doubt they are both very Good Humour'd.
Luc.: Just the Reverse, for their present Unison is owing to no other cause, than their both being Devils alike.
An.: How can that be?
Luc.: When they came first together, they Fell out, and Fought every Day like Dogs and Cats, and did one another abundance of Mischief. But as every one feels his own Hurt best, so both perceiving the ill conveniences they got by every quarrel, being equally Match'd, they became so terrible one to another, that at last they lived Peaceably, in Dread only of provoking one another's Anger.[29]

---

[29] B. Mandeville, *The Virgin Unmask'd: or Female Dialogues betwixt an elderly Maiden Lady and her Niece, on several Diverting Discourses on Love, Marriage, Memoirs, Morals, etc., of the Times*, 1709, p. 73 (Fourth Dialogue).

Mandeville's convert and spokesman, Cleomenes, is much more serious about it:

Cleomenes seemed charitable, and was a Man of strict Morals, yet he would often complain that he was not possess'd of one Christian Virtue, and found fault with his own Actions, that had all the Appearances of Goodness; because he was conscious, he said, that they were perform'd from a wrong Principle. The Effects of his Education, and his Aversion to Infamy, had always been strong enough to keep him from Turpitude; but this he Ascribed to his Vanity, which he complain'd was in such full Possession of his Heart, that he knew no Gratification of any Appetite from which he was able to exclude it . . . He was sure, that the Satisfaction which arose from worldly Enjoyments, was something distinct from Gratitude, and foreign to Religion; and he felt plainly that, as it proceeded from within, so it center'd in himself. The very Relish of Life, he said, was accompanied with an Elevation of Mind, that seem'd to be inseparable from his Being. Whatever Principle was the Cause of this, he was convinced within himself, that the Sacrifice of the Heart, which the Gospel requires, consisted in the utter Extirpation of that Principle; confessing at the same time, that this Satisfaction he found in himself, this Elevation of Mind, caused his chief Pleasure; and that in all the Comforts of Life, it made the greatest Part of the Enjoyment.[30]

Men are not naturally good: on the contrary, they cannot be virtuous without conquering their natural impulses. And, however we may delude ourselves, this is something we very rarely do:

Horatio: But are there no Persons in the World that are good by Choice?
Cleomenes: Yes, but then they are directed in that Choice by Reason and Experience, but not by Nature, I mean, not by untaught Nature: But there is an ambiguity in the Word Good which I would avoid; let us stick to that of Virtuous, and then I affirm that no Action is such, which does not point at some Conquest or other, some Victory great or small over untaught Nature; otherwise the Epithet is improper.
Hor.: But if by the help of a careful Education this Victory is obtain'd, when we are young, may we not be virtuous afterwards voluntarily and with Pleasure?
Cleo.: Yes, if it really was obtain'd: But how shall we be sure of this, and what Reason have we to believe it ever was? When it is evident, that from our Infancy, instead of endeavouring to conquer our Appetites, we have always been Taught, and have taken pains ourselves

---

[30] *Fable of the Bees*, ed. Kaye, vol. 2, pp. 18-19 (Preface to Part 2).

to conceal them; and we are conscious within, that whatever Alterations have been made in our Manners and Circumstances, the Passions themselves always remain'd?[31]

The worldliness, the hypocrisy, the backsliding are not, then, accidental: they are the necessary consequences of man's nature. Virtue, it would seem, is impossible. At least, it is impossible to corrupt and unregenerate man: 'when I say Men, I mean neither Jews nor Christians; but meer Man, in the State of Nature and ignorance of the true Deity.'[32] 'Devout Christians, who alone are to be excepted here, being regenerated and preternaturally assisted by the Divine Grace, cannot be said to be in Nature.'[33] But good Christians, Mandeville adds, 'have always been very scarce and there are no Numbers of them any where, that one can readily go to'.[34]

There seems, then, to be a good deal to support Mandeville's claim that *The Fable of the Bees* 'is a Book of severe and exalted Morality'.[35] Mandeville himself appears as a quite uncompromising ascetic, disgusted by the materialism, the selfishness, the lust, and the vanity of mankind, detecting the wickedness in the hearts of even the respectable and apparently upright, horrified at the worldliness and hypocrisy of institutionalized religion, and preaching spiritual regeneration as the only possible remedy.

One might expect such a man to be unpopular, especially for what he said about the churches and about the corruption on which every powerful and prosperous state was built. One might even expect him to be accused of cynicism, of scoffing at some of the finer things in life, of traducing good and pious men. That is what the boosters usually say about the knockers; and Mandeville was undoubtedly a knocker. But why should he be accused of godliness, of materialism, of licentiousness, of moral nihilism? Why should he be linked, not only with Sandeman, but with Hobbes, Machiavelli, Voltaire, Tindal, and the Devil?

The explanation is put very neatly by Richard Whately. Mandeville, he suggests, is merely putting forward a hypothetical

---

[31] Ibid., p. 109 (Third Dialogue).
[32] Ibid., vol. 1, p. 40 (Introduction to *An Enquiry into the Origin of Moral Virtue*).
[33] Ibid., p. 166 (Remark O).
[34] *Origin of Honour*, p. 56 (Second Dialogue).
[35] *Fable of the Bees*, ed. Kaye, vol. 1, p. 404 (*A Vindication of the Book from the Aspersions*, etc.).

argument. If virtue consisted in self-denial, as was taken for granted by all the moralists and theologians, and if national wealth and greatness were desirable, as was taken for granted by everybody, then the public happiness depended on the vices of individuals. National virtue and national wealth must be irreconcilable. 'Of two incompatible objects we must be content to take one, or the other. Which of the two is to be preferred he nowhere decides in his first volume: in his second, he solemnly declares his opinion that wealth ought to be renounced, as incompatible with virtue.'[36]

The argument, that is to say, cuts both ways. One might draw the conclusion that the world ought to be renounced. But one might also decide that virtue should be. Or at least that the virtue of the theologians, which consisted in self-denial, was not really virtue at all. Why not adopt the utilitarian criterion, and count as virtuous any action that contributed to the welfare of society in the long run? In that case the 'vices' on which the national prosperity depended were really not vices, but virtues. Perhaps that was what Mandeville was really getting at? When one then remembered that in *The Fable of the Bees* not only luxuriousness and worldly enjoyment were shown to contribute to the nation's prosperity, but also the activities of cheats and highwaymen, this became a very shocking conclusion indeed.

Was there anything to suggest that this was Mandeville's real meaning, in spite of his denials? There was a great deal.

To begin with, there was Mandeville's personality. His early opponents accused him of dissolute habits. There is however very little reason to believe them; Mandeville somehow managed to sustain a medical practice as well as writing a good many books, which could hardly have left him much time for debauchery. Leslie Stephen says: 'Mandeville is said to have been in the habit of frequenting coffee-houses and amusing his patrons by ribald conversation. The book smells of its author's haunts. He is a cynical and prurient writer, who shrinks from no jest, however scurrilous, and from no paradox, however grotesque . . .'[37] But Mandeville is no coarser than Swift, who was after all a Dean.

---

[36] R. Whately, *Introductory Lectures on Political Economy*, 2nd ed., 1832 (Reprints of Economic Classics, New York, Augustus M. Kelley, 1966, p. 44).

[37] L. Stephen, 'Mandeville's *Fable of the Bees*', in *Essays on Freethinking and Plainspeaking*, London, 1907, p. 279.

Stephen's contemporaries might have thought Bunyan coarse, if they had read all of him.[38] There is a different way, however, in which the quality of Mandeville's prose tells against the view that he was a pious ascetic. His tone is too detached, too amused. When, in *Free Thoughts on Religion*, he recounts the enormities committed by churchmen in the name of Christianity, it is much in the tone of Voltaire, or Gibbon, or Anatole France:

In the time of *Theodosius* junior, they [Christians] enjoy'd a full liberty of conscience in *Persia*, when *Abdas*, a zealous bishop, had the courage to pull down one of the temples where the Persians worship'd the fire. The *Magi* made their complaints to the King, who sent for *Abdas*, and demanded no other satisfaction than the rebuilding of the temple: *Abdas* refus'd it with scorn, tho' that prince had declar'd to him that in case of disobedience he would cause all the christian churches to be pull'd down; which he did, and began a terrible persecution, in which the valiant *Abdas* fell the first martyr.

The brave remainder of the faithful, that could escape the fury of the *Persian* priests, were not so dejected at their loss, but that, animated with the hopes of a noble revenge, they implored the assistance of the emperor, which kindling a long war between *Romans* and *Persians*, occasion'd a second deluge of blood in vindication of the gospel.[39]

Or again:

Nothing is more diverting than to read the various and noble struggles the popes have had with the princes of christendom, till *Gregory* the seventh, with the utmost intrepidity, and equal hazard and difficulties, establish'd his superiority over their temporalities: that able and stately prelate, who, in the midst of winter made an emperor barefoot wait unattended in a hall, fasting from morning till night, for three days together, before he would admit him to his presence; and was the first, who undertook to deprive his lord and master of the imperial dignity.[40]

Then there is the actual subject-matter of some of his books. One would after all be surprised to learn that Savonarola, say, had written a tract called *A Modest Defence of Public Stews* (subtitle: an Essay upon Whoring) in which he argued strongly for the

---

[38] For example, his comparison of the evangelist to the father of a family ridding his children's hair of lice. See W. Y. Tindal, *John Bunyan. Mechanick Preacher*, New York, Russell & Russell, 1964.
[39] *Free Thoughts on Religion*, pp. 143-4.
[40] Ibid., pp. 145-6.

establishment of state-owned brothels, and worked out all the practical details, including charges. One would be only a little less surprised if he published an attack on free schools for the poor, on the ground that education would make the poor discontented with their lot and lead to a scarcity of servants and a rise in the wages masters would have to pay. One can hardly regard the author of these works as excessively unworldly.

None of this is, of course, conclusive. Obviously Mandeville did not correspond to popular stereotypes of an austere moralist; he was certainly a wit who sometimes found men's follies amusing. It may still be true that he also found them horrifying and was sincere in denouncing them. As for the *Modest Defence* and the *Essay on Charity and Charity-Schools*, a firm belief in human corruption and the final inefficacy of any remedy short of spiritual regeneration with miraculous assistance need not rule out an interest in palliatives. Charity schools, Mandeville argued, only made social conditions worse; public brothels, as a means of regulating and controlling sexual irregularity, might make them at least a little better. Nevertheless, it is not very easy to see Mandeville as the kind of pious Christian he declares himself to be.

More significant than any of this is the equivocal note which creeps into Mandeville's most earnest preachments, and even into his very denials of the charges against him. I have already quoted one exchange between Horatio and Cleomenes:

Hor.: How long, pray, do you intend to go on with this Cant?
Cleo.: If I am to personate a Christian Divine, who is a sincere Believer, you must give me leave to speak his Language.

If Cleomenes is really Mandeville's spokesman here, we may well conclude that he, too, is merely personating a Christian. But of course Mandeville could point out in reply that Cleomenes, though a convert to the ideas of *The Fable of the Bees*, is also represented as a member of the *beau monde*, along with Horatio. In a discussion between gentlemen the phrases of the pulpit would be a little out of place, and it was after all only the phraseology, and not the actual arguments, that Cleomenes was disclaiming.

There are, however, other passages less easy to explain away. 'If I have shown the way to worldly Greatness', Mandeville says in his own defence, 'I have always without Hesitation preferr'd the Road that leads to Virtue.' He then goes on to tell us how to travel along that road:

Would you banish Fraud and Luxury, prevent Profaneness and Irreligion, and make the generality of the People Charitable, Good and Virtuous, break down the Printing Presses, melt the Founds, and burn all the Books in the Island, except those at the Universities, where they remain unmolested, and suffer no Volume in private Hands but a Bible: Knock down Foreign Trade, prohibit all Commerce with Strangers, and permit no Ships to go to Sea, that ever will return, beyond Fisher-Boats. Restore to the Clergy, the King and the Barons their Ancient Privileges, Prerogatives, and Possessions: Build New Churches, and convert all the coin you can come at into Sacred Utensils: Erect Monasteries and Alms-houses in abundance, and let no Parish be without a Charity-School. Enact Sumptuary Laws, and let your Youth be inured to Hardship: Inspire them with all the nice and most refined Notions of Honour and Shame, of Friendship and of Heroism, and introduce among them a great Variety of imaginary Rewards: Then let the Clergy preach Abstinence and Self-denial to others, and take what Liberty they please for themselves; let them bear the greatest Sway in the management of State-Affairs, and no Man be made Lord-Treasurer but a Bishop.
By such pious Endeavours, and wholesome Regulations, the Scene would be soon alter'd; the greatest part of the Covetous, the Discontented, the Restless and Ambitious Villains would leave the Land, vast Swarms of Cheating Knaves would abandon the City, and be dispers'd throughout the Country: Artificers would learn to hold the Plough, Merchants turn Farmers, and the sinful over-grown *Jerusalem*, without Famine, War, Pestilence or Compulsion, be emptied in the most easy manner and ever after cease to be dreadful to her Sovereigns ...

And so on, ending with a quite indubitable sneer: '... an harmless, innocent and well-meaning People, that would never dispute the Doctrine of Passive Obedience, nor any other Orthodox Principles, but be submissive to Superiors and Unanimous in religious Worship'.[41]

Mandeville cites this passage, or at least the sentence preceding it, about preferring the road that leads to virtue, in both the *Vindication* attached to later editions of the *Fable* and *A Letter to Dion*, in which he replies to Berkeley's attack on him. Yet it hardly reassures the reader who suspects him of scoffing at both virtue

[41] *Fable of the Bees*, ed. Kaye, vol. 1, pp. 231–2 (Remark T).

and religion. It is true that one recent defender of Mandeville finds in this passage 'proof of his ferocious seriousness'. Mandeville, he suggests, is

> mocking his own hopes for salvation as well as ours. The program horrifies him as much as it was calculated to horrify the newly liberated middle-class readers or us, their liberal heirs ... We may hope for reformation within individual men ... but if some miracle were to effect a wholesale conversion to virtue, could we bear it? It would be as hard for Mandeville as anyone; the peculiar honesty of his method requires that he be as vulnerable as his readers ... The point is that whole-hearted Christianity is rare, to say the least, and Mandeville would not claim it for himself any more than he will allow it to most other men.[42]

This is hardly convincing. No doubt Mandeville did regard some Christian virtues as desirable, but too hard for unregenerate men; but no reader of his *Free Thoughts on Religion* can suppose that he felt that about the participation of the clergy in politics, or the doctrine of passive obedience, to say nothing of charity schools. The Utopia described in the passage we are considering seems to be a curious mixture of what, in Mandeville's view, the clergy say they want but really do not, and what they really want but say they do not. Mandeville is not only saying that real virtue would be incompatible with national power and prosperity; he is also saying that what the clergy call virtue is a sham, and a cloak for their avarice and their thirst for power.

Mandeville may well have believed both propositions. Neither is inconsistent with a genuine concern for morality and religion. But here the two are so confused that the reader can hardly escape the conclusion that it is only the sham and not the real virtue that cannot coexist with national greatness.

This impression may well be confirmed by the Preface to Part I of the *Fable*, in which Mandeville says that his object is

> to expose the Unreasonableness and Folly of those, that desirous of being an opulent and flourishing People, and wonderfully greedy after all the Benefits they receive as such, are yet always murmuring at and exclaiming against those Vices and Inconveniences, that from the Beginning of the World to this present Day, have been inseparable

---

[42] Thomas R. Edwards, Jr., 'Mandeville's Moral Prose', *ELH* 31 (1964), 208.

from all Kingdoms and States that ever were fam'd for Strength, Riches and Politeness, at the same time.[43]

It is true that Mandeville merely says here that it is inconsistent to expect a state to be opulent and virtuous at the same time. As he puts it in the *Fable* itself:

> Then leave Complaints: Fools only strive
> To make a Great an Honest Hive.

This leaves it an open question whether greatness or honesty should be abandoned. But the emphasis is on the folly of complaining about the necessary accompaniments of opulence, not on the folly of pursuing opulence in the first place. Of course this may be meant ironically; but there is at least ground for suspicion that Mandeville is really saying: 'Why make all this fuss about vice? We could not get on without it, and, besides, those who make most fuss about it are really only trying to hoodwink us so that they can gain control of the state and set up a theocracy like Cromwell's.'

William Minto, indeed, in an *Encyclopaedia Britannica* article on Mandeville, suggested that *The Fable of the Bees*, or at least its nucleus, the poem called *The Grumbling Hive, or Knaves Turn'd Honest*, was originally published as an election pamphlet.

It appeared during the heat of the bitterly contested elections of 1705, when the question before the country was whether Marlborough's war with France should be continued. The cry of the high Tory advocates of peace was that the war was carried on purely in the interests of the general and the men in office; charges of bribery, peculation, hypocrisy, every form of fraud and dishonesty were freely cast about among the electors.[44]

In *Free Thoughts on Religion* Mandeville tells us: 'I despise the very thoughts of a party-man and desire to touch no man's sore, but in order to heal it.'[45] But that book itself contains a fairly orthodox statement of whig political theory: he was certainly no friend to the Tories. Minto does not, however, suggest that the intention of *The Grumbling Hive* was to defend Marlborough by defending vice; he sees the poem as merely 'a political *jeu d'esprit*, full of the

---

[43] *Fable of the Bees*, ed. Kaye, vol. 1, p. 7 (Preface).
[44] *Encyclopaedia Britannica*, 9th ed., Edinburgh, A. & C. Black, 1875–87, vol. 15 (1883), p. 472.
[45] *Free Thoughts on Religion*, p. 169 (Chapter 7).

impartial mockery that might be expected of a humorous foreigner'. This need not prevent the *Fable* from being also 'a Book of severe and exalted Morality'; but it is at least consistent with, and perhaps tends to suggest, a quite different interpretation.

Once Mandeville was taken seriously as a defender of vice, it was easy to see his attacks on the ideal of Honour, and on duelling and war, as simply deriding the values which good citizens held dear. Horatio complains to Cleomenes that Mandeville 'ridicules War and Martial Courage, as well as Honour and everything else'.[46] Alternatively, Mandeville could be taken to be defending duelling, at least by those who read only Part 1 of the *Fable*. He says there that the practice of duelling

polishes and brightens Society in general. Nothing civilizes a Man equally as his Fear . . . the dread of being called to an Account keeps abundance in awe, and there are thousands of mannerly and well-accomplish'd Gentlemen in *Europe*, who would have been insolent and insupportable Coxcombs without it; besides if it was out of Fashion to ask Satisfaction for Injuries which the Law cannot take hold of, there would be twenty times the Mischief done there is now, or else you must have twenty times the Constables and other Officers to keep the Peace . . . It is strange that a Nation should grudge to see perhaps half a dozen Men sacrific'd in a Twelvemonth to obtain so valuable a Blessing, as the Politeness of Manners, the Pleasure of Conversation, and the Happiness of Company in general, that is often so willing to expose, and sometimes lose as many thousands in a few Hours, without knowing whether it will do any good or not.[47]

In Part 2, Cleomenes has to tell Horatio that this passage is meant ironically.[48] He was certainly not the only reader to take it seriously. His contemporary George Bluet did, for one. Mandeville's genuine dislike of duelling does, I think, shine through the discussion in the *Origin of Honour*, but even here it might be pointed out that his chief argument is that duelling is opposed to Christian principles. It could be alleged that he was saying, *sotto voce*, so much the worse for those principles. It was, after all, claimed that in *The Fable of the Bees* Mandeville was really saying: if Christianity and national prosperity are incompatible, so much

---

[46] *Fable of the Bees*, ed. Kaye, vol. 2, p. 103 (Third Dialogue).
[47] Ibid., vol. 1, pp. 219–20 (Remark R).
[48] Ibid., vol. 2, p. 101 (Third Dialogue).

the worse for Christianity. It is true that in the *Free Thoughts on Religion* Mandeville attacked the clergy on the ground that their principles were incompatible with Christianity, and here no one doubted that it really was the clergy he was attacking. But, it might be argued, what he really objected to was their hypocrisy, not their worldliness, though it was the worldliness that he ostensibly attacked.

But it was Mandeville's views on human corruption that drew most of the fire. For what he is saying here is that it is simply not in human nature to behave in the ways commonly called virtuous. Virtue, then, is neither desirable (if national prosperity and happiness are) nor even possible. Men are bound to act from self-interest, however much they delude themselves that they have other motives. The conclusion seems irresistible: why not, then, abandon all this fuss about virtue, accept man as he is, and make the best of what we have got?

Mandeville, Leslie Stephen tells us,

will not be beguiled from looking at the seamy side of things. Man, as theologians tell us, is corrupt, nay, it would be difficult for them to exaggerate his corruption; but the heaven which they throw in by way of consolation is tacitly understood to be a mere delusion, and the supernatural guidance in which they bid us trust, an ingenious device for enforcing their own authority. Tell your fine stories, he says in effect, to school girls or to devotees; don't try to pass them off upon me, who have seen men and cities, and not taken my notions from books or sermons. There is a part of our nature that is always flattered by the bold assertion that our idols are made of dirt; and Mandeville was a sagacious sycophant of those baser instincts.[49]

Mandeville's doctrine was, he adds a little later: 'Virtue is an empty pretence . . . To feather our own nests as warmly as may be is our only policy in this pitiless storm. Lust and pride are realities; to gratify them is to secure the only genuine enjoyment.'[50]

There is, then, a plausible case to be made for either interpretation of Mandeville. A glance at the bibliography at the end of this book will show that each of them still has its champions. Which is the right one? Which of the two Mandevilles really existed?

---

[49] L. Stephen, *Essays on Freethinking and Plainspeaking*, 1907, pp. 281-2.
[50] Ibid., p. 314.

Perhaps the best way of arriving at an answer to that question will be to forget it for a while, and look more closely at some other aspects of Mandeville's work. We may even discover more Mandevilles than two.

2
THE WIT

In his *Britannica* article on Mandeville, Minto says that he is 'at least as much of a humorist as a philosopher', and that 'his purpose was rather the invention of humorous paradoxes than the elaboration of serious theory . . . to entertain himself and others at the expense of more serious but less quick-witted theorizers.'[1] He amused himself by pointing out the paradoxes that could result from some of the current accounts of the virtuous life: the denunciation of luxury and worldliness in general, for example, or the insistence on self-denial; but he was not really very interested in the moral, theological, or philosophical implications.

There is certainly something to be said for this view. It might explain, for example, the passage that puzzled us in Remark T of the *Fable*, in which Mandeville gives such an equivocal account of 'the road that leads to virtue'. We might simply suppose him to have been unable to resist the temptation to have some more fun at the expense of the clergy and the universities, even if it was also at the expense of his own consistency.

Perhaps, then, it is a mistake to approach Mandeville as a philosopher when all he set out to write was an entertaining commentary on the social scene. His genre might perhaps be described as the comedy of social manners. I imagine that a painstaking researcher (or a suitably programmed computer) could find inconsistencies easily enough in, say, Laurence Sterne; but nobody would worry very much. Even Swift or Pope or Samuel Butler, though as satirists they are expected to have a fairly consistent general point of view, are allowed to lash out at an assortment of whipping-boys without taking too much care to see that what they say about one never conflicts in the smallest particular with what they say about the others.

The Fable of the Bees, after all, began as *The Grumbling Hive*, a satirical poem. And it was not Mandeville's only attempt at comic verse. When it appeared in 1705 he had already published

[1] *Encyclopaedia Britannica*, 9th ed., vol. 15.

Some Fables after the Easie and Familiar Method of Monsieur de la Fontaine (1703), reissued in the following year, with some additions, as *Aesop Dress'd*. In 1704 he also published, *Typhon, or the Wars between the Gods and Giants: A Burlesque Poem in Imitation of the Comical Monsieur Scarron*. It is clear that Mandeville is imitating literary models. The Aesop poems indeed are, with two exceptions, faithful translations of La Fontaine. His models are, it is true, didactic; but the interest in a fable of Aesop's does not, after all, lie in the profundity of the thought, which is trite enough, but in the aptness and ingenuity of the story which illustrates it.

The morals of the fables are indeed, at least at first sight, not entirely consistent. The poem called 'Belly, Hand and Foot', which tells the story of the limbs which refuse to work to feed the belly, with the result that they perish themselves, is explicated in this way by Mandeville:

> The Belly is the Government
> From whence the Nourishment is sent
> Of Wholesome Laws for Mutual Peace
> For Plenty, Liberty and Ease
> To all the Body Politick
> Which where it fails the Nation's sick.

If he had been very anxious to teach this lesson, however, Mandeville would hardly have also translated 'The Plague among the Beasts', in which the harmless ass is the scapegoat who is killed to expiate the crimes of the king of the beasts:

> The Fable shews you poor Folks fate
> Whilst Laws can never reach the Great

The two assertions may, of course, be reconciled. It is not unlikely that Mandeville believed, both that social inequality was inevitable and better than any possible alternative, and that the rich and great would take advantage of their privileged position, at least on occasion, to oppress the poor. Even so, it would seem to be overstating this case to exclaim

> How necessary for the State
> It is that Princes should be great
> Which, if their Pomp and Pow'r were less,
> Could not preserve our Happiness.

The ass's happiness after all was not preserved. It is possible, of course, to read these lines ironically: the modern reader may well be reminded of Belloc's:

> When Science has discovered something more
> We shall be happier than we were before.[2]

Mandeville's lines strike exactly the same note of naïve optimism; and Mandeville was not of course really a naïve optimist any more than Belloc was. Moreover, there seems to be irony elsewhere in the fables: for example, in the moral to 'The Frogs asking for a King', which tells the story of King log and King stork:

> Thank God, this Fable is not meant
> To Englishmen; they are content
> And hate to change their Government

But this has, of course, been added to La Fontaine's original. The moral of 'Belly, Hand and Foot' is quite close to the original. Moreover, it is hard to see what other moral the story could have.

Mandeville translated only a few of La Fontaine's 240 fables. He was, therefore, in a position to pick and choose. His selection does not seem to have been guided by any particular political or other didactic purpose. Didacticism does indeed intrude rather oddly in 'The Satyr and the Passenger', in which the indignant satyr kicks out a traveller to whom he has given food and shelter when he sees him blow, first on his hands to warm them, and then on his broth to cool it.

> I hate such juggling company
> What! Out of the same Mouth to blow
> Both hot and cold! Friend, prithee go!
> I thank the Gods my roof contains
> None such as you. The Fable means
> > The Moral
> None are more like to do us wrong
> Than those that wear a double Tongue.

La Fontaine ends his fable with the speech of the satyr:

> Ne plaire aux Dieux que je couche
> Avec vous sous même toit!

---

[2] H. Belloc, 'Lambkin's Newdigate', in *The Aftermath, or Gleanings from a Busy Life*, called on the cover, for purposes of sale, *Caliban's Guide to Letters; and Lambkin's Remains*, London, Duckworth, 1927, p. 190.

> Arrière ceux dont la bouche
> Souffle le chaud et le froid!

Mandeville's addition would seem to be not only gratuitous but wrong. The joke is surely on the satyr and his superstitious fears. Since what the traveller has done is perfectly sensible, his conduct can hardly be regarded as a condemnation of those who blow hot and cold in the metaphorical sense.

This flat-footedness is not however usual in Mandeville. J. S. Shea is no doubt right when he says that Mandeville is less subtle and more direct than La Fontaine;[3] but he is not as a rule imperceptive. The two original fables, 'The Carp' and 'The Owl and The Nightingale', are not noticeably inferior in plot or point to the translations, though in 'The Carp' the pretence that the story is about fish and not men is very thin indeed. (Much the same may be said of *The Grumbling Hive*.) Both are aimed at typical eighteenth-century targets: the young spark who makes the Grand Tour and learns nothing from it but debauchery, and the man of letters seeking patronage who overplays his hand.

The carp leaves his native river and sets out to sea. He cannot understand the speech of the ocean fishes, and when he meets a herring who speaks his own language, he cannot answer his questions about his own country. Eventually

> He meets a Country Fish of his
> One used to sea, a subtle Spark,
> A Pike that's served his time t'a Shark

who leads him into riot and debauchery. Finally

> Half of his Tail, and Snout, are gone
> And he lean, shabby and undone
> Sneaks home as vain and ignorant
> As e'er he was before he went.

The moral, we are told, is

> Strange Countries may improve a Man
> That knew the World before he went
> But he that sets out ignorant
> Whom only Vanity intices
> Brings Nothing from 'em but their Vices

---

[3] In his introduction to the reissue of *Aesop Dress'd* in the Augustan Reprints, Los Angeles, Calif., 1966.

In 'The Nightingale and the Owl', the king of the birds

> The Bird of *Jove* who was all Day
> As much intent upon his Prey
> As any Prince in Christendom

(the eagle in short) wants a night watchman who will sing all night in order to show that he has not fallen asleep on the job. The nightingale realizes that he alone has all the necessary qualifications:

> Says he, it hits so luckily
> As if it was contriv'd for me

and is delighted; but instead of offering his services he plays hard to get in the hope of getting a higher reward. In the meantime the owl gets the job. His voice is poor but he keeps watch conscientiously:

> So, though his Owlship could not sing,
> His Watchfulness had pleas'd the King.

When the nightingale finally condescends to go to court, he is ordered to watch and sing with the incumbent, and is affronted:

> But who has so much Vanity
> That dares pretend to sing with me?

On learning who it is:

> A King! a Devil, stupid Fowl
> That can compare me to an Owl!

Naturally enough, the king decides to stick to his faithful owl, and

> The Nightingale is kick'd from Court
> And serv'd the little Birds for Sport.

Mandeville adds the moral:

> Princes can never satisfy
> That Worth that rates itself too high.

In these fables, Mandeville is writing neither as a Savonarola nor as a cynic, but simply as an amused and intelligent observer of the human scene. His gaze falls on writers as well as on politicians: his Preface consists of an amusing attack on prefaces:

> Prefaces and Cuts are commonly made use of much to the same Purpose; to set off, and to explain. The latter, being too expensive, are pretty well out of date, in an Age where there are abundance of fine things to be bought besides Books. But the first by wicked Custom has become so necessary, that a Volume would look as defective without it as if it wanted the very Title Page. Though it is hard I should be compelled to talk to my Reader, whether I have any thing to say to him or not. Nay, what is worse every Body thinks a Man should be more lavish here of his Skill and Learning, than any where else: Here they would have him shew his Airs, and therefore most Authors adorn their Prefaces, as if they were triumphal Arches; there's nothing empty to be seen about 'em, and from top to bottom they are to be crowded with Emblems and pretty sayings, judiciously interwoven with Scraps of Latin; though they should borrow 'em from the Parson of the Parish.

(There is a similar attack on prefaces in the preface to *The Virgin Unmask'd*.) All this confirms the impression that Mandeville's motives are mainly literary: he is looking for the pithy phrase, the entertaining story, the contemporary illusion. 'If any like these Trifles,' he says at the end of the preface to *Aesop Dress'd*, 'perhaps I may go on: if not, you shall be troubled with no more of 'em.'

He did go on. *The Grumbling Hive* is, after all, just a longer and rather more ambitious poem in the style of the Aesop verses. The moral is, in effect: don't grumble too much at what you've got; what you are asking for might be worse, if you only realized it. And Mandeville has thought of a particularly ingenious application.

His first prose work, *The Virgin Unmask'd: or, Female Dialogues betwixt an Elderly Maiden Lady and her Niece*, is not altogether different in conception. There is some argument, and various positions are taken up, mainly by Lucinda, the aunt; but six of the ten dialogues which make up the book are given up to two lengthy illustrative anecdotes, each told with enough animation, elaboration of detail, and skill in characterization to give Mandeville some claim to a place among the ancestors of the novel. And at this time Mandeville seems to have intended to go on writing fiction: his preface ends with the sentence: 'By leaving the Story of *Leonora* unfinished, you may expect I intend to go on.'

The book begins with Lucinda's strictures on the immodesty of her niece's dress:

Lucinda: Here, Niece, take my Handkerchief, prithee now, if you can find nothing else to cover your Nakedness: If you knew what a Fulsome Sight it was, I am sure you would not go so bare: I cann't abide your Naked Breasts heaving up and down; it makes me sick to see it.
Antonia: 'T in't clean, Aunt: besides, 'tis so hot I cann't endure any Thing about my Neck; I hate to be stifled up so.
Lu: Harkee, *Antonia*, those little Pretences won't pass upon your Aunt; 'tin't the Heat of the Weather, 'tis the Heat of your Blood, your Wantonness, and Lascivious Thoughts, 'tis they that are the Cause of all your immoderate Behaviour . . . Yesterday 'twas as hot again as it is now, then all the while we were in the Garden, rather than to have your White Skin Tann'd you could endure your Handkerchief, and your Mask, both; then you was close muffled up, and I did not hear you once complain of being stifled.
Ant.: As long as I use no Art to make my skin White, I hope 'tis no Sin, Aunt, to keep it from being Sun burnt.
Luc.: Yes; and for what Reason do you keep it white? To raise up sinful Thoughts in others: If your Breasts were Yellow or Freckled, you know they would not be so inviting to the Fellows . . .[4]

The first dialogue goes on like this, with Antonia answering pertly enough at first, but finally reduced to tears. Lucinda then (in the second dialogue) softens, and explains that she scolds Antonia only because she wants to protect her from men: partly because she does not wish to lose Antonia, an orphan, whom her aunt has cared for since infancy; and partly because she dislikes and distrusts men. The elderly man-hating maiden virago is a more or less stock comic character; but Mandeville treats Lucinda quite sympathetically. Her character emerges quite clearly: she is tart and frank in speech, without sentimentality but not without feeling. She has no illusions about either men or women, and observes their behaviour with wry amusement, and certainly not without insight.

Consider, for example, her account of courtship:

What your Opinion of Wooing may be, I cann't tell, but I always thought it very ridiculous; tell me, pray, *Antonia*, which is more unaccountable, the Pride of the Woman, or the Humility of the Man? She is resolved to be very cross, and with abundance of Coyness sits

---
[4] *The Virgin Unmask'd*, 1709, pp. 1-2 (First Dialogue).

in State, insults over the Man, and treats him with as much Scorn, as if he was not worthy to wipe her Shoes; and why does she do all this? For no other Reason, but because she designs to make him her Master, and give him all she has in the World. The Man, on his Side, takes all these Indignities in good Part, seems to be fond of being ill treated, and with the most profound Veneration to his Idol, begs on his Knees, that a certain modest Petition may be granted him; the upshot of which is, that the Person, to whom he pays his Devotion, would be so kind, as to oblige herself solemnly, before Witnesses, upon the Penalty of being damn'd, to be his Slave as long as he lives, unless he should happen to die before her.[5]

Lucinda is a man-hater largely because she is indignant about the subjection of women: to their fathers when they are single, and to their husbands when they are married. When Antonia protests that women in England are 'treated very Respectfully, as well as Tenderly', she answers:

Lu.: 'Tis that Respect, and Tenderness I hate, when it consists in outward shew: in *Holland* Women sit in their Counting-houses, and do Business or at least are acquainted with every thing their Husbands do. But says a Rascal here, no, my Dear, that is too much Trouble; those Butter-Boxes don't know, how to treat Ladies; Men should only study, how to give 'em Pleasure: With this he sends her to the Play-House; and when she comes Home, there's an Extent out against her Husband, all what they have in the World is gone, and they tear the very Rings from the Lady's Fingers, that was so respected an Hour ago. Is not this enough to make a Woman run Mad.[6]

Unlike many champions of an oppressed group, Lucinda does not suppose that the oppressors have all the vices, and the oppressed all the virtues. On the contrary, the oppression itself is bound to damage the characters of the victims. Women are often silly, because they have been bred to be silly. Girls at boarding-schools 'may be taught to Sing and Dance, to Work and Dress, and, if you will, receive Good Instructions for a Genteel Carriage, and how to be Mannerly: but these Things chiefly concern the Body, the Mind remains uninstructed.'[7]

Men, on the other hand, have 'all manner of Knowledge, as it were, beat into their Brain, with all the Application imaginable, while we are pricking a Clout'. As a result: 'Women are shallow

---

[5] *The Virgin Unmask'd*, 1709, p. 30 (Second Dialogue).
[6] Ibid., p. 128 (Sixth Dialogue).   [7] Ibid., p. 48 (Third Dialogue).

Creatures; we may boast of Prattling, and be quick at Jest, or Repartee, but a sound and penetrating Judgment only belongs to Men, as the Masters of Reason and Solid Sense.'[8] Lucinda admonishes Antonia that women are in most danger when they 'can be calm, and hear a Man sedately; then, they'll sit down and hearken to Reason.'

Ant.: And should they not?
Luc.: No, by no means, never, if they would keep their Virginity unspotted: No, Niece, she that listens to them, is ruined, and her Liberty is lost. In Reasoning, Women never can cope with Men . . .[9]

Lucinda (and, one suspects, Mandeville) is however quite sure that this inferiority is not natural, but socially engendered: 'our Wit may be equal with theirs.' Mandeville, indeed, makes Cleomenes go much further than Lucinda:

The generality of Women are quicker of Invention, and more ready at Repartee, than the Men, with equal helps of Education . . . The Workmanship in the Make of Women seems to be more elegant, and better finish'd: the Features are more delicate, the Voice is sweeter, the whole Outside of them is more curiously wove, than they are in Men; and the difference in the Skin between theirs and ours is the same, as there is between fine Cloth and coarse. There is no Reason to imagine, that Nature should have been more neglectful of them out of Sight, than she has where we can trace her; and not have taken the same care of them in the Formation of the Brain, as to the Nicety of the Structure, and superior Accuracy in the Fabrick, which is so visible in the rest of their Frame.[10]

There is another matter, too, in which the differences between men and women, so widely advertised, are due to nurture rather than nature. Women, Lucinda insists, are quite as lustful as men. She gives us a vivid description of Antonia's adolescence:

About Seventeen you was at the Worst; then you never kept Two Minutes in one Posture: if you walk'd through the Room, it was with as much Faintness as if your Back had been broke; and if you stood still, it was always leaning against something or other, and seldom on both Legs, whilst the Small of the one would be continually hitting the Calf of the other: A Hundred Pranks you would play with your Legs; when you sat down, the Heel of one Foot would always be rubbing

---

[8] Ibid., p. 28 (Second Dialogue). [9] Ibid., p. 27 (Second Dialogue).
[10] *Fable of the Bees*, ed. Kaye, vol. 2, pp. 172–3 (Fourth Dialogue).

and pressing the other's in Step: Sometimes when you thought you was not observ'd, how passionately would you throw yourselves backward, and clapping your Legs alternatively over one another, squeeze your Thighs together with all the Strength you had, and in a Quarter of an Hour repeat the same to all the Chairs in the Room? Many times, *Antonia*, have I seen you sit in that Careless Manner, and half shutting your Eyes, whilst your Head would slowly drop down to one Shoulder, bite on your Lip with so Craving and so Begging a Look, that I have pitied you my self, and spoke, to make you think on something else: Every Action, and every Limb, betray'd your Desires, your Tongue only excepted: Nay, I have often fear'd that that likewise would have been drawn into the Plot, and ask'd for Man as loud as they.[11]

Lucinda adds, however: 'What disorders young Women so much at the Sight of Man, is the Conflict between their Natural Wishes, and the Inborn Modesty of Virgins';[12] and, a little further on, tells Antonia that 'Women have . . . an Innate Reservedness, and a Kind of Horror against losing their Virginity more than the Females of any other Creature.'[13]

So far what has been said may seem to give little support to the thesis that Mandeville is a humorist rather than a philosopher: Lucinda, it may appear, is just another mouthpiece for Mandeville's opinions, like Cleomenes. It might be said in reply that many of Antonia's speeches could hardly have been made by Mandeville in his own person. For example:

But if Man was not a Venomous Creature, how would it be possible, that a Hail, Plump Girl, of a good Complexion, should in so little a time, after Conversing with him, turn thin Visaged, Pale, Yellow and look as if she was Bewitch'd? Not be able to endure the sight of Bread, Loath the best of Food, and in an Instant, get an Aversion to twenty things, which she used to admire before: whilst she'll run Raving Mad for strange, nasty, and unnatural Messes, that no Human Stomach, of People in their Senses, ever craved; with an Appetite so uncommon, and unaccountable, that if it be not satisfied, or she is denied, or any ways hindered in her Frentick Lusts, she'll Swoon away, be thrown into Convulsions, and such Agonies, as have often proved Fatal: Are not these Signs, that the Venom flies up to the Head? Does it not come up to Demonstration, that the Sting of Man comes up to that of the *Tarantula*?[14]

---

[11] *The Virgin Unmask'd*, pp. 21–2 (Second Dialogue).
[12] Ibid., p. 25 (Second Dialogue).   [13] Ibid., p. 31 (Second Dialogue).
[14] Ibid., pp. 120–1 (Sixth Dialogue).

It might also be pointed out that Lucinda's vivid description of an adolescent's physical uneasiness, or her sardonic account of a proposal of marriage, goes beyond what is needed to make a point in an argument. But in any case the argument itself merely forms the introduction to a novella, or rather two novellas. Lucinda and Antonia dispute about whether wives or old maids have the happier lives; and Lucinda challenges her niece to name a married woman she would be prepared to change places with. Antonia names their acquaintance Aurelia; whereupon Lucinda spends some seventy pages in telling the story of Aurelia's life.

It turns out to be a horrifying story. Aurelia elopes with Dorante, a young army captain, largely to escape from the wealthy but uncongenial suitor her father has tried to force upon her. Her father then disowns and disinherits her, to the dismay of her husband, who has married her for her money. He is, it turns out, an Irish adventurer, a professional card-sharper, who has, through getting a nobleman into his debt, managed to secure a commission in the army: a useful defence against inquisitive people who are suspicious of affluent gamblers with no visible means of support. On his marriage he flees to Dublin; but in a smaller city his winnings at cards become notorious, and his source of income vanishes. In these straits, he 'threw his Eyes on her Beauty and was resolved, if one Way he could not get Money with her, he would have it another'; he resolves to make his wife the mistress of a nobleman. Aurelia refuses, in spite of Dorante's arguments: 'If your Conscience be so foolishly Scrupulous, as to boggle at Sin, there is no occasion of committing any, unless you have a mind to it; for it being an Act of Soul, it is in your power to prevent it, by having no Lustful thoughts.'[15]

Disappointed in his hopes of making money as Aurelia's ponce, Dorante goes to live in England, leaving Aurelia with his mother, who ill-treats her. So does Dorante, who returns at intervals. Her little boy dies, after a fit brought on apparently by fright at seeing his father's drunken harassment of his mother. Her mother-in-law treats her as an unpaid servant, giving her only cast-off clothes to wear: she is unable to leave the household because if she did her daughter, her only remaining child, would be taken from her. Eventually Dorante is killed in a duel.

Aurelia is now left destitute; but money is sent her by a

[15] Ibid., p. 66 (Fourth Dialogue).

mysterious benefactor in England, together with a letter asking her to come to London. She does so; and when she gets out of the coach

... a Handsome Young Gentleman of Eight and Twenty, or Thirty Years of Age, made up to her, and without asking any Questions, Saluting her, and calling her by her Name, bid her welcom to *England*; *Aurelia* was Amazed, and Blushing, beg'd his Pardon for not knowing him; the Gentleman replied Smilingly, that he hoped shortly, to have the Honour of being better acquainted with her: And having taken care of a Trunk she had, Handed her and her Daughter into a Gentleman's Coach, that waited for him in the Yard, then got in himself, and bid the Fellow drive Home.

Ant.: And so I suppose she got a second Husband. He found very little Opposition my thinks, and certainly no Body ever wanted less Courtship than Aurelia.

Lu.: I thought you would Censure her, but think you are in the Wrong; I can't see what she has committed, that you find so much fault with.

Ant.: I don't blame her for committing any thing, but for omitting, what she ought to have done, when she had told him, that he was a Stranger to her; and he seeing her in that incertitude, instead of telling her who he was, made her that familiar Compliment, by which he shew'd himself Cock-sure of her; she ought to have broke off all Conversation with him; but not suffer'd her self without speaking a word, like a Natural, to be led into a Coach, not knowing whose it was, or whither it was to go.[16]

In spite of Aurelia's behaviour, Antonia is disappointed when it turns out that the handsome young man is married, with three children, and has no designs on Aurelia, whose benefactor turns out to be an elderly relative of her mother's. He takes Aurelia into his household and her life now becomes comfortable enough for Antonia to have been misled into giving her as an example of a happy matron, with a charming daughter, 'well disposed of to a Baronet, a Gentleman of Three Thousand a Year', and four delightful grandchildren. But even the daughter's happiness, Lucinda hints dourly, is not likely to last long; she and her husband have extravagant tastes and are living beyond their means.

The second novella is a study in seduction. Antonia remarks that 'it is impossible for a really virtuous woman to lose her

[16] *The Virgin Unmask'd*, pp. 104–5 (Fifth Dialogue).

Honour, unless she be ravish'd;' in which case she can hardly be said to lose it. Lucinda replies that 'no woman, tho' of the most exemplary Virtue, is able to withstand the Treachery of some Men'[17] and, by way of illustration, tells the story of Leonora.

Leonora, who is married to a man she has never loved and who has become indifferent to her, falls victim to a particularly patient and painstaking seducer, who prefers his prey to be hard to catch:

> He despis'd every Thing that was easy, and only lay in Wait for such as were counted cunning and difficult, and commonly for Women of a very good Reputation. Having heard of *Leonora's* exemplary Vertue and Reservedness, as well as dazling Beauty, he thought attacking her would be a noble Enterprize.[18]

He makes the acquaintance of Leonora's husband, and contrives to become a lodger in the household. He professes to have no interest in love, though full of esteem for women.

> She had never yet been in a Man's Company, but more or less, in either his Countenance, Speech, or Actions, she had observ'd, that the piercing Lustre of her Eyes made some Impression upon his Soul; but only Mincio, with an unaffected Freedom, could gaze on 'em, and doing Justice to her Beauty, speak of her Charms as unconcernedly, as the Minute after he would extol the happy Features of her little Son. What strange perverse Creatures we Women are! The chast and wary *Leonora*, who would so bravely have resisted him, in Case he had assaulted her with Love; she that prepar'd herself for a vigorous Defence, whilst she dreaded the Danger of Vice, was foil'd by well dissembl'd Vertue, and envying his cold Indifferency, was ready to quarrel at the Weakness of her Charms, 'till, quite disarm'd of all her Fear, she almost could have wish'd him less insensible.[19]

They are on brother and sister terms. After six months, Mincio suddenly becomes melancholy, and makes Leonora believe that he has reluctantly fallen in love with her and is struggling to conceal his passion. He says that he had better go away, but is prevented by a feigned illness. He now pretends to be on the point of death, and all for the love of Leonora.

At this point, rather oddly, *The Virgin Unmask'd* comes to an end, with Lucinda saying: 'Now, *Antonia*, tell me where you

[17] Ibid., p. 183 (Ninth Dialogue).
[18] Ibid., p. 205 (Tenth Dialogue).
[19] Ibid., pp. 208–9 (Tenth Dialogue).

can blame *Leonora* yet? Consult your Pillow upon it, and to Morrow you shall know all.'

As is indicated in the preface, Mandeville obviously intended to continue the story. It would be interesting to know why he did not. We may suppose Leonora to have been seduced and Lucinda to have made her point. It is a characteristic Mandeville point: the way to men's (and women's) hearts is through their vanity. (But also, it should be noted by those who find Mandeville's view of human nature entirely cynical, through their pity.) Yet the point might have been made without telling the story in such detail. Before Mincio appears on the scene at all there is an account, twenty pages long, of Leonora's life before her marriage, and of her separation from her girlhood sweetheart, the only man she ever loved. Even when Mincio has been introduced the action is delayed while we are told at some length about his education and the way in which his character was formed. These details are not irrelevant: they establish Leonora's character as a woman of unflagging chastity who has already resisted the wicked Duke of B—, they explain why she had accepted a loveless marriage, and they help to make Mincio's behaviour credible. They are, however, quite excessive if Mandeville's only object was to point a moral and to let Lucinda win the argument. In telling Leonora's story it is clearly the novelist's impulse that is moving him: one may guess that he intended to bring Leonora and her first lover together again in the sequel.

On the other hand, he may have intended to avoid doing that, just because it was what would have happened in a conventional romance. In two or three places in *The Virgin Unmask'd* Mandeville glances at the romances of the day: Antonia expects the characters in Lucinda's stories to behave like the heroines in her favourite reading, and is disappointed when they do not.

The novelist's impulse does not of course exclude the moralist's: one may find sermons in novels far more readily than in stones, and with much more assurance that a creator has actually put them there. As a philosopher, Mandeville's main interest was probably what would now be called the philosophy of mind, which comes even closer to the novelist's preoccupations. It might be said that in Mandeville's fiction the philosopher continually intrudes upon the novelist: when he tells a story it is to illustrate a general thesis; even in *The Virgin Unmask'd* Lucinda and Antonia continually make general reflections on the behaviour and motives of the characters. If there is some truth in this claim, it is also true that, when Mandeville sets out to expound a general thesis, the novelist continually intrudes upon the theorist.

He cannot write a philosophical dialogue without furnishing each participant with a character sketch that might have done for the *Tatler* or the *Spectator*: often enough he does the same when he merely wants to illustrate a point by means of an anecdote. When he writes a pamphlet about penal reform he introduces so many vivid and lively descriptions of the scenes attending public executions at Tyburn that they were 'pirated by authors of guide-books, etc.' for the next fifty years, and continue to be quoted by social historians.[20] Here is Newgate:

> The horrid Aspects of Turnkeys and Gaolers, in Discontent and Hurry; the sharp and dreadful Looks of Rogues, that beg in Irons, but would rob you with greater Satisfaction, if they could; the Bellowings of half a dozen Names at a time, that are perpetually made in the Enquiries after one another; the Variety of strong Voices that are heard, of howling in one Place, scolding and quarrelling in another, and loud Laughter in a third; the substantial Breakfasts that are made in the midst of all this, the Seas of Beer that are swill'd; the never-ceasing Outcries for more; and the bawling Answers of the Tapsters as continual; the quantity and Varieties of more entoxicating Liquors, that are swallow'd in every Part of *Newgate*; the Impudence, and unseasonable Jests of those, who administer them; their black Hands, and Nastiness all over, all these, joined together, are astonishing and terrible, without mentioning the Oaths and Imprecations, that from every Corner are echo'd about, for Trifles; or the little light, and general Squallor of the Gaol itself, accompany'd with the melancholy Noise of Fetters, differently sounding, according to their Weight: But what is most shocking to a thinking Man is the Behaviour of the Condemn'd whom (for the greatest Part) you'll find either drinking madly or uttering the vilest Ribaldry, and jeering others that are less impenitent; whilst the Ordinary bustles among them, and shifting from one to another, distributes Scraps of good Counsel to unattentive Hearers; and near him the Hangman, impatient to be gone, swears at their Delays; and, as fast as he can, does his Part, in preparing them for their Journey.[21]

---

[20] See Gerald Howson, *Thief-taker General: the rise and fall of Jonathan Wild*, London, Hutchinson, 1970, p. 294.
[21] B. Mandeville, *An Enquiry into the Causes of the Frequent Executions at Tyburn*, 1725, pp. 18–19.

And here are the crowds lining the streets:

> All the Way, from *Newgate* to *Tyburn*, is one continued Fair, for Whores and Rogues of the meaner Sort. Here the most abandon'd Rakehells may light on Women as shameless: Here Trollops, all in Rags, may pick up Sweethearts of the same Politeness; and there are none so lewd, so vile, so indigent, of either Sex, but at the Time and Place aforesaid, they may find a Paramour. Where the Crowd is the least, which, among the Itinerants, is nowhere very thin, the Mob is the rudest; and here jostling one another, and kicking Dirt about are the most innocent Pastimes. Now you see a man, without Provocation, push his Companion in the Kennel; and two Minutes after, the Sufferer trip up the other's Heels, and the first Aggressor lies rolling in the more solid Mire: And he is the prettiest Fellow among them, who is the least shock'd at Nastiness, and the most boisterous in his Sports. . . .[22]

The description is not, of course, irrelevant: the more vividly Mandeville's readers realized what Newgate and Tyburn were really like, the more readily would they agree that reforms were needed. But there is little doubt that Mandeville also enjoyed exercising his literary skill. 'The Pleasure there is in imitating Nature in what shape soever,' he tells us in the Preface, 'is so bewitching that it over-rides the dictates of Art, and often forces us to offend against our own judgment.' The remark is, of course, meant to appease those readers who found his realism coarse; but Mandeville did take genuine pleasure in 'imitating Nature', perhaps in improving on her. Consider, for example, another lively piece of description, this time in comic vein, from one of Mandeville's contributions to the *Female Tatler*. There is no reforming purpose here, but only one of those literary family jokes typical of the eighteenth century. A lady has swooned on hearing the (false) news of the death of Isaac Bickerstaff, the alleged author of the other, male *Tatler*:

> She was held upright in a Chair, had her Eyes shut and, without either Colour or Motion, looked like Death itself. Two Ladies rubb'd her Temples with *Hungary Water*, as many held *Hartshorn* to her nostrils; one threw Vinegar in her Face, another half drowned her with Cold Water and a Third on her Knees was cutting the Lace of her Stays behind her whilst Old Nurse plyed her with the burning Tape,

[22] B. Mandeville, *An Enquiry into the Causes of the Frequent Executions at Tyburn*, 1725, pp. 20–1.

and made Smoak enough, if some body had not opened one of the Sashes, to have stifled us all.[23]

That Mandeville should have written for the *Female Tatler* at all is perhaps the most obvious piece of evidence that his purpose as a writer was often simply literary (not to say journalistic). The paper was in part an imitation, and sometimes a conscious parody, of Steele's *Tatler*, and in part something of a scandal sheet. The earlier numbers purported to be 'by Mrs. Crackenthorpe, a Lady that knows every thing'. The nature of her knowledge may be gathered from a notice in nos. 44 and 45:

Mrs. Crackenthorpe has received Intelligence from several People, that there is a Scandalous Fellow about Town, that makes it his Business to impose on People by extorting Money from them, under the pretence of producing sham Letters, etc., that unless they deposite such Sums of Money as he villainously demands, they shall be expos'd in this Paper; this is to give Notice that she is in no way directly or indirectly privy to or concern'd in those his Rascally and Knavish Impostures . . .

After no. 51, Mrs. Crackenthorpe handed over the paper to 'a Society of Modest Ladies, who in their turns will oblige the Publick with whatever they shall meet with, that will be Diverting, Innocent or Instructive'. Two of these, Lucinda and Artesia, were in fact Bernard Mandeville. Between them they wrote about half the issues from nos. 52 to 111, when the paper ceased publication.

Before long Lucinda is telling us that readers are complaining that she publishes no scandalous stories about real people.

You may keep your musty Morals to yourself; all the Instruction we want from you, is from Example, by seeing Vice lash'd, and nothing can be a greater Diversion, than to see others handsomely exposed; railing at the Vices and Follies of the Age in general is insignificant . . . for none of all my Acquaintances would give a Pin for Scandal where the Parties are not sufficiently described to be known.[24]

Lucinda replies that she will not stoop to spreading scandal about identifiable individuals.

As a doctor, Mandeville may have been worried about other features of the *Female Tatler* as well as its scandal. The advertise-

[23] *Female Tatler*, no. 72, 24–6 Dec. 1709.
[24] Ibid., no. 60, 21–3 Nov. 1709. See also no. 56.

ments frequently extolled the Grand Chymical Anti-Scorbutick Drops for the Scurvy; or Purging Sugar Plumbs for Children, which killed Worms and cured Green sickness in Maids, pale Looks in Children, Rickets, Stomach Pains, King's Evil, Scurvies, Rheumatisms, etc.; or a Fam'd Elixir for the Wind, which expelled it to Admiration; or most excellent Tablets of a delightful Flavour and Taste, one of which at a time being only chewed or held in the Mouth, rowling it about with the Tongue, wonderfully (without the least offence or hindrance of Business) purged the Head and Brain, curing all the Diseases thereof; or the highest Compounded Spirit of Lavender, of the most Glorious (if the expression might be used) enlivening Scent and Flavour that could possibly be, which, when either smelt or dropt on a bit of Loaf Sugar, or eaten or dissolv'd in Wine, Coffee or Tea, so raptured the Spirits, delighted the Gust, and gave such Airs to the Countenances of those subject to Sick Fits or Vapours, as were to be imagin'd but by those who had tryed it. At any rate, Artesia devotes no. 58 to quack advertisers, whom she praises ironically for their unflagging and disinterested zeal in advancing knowledge and enlightening mankind. No. 58 itself contains eight such advertisements—the entire advertising for the issue—and there was no falling off in later numbers.

Even Mrs. Crackenthorpe had claimed that the *Female Tatler* was 'a Serious, Reforming Paper, tho' loaded with Jests, Epigrams and pleasant Tales'; in Lucinda's and Artesia's pages the readers were treated to discussions of the morality of duelling, the nature of Honour, and the defects in women's education, and were introduced to 'a gentleman from Oxford' who maintained that

Humility, Temperance, Contentedness, Frugality, and several other Virtues are very insignificant, as to the Publick, and so far from making a Country flourish, that no Nation ever yet enjoy'd the most ordinary comforts of Life, if they were not Counter-ballanc'd by the opposite Vices.

He would have gone on, but seeing by our Countenances that no body admired his Doctrine, he said no more.[25]

There are plenty of jests, epigrams, and pleasant tales. There is also one somewhat unpleasant tale, a sop perhaps to Mrs. Crackenthorpe's followers, about the exposure of a prude who sleeps in

[25] *Female Tatler*, no. 62, 25–7 Nov. 1709.

secret with her gardener.²⁶ Three of the fables from *Aesop Dress'd*, including 'The Carp', are reprinted in different issues, possibly to fill up the page. The mingling of entertainment and instruction suited Mandeville's temperament and talents very well. Less sentimental than Steele and less school-ma'amish than Addison, he was a bolder, a more original, and, one may add, a more dedicated thinker than either. He took his ideas seriously; but he also enjoyed playing with them. As Lucinda tells us: 'I often serve my Arguments as I do my Tea, which I make pretty strong at first, but because I would have all the goodness out of it, I generally Drink it weaker at last than I really love it.'²⁷

After the *Female Tatler* Mandeville's writings are, at least in appearance, more serious in tone: instead of verse fables and articles for a slightly scurrilous paper, he takes to writing a medical treatise and a fairly long book on religion and the churches, as well as transmogrifying *The Grumbling Hive* into *The Fable of the Bees*, with its bulky appendage of more or less serious argument. Yet even the medical treatise is in dialogue form (between a doctor and his patient) and is not without its quota of jests, epigrams, and pleasant tales. Mandeville's fondness for dialogue is indeed one reason why it is hard to know what his own beliefs are.

I have already mentioned the character sketches. The 'character' was a recognized literary form of the day. When Cleomenes, in Part 2 of the *Fable*, draws his 'Picture of a fine Gentleman', Horatio comments: 'This is a study'd Piece', and Cleomenes replies: 'I have thought of it before, I own.'²⁸ It is one of many. In *Free Thoughts on Religion*, for example, Mandeville wants to make the point that a devout attention to the outward forms of religion may accompany quite unworthy motives: he does it by 'presenting the reader with two or three characters', which almost become short stories. I shall quote one in full:

EMILIA had a great share of wit and beauty, but pride enough to outweigh both: she was every way well accomplish'd, and her discretion hid the greatest part of her frailty: she hated all female acquaintance, and yet shew'd no fondness to men: she was a pattern of modesty, and

---

²⁶ Ibid., no. 102, 8–10 Mar. 1710.
²⁷ Ibid., no. 81, 9–11 Jan. 1710.
²⁸ *Fable of the Bees*, ed. Kaye, vol. 2, p. 68 (Second Dialogue).

remain'd virtuous, till she was five and twenty; at which time, her father, who was a merchant, dying insolvent, Emilia was left destitute to the wide world. Two months after she grants the last favour to a Jew, and gets five hundred pounds by the bargain. She soon discards him, admits another, and abates of her price. She had six gallants in less than a month; and in half a year's time, *Emilia* became a common miss of the town. As she was a well-bred woman, that never drank to excess, and guilty of no other crimes besides prostitution, she had a very good income, and no rakish customers; being expensive in nothing but cloaths and furniture she hoarded up money. All the women of the profession hated her, and she them more inveterately. At three and thirty she had a fit of sickness, which alter'd her much for the worse; upon which, finding her trade to fall off, she left it, and retir'd with five thousand pounds in her pocket. She went a hundred miles off, changed her name, and was married to an old knight, who had little or nothing, and spent her above half of what she had.

HER husband has been dead these two years, and *Emilia* is now turn'd of fifty. She is grave in her dress, and solemn in her gate: She has left off house-keeping, lives within compass, and, with her woman and foot-boy, boards in a very sober family. She appears very devout, is never absent from prayers, and has for some years read nothing but divinity, she delights in controversy, and is well versed in ecclesiastical history, and so good a disputant that, all around her, there is no body able to cope with her. Since she left her first employ, she has not been guilty of one act of incontinence; but as she commits no fault herself that way, she is resolved not to connive at the least shadow of it in others. She talks very well, and passes not a day without telling lies, either of her birth and family, or else the virtues of her youth. She never had a child; and the hatred to her sex, especially those of merit, continues. She is the most censorious woman in the world; and, in the seventeen years she has been in the country, she has broke off above twenty matches, that, in all probability, would have been happy ones, and ruin'd above fifty reputations, that never deserv'd it; yet she is so circumspect, as well as sly in her insinuations and manages her slander with so much dexterity, that she has never been detected.

EMILIA is fam'd both for wisdom and piety; the parson of the parish extols her to the skies but is afraid of her in his heart; every body admires and stands in awe of her, and no woman in the country has more respect paid her. Half a year ago she made her will and left every farthing she has, to rebuild the front of a little alms-house, that has a very little income, and stands about a mile off from where she lives. Over the porch is to be her effigy in stone, with an inscription of her own indicting underneath it. Since she has had this design, she often visits the poor inhabitants, to whom she gives what charity she can spare, and who, in return, take her to be a saint, and trumpet her praise all over the country.

WHAT *Emilia* thinks of her self is worth any man's notice. Her prostitution she is sure never proceeded from lust, but from necessity, *ergo* no sin. The mischief she does with her slander, she ascribes to the aversion she has to vice. When she reflects on the hours she spends at church, and in reading, and then thinks on the will she has made, she flatters her self with having perform'd every christian duty, and her conscience is entirely clear. Is it not strange, that *Emilia*, with all her cunning, never suspected her self to be an ill woman, and knows not to this hour, that envy and vanity are her darling vices?[29]

A highly moral tale, certainly; but quite as much a tale as a moral. Even Mandeville's use of argument has this double character. Argumentation is one of the tricks of the humorist's trade from the melancholy Jacques to W. S. Gilbert. Whately's proof that Napoleon did not exist, or Ronald Knox's proof that Queen Victoria wrote *In Memoriam*, though they have a serious satirical point, are funny just as pieces of ingenious if wrongheaded reasoning. At least some of Mandeville's arguments are of this kind. Examples have already been given in discussing *The Virgin Unmask'd*. Lucinda's proof that 'Man is a Venomous Creature' may be regarded in this light, and so may Dorante's recipe for committing adultery without sin. Each argument has its point, as helping to build up the characters of Lucinda and Dorante respectively, and perhaps another point as well: Lucinda has after all laid her finger on one of the ways in which men frequently exploit women, and Dorante is glancing at some quite eminent theologians. But the arguments can also be enjoyed, and one imagines were enjoyed by Mandeville, just for their own sake. In the Preface Mandeville thinks it necessary to warn his readers that he is not to be taken to endorse 'the wicked Sophistry of Dorante', who brings further arguments to bear on Aurelia:

He told her, how little he could ever be guilty of Jealousie; and that Friends might be communicative in every thing; that it must be a great Churl, or a Fool, that should like his own Garden the worse, because another had been there, tho' he had robb'd it of nothing, nor left so much as a Footstep behind him: As for his Part, he thought no more Harm in it, than in drinking with a man out of the same Cup.[30]

---

[29] *Free Thoughts on Religion, the Church, and National Happiness*, 2nd ed., 1729, pp. 31-5.   [30] *The Virgin Unmask'd*, p. 53 (Third Dialogue).

It is possible, though not quite certain, that when Mandeville makes Cleomenes argue to the superior intellect of women from the finer texture of their skins, he is once again developing an ingenious argument for the fun of it, and not because he endorsed it.

Was Minto, then, right, and is Mandeville primarily a framer of paradoxes and *jeux d'esprit*? Even from what has already been said, it seems clear that this is not true or not the whole truth. The thesis has some plausibility if it is confined to *The Grumbling Hive*, or even to everything Mandeville wrote down to 1710, when the *Female Tatler* ceased publication. Even *The Fable of the Bees*, Part 1, might be an elaborate joke: we might suppose that Mandeville, amused and perhaps nettled by the solemn outcry against *The Grumbling Hive*, set himself, in the spirit of a barrister doing his best with a hopeless brief, to see what could be said in defence of his paradoxes. The *Enquiry into the Origin of Moral Virtue* and the *Essay on Charity and Charity-Schools* might just conceivably be elaborate leg-pulls. But already the hypothesis is becoming strained; and one can hardly imagine that Mandeville would have persevered with the joke, if that was all it was, throughout the quite lengthy books that followed.

Mandeville was never solemn, but he was usually serious, or at least partly serious. In spite of the fun he poked at Shaftesbury, he would probably have agreed that humour is the only test of gravity, and gravity of humour: a joke should have a serious point, and a doctrine or theory is not worth much if it can be punctured by a little levity. Throughout his writings Mandeville recurs to the same themes: the prevalence of self-deception (even his medical treatise is about hypochondria and hysteria), the ceaseless striving of mankind for praise and esteem, the disparity between what men say and what they do. There is very little doubt that he took them seriously. Moreover, a good deal of what he said about them deserves to be taken seriously.

At the same time, Minto's remarks are worth noticing. Mandeville was a many-sided man. If one thinks of him just as a preacher, or even just as a cynic, one is likely to misinterpret much of what he says. It is as well to remember that he began as a writer of light verse, and of entertaining pieces for the *Female Tatler*; that he continued to write dialogues; that his interests were literary as well as philosophical or sociological, so that he was quite capable of depicting a scene, telling a story, or sketching a character at least partly for its own sake; that he liked to treat an argument like a pot of tea, wringing the last drops out of it even when that meant that it lost some of its strength. Some of the diverse interpretations of him may have resulted from forgetting these facts. In interpreting Mandeville one must always remember that he is a satirist. Satirists do, and perhaps must, have serious convictions, but their convictions will not always appear on the surface. And, quite apart from understanding him better, we may come to appreciate him better if we think of him, not merely as a crude and misty anticipator of economists like Adam Smith or psychologists like Freud, but as a satirist and (in both the modern and the eighteenth-century senses) a wit.

3
THE DOCTOR

The title-page of Mandeville's medical treatise is worth quoting in full:

A TREATISE OF THE HYPOCHONDRIACK AND HYSTERICK PASSIONS, Vulgarly call'd the HYPO in MEN and VAPOURS in WOMEN; in which the SYMPTOMS, CAUSES, and CURE of those DISEASES are set forth after a Method intirely new. The whole interspers'd with Instructive Discourses ON THE Real ART OF PHYSICK it self; And Entertaining Remarks on the Modern Practice of PHYSICIANS AND APOTHECARIES: Very useful to all, that have the Misfortune to stand in need of either. In Three Dialogues. By B. DE MANDEVILLE, M.D. *Scire potestates herbarum usumque medendi Maluit, et Mutas agitare inglorius artes.* Aeneid. Lib. XII. London: Printed and Sold by *Dryden Leach*, in *Elliott's Court*, in the *Little-Old-Baily*, and *W. Taylor*, at the *Ship*, in *Pater-Noster-Row*. 1711.

The revised edition, published in 1730, changes 'passions' to 'diseases'.

The book takes the form of a series of discussions between a physician, Philopirio, and a patient, Misomedon. Philopirio is Mandeville, quite explicitly:

In these Dialogues, I have done the same as *Seneca* did in his *Octavia*, and brought my self upon the Stage; with this difference, that he kept his own Name, and I changed mine for that of *Philopirio*, a Lover of Experience, which I shall always profess to be: Wherefore I desire my Reader to take whatever is spoke by the Person I named last, as said by my self; which I entreat him not to do with the Part of *Misomedon*, whom the better to illustrate his Distemper, I have made guilty of some extravagant Sallies, that in strictness I would not be accountable for.[1]

Since the reader is left with the impression that Philopirio will be able to cure Misomedon when all other doctors have failed, the book might easily be construed as a piece of advertising. Mandeville is quite unrepentant about this: 'If a Regular

[1] *Treatise of the Hypochondriack and Hysterick Passions*, 1711, p. xi.

Physician writing of a Distemper, the Cure of which he particularly professes, after a manner never attempted yet, be a *Quack*, because, besides his Design of being instructive and doing good to others, he has likewise an aim of making himself more known by it than he was before, then I am one.'[2] And, as a final piece of defiance: 'neither would I have scrupl'd to direct the Reader to my Habitation, if I made my constant abode in the City; but as I live with my Family out of Town, instead of dating this Epistle from my own House, I shall refer him to the Booksellers and Printer, named at the bottom of the Title-Page, from whom any one may always learn where to find me.'[3] (In the second edition he gives an address in Westminster; in the third edition he omits the passage altogether.)

Misomedon, as his name indicates, has, through long and painful experience, come to dislike doctors and their medicines. The preface to the 1730 edition includes a sketch of his character. Originally gay, friendly, and even-tempered, his illness has made him peevish, fickle, censorious, and mistrustful. He is biased, captious, and given to satire. This is obviously very convenient for Mandeville, who, having cautioned the reader that he is not to be held responsible for Misomedon's opinions, can proceed, at the expense of his colleagues, to indulge his taste for ridicule. It is hardly surprising that Misomedon's temper has been soured, since he has been afflicted with hypochondria in almost all of its many forms: necessarily, since his fellow sufferers are to be assured that they are bound to find their own symptoms somewhere in the book.

Misomedon, however, could hardly be expected to suffer from the feminine form of the disease, hysteria or the vapours. Consequently, a third character is introduced, his wife Polytheca, who has also lost her former gaiety and sprightliness, and can now talk of nothing but her ailments. Unlike her husband, she believes in physic, and is constantly swallowing pills and potions (or, as she would be more likely to say, boluses and electuaries). Since hysteria affects young girls and mature women differently, the couple have a suffering daughter, who does not actually appear but whose symptoms are described to Philopirio by her parents.

Misomedon, the preface tells us, is a man of some learning who

[2] Ibid., p. xiii.
[3] Ibid., p. xiv.

is over fond of sprinkling his conversation with Latin proverbs. Humouring his patient, Philopirio occasionally answers him in the same language. Each of the three dialogues ends with an interchange in Latin. Evidently proud of his artistry, Mandeville calls upon us to notice that Philopirio knows only the stock tags, whereas Misomedon's quotations are less trite. He often 'says things on purpose to make room for a proverb, which Philopirio never does'.[4] Clearly the novelist in Mandeville intrudes upon the doctor no less than upon the philosopher. This is most noticeable in his handling of Polytheca. Having come ostensibly to consult Philopirio about her daughter, she launches into a lengthy monologue about her own symptoms, interrupted only by her husband's snide comments on her drug-taking. It is only after fifteen pages that Philopirio is able to get a word in, and comment on her first sentence.

Mandeville's chief criticism of his medical colleagues is indicated in his choice of the name Philopirio, 'lover of experience'. They are too fond of what he calls 'hypotheses': *a priori* conjectures about the causes and the cures of disease which they do not take the trouble to test by careful observation. He makes Misomedon, indeed, go so far as to declare that the science of medicine is itself fallacious, 'and no more to be depended upon than that of Astrology'.[5] Misomedon bases this conclusion on the notorious differences of opinion among doctors, 'how various and opposite to each other their Hypotheses have been on which they have built all the rest, how precarious the best of them are, yet how strenuously they have all been defended by their several Authors',[6] and on their frequent failures to effect the cures they confidently promise. Philopirio replies that there is 'abundance of difference between the Art of Physick and the Practice of Physicians'.[7]

Some doctors, he concedes, are simply lazy and far more interested in getting patients than in curing them:

... rather than that you should spend your Time before the squallid Beds of poor Patients, and bear with the unsavoury smells of a crowded Hospital, shew your self a Scholar, write a Poem, either a good one, or a large one; Compose a *Latin* Oration, or do but Translate some-

---

[4] *Treatise*, 3rd ed., 1730, p. xv. [5] *Treatise*, 1st ed., 1711, p. 30.
[6] Ibid., p. 29. [7] Ibid., p. 37.

thing out of that Language with your Name to it. If you can do none of these, Marry into a Good Family, and your Relations will help you into Practice: Or else cringe and make your court to half a dozen noted Apothecaries, promise 'em to prescribe loads of Physick, never to forget the Melodious sound of *Bolus*, and always to make your Bills like the Chimes of the *Exchange*, ring with a *repetatur tertia quaque hora*: Nay, get but in favour with one that has great Business and yours is done. Otherwise be a rigid Party-Man, it is all one, *Whig* or *Tory*, so you are but violent enough on either side; or if you can Chat, and be a good Companion, you may Drink yourself into Practice; but if you are too dull for what I have hitherto named, and in reality good for nothing, you must say little and be civil to all the World, keep a set of Coffee Houses, observe your certain Hours, and take care you are often sent for where you are, and ask'd for where are you not; but tho' in them you are forc'd to sit idle and loiter away your time all day long, yet out of 'em always Counterfeit a Man that is in haste and wanted in a great many places; as for the rest study what *Demea* said of his Brother, to be *Clemens, placidus, nulli os laedere, arridere omnibus*; contradict no body, never open your Lips without a Smile, and give no peace to your Hat.[8]

Not all doctors are incompetent careerists on the make; but their training disposes them to confine themselves to theory:

A Young Gentleman, that understands Latin, takes his Pleasure at some University or other, for Six or Seven Years, in which having at his leisure Hours gone through the usual Stages of Logick, natural Philosophy, Anatomy, Botany and perhaps Chymistry, he learns by heart all the Distempers from Head to Foot, incident to humane Bodies, a few signs by which they are known, and distinguish'd from one another, and what Prognostication is commonly made upon every one of them, with the Method of Cure and such Remedies, as the Author he reads is pleas'd to insert and recommend.[9]

These studies, Philopirio says, are necessary for beginners, 'but they only make up the Easie, the Pleasant, the Speculative part of Physick'. Real medical skill can only be gained by practice: which means 'an almost everlasting attendance on the Sick, unwearied Patience, and Judicious as well as Diligent Observation'.[10] The temptation is to suppose that the pleasant and easy part will do as a substitute for the tedious and difficult one;

[8] Ibid., pp. 36–7.
[9] Ibid., p. 31.
[10] Ibid., p. 32.

especially as a successful practice may be built up in this way, as well as by the dodges already described.

As the World grows wiser, Physicians of later times have found out more Compendious ways to Renown and Riches: By applying themselves particularly to Anatomy, Chymistry, etc., and writing of, or performing something with accuracy in any one of the shallow auxiliary Arts, that all together Compose the Theory of Physick, they know how to insinuate themselves into the publick Favour; and from their giving proofs of their understanding one inconsiderable branch of their Art, are stupidly believ'd to be equally skill'd in the whole. The great Anatomist that Artfully Dissects the Dead Body of a Malefactor shall be trusted with the live one of the Judge, till he has fitted it for his purpose. The witty Philosopher who can so exactly tell you, which way the World was made, that one would think he must have had a hand in it, Cures all Diseases by Hypothesis, frightens away the Gout with a fine Simile, but oftner reasons a trifling Distemper into a Consumption. But says the Botanist, *non verbis sed herbis*: He that by the colour and shape of Seeds can foretell what Leaves and Flowers the Plants will produce is no small Physician, and must have a great insight into the Seeds of Diseases: Being so well acquainted with the Virtues of all the Simples, he knows, without doubt, what will Cure you, if God has created it. The boasting Chymist values himself above the rest, since by the force of Fire (he'll tell you) and his *Menstruum* he exalts the Minerals to a higher pitch of perfection than their Soil or Climate could ever have rais'd them, and, despising the efficacy of Simples, puts Nature herself upon the rack to make her confess, what Medicines she has within her.[11]

What is needed is the collection and collation, in minute detail, of the symptoms and progress of a very large number of patients. This will be more practicable if, as far as possible, doctors specialize, each confining himself to one disease. Hypotheses are to be avoided.

Misom. . . . . You are without doubt acquainted with all the Hypotheses of Note, and so am I. Wherefore, that I may understand you the better, I beg to know before-hand, whose it is you go by in the explication of *Hypochondriacism*, or else whether you have a peculiar one of your own.
Phil. Indeed, *Misomedon*, I don't make use of any.
Misom. How is that possible? Which way can you reason about the Causes and Seat of the Distemper, or so much as solve the least of the Symptoms that attend it?

---

[11] *Treatise*, 1st ed. pp. 33–4.

Phil. I don't pretend to reason about either the one or the other; nor did I ever strive to solve any of its Symptoms, otherwise than by removing them.
Misom. Would ever Man of Learning offer to cure Distempers of that complicated difficulty as the Hypochondriack Passion immethodically after the manner of Ignorant Quacks! . . . What! are you an *Empyrick*?[12]

Philopirio admits that he is, adding that the classical empirics were no doubt maligned when they were said to dispense with all generalizations, since without generalizations observation would be of no use. *A posteriori* reasoning, which attempts to find an explanation for a cure which has been found to work, can do no harm, and may help us to understand what is going on. What he objects to is *a priori* reasoning from a speculative theory about the nature of the body to a treatment which it is assumed must work. For example, if the doctrine of the four humours is erroneous, as it may well be, the practice of prescribing a separate purge for each humour is useless.[13]

When Misomedon reads a passage from Thomas Willis (Oxford professor, physician to Charles II, pioneer of experimental medicine, brother-in-law of the antipathetic Dr. Fell of the rhyme) in which the body is compared to a still, the brain being the 'little Head or Glass Alembick with a Spunge laid upon it', the spleen the vessel which draws off the dregs, and so on, Philopirio comments:

These *Similes*, I confess, are very diverting for People that have nothing else to do: In some of our Modern Hypotheses there is as much Wit to be discover'd as in a tollerable Play, and the Contrivance of them costs as much Labour; what Pity it is they won't cure Sick People.
Misom. Is it not very natural? What d'ye think of it?
Phil. Yes, it is very natural, and what I think of it I'll tell you. You have seen without doubt a pretty *Simile*, between a yielding Mistress and a green Faggot that's laid upon the Fire; the weeping, and crackling in the Flame of both is a happy thought; and so are the Spunge of the Brain, and the Nerves for Snouts in the Alembick of *Willis*; but sure no mortal would lay any stress upon, or look for any real application in either.[14]

The truth is that we just don't know enough yet for our hypotheses to be very fruitful.

[12] Ibid., pp. 47-8.   [13] Ibid., p. 79.   [14] Ibid., pp. 86-7.

We are altogether in the Dark as to the real use the Liver, the Milt, and the Pancreas are of to our Bodies; nay, wholly ignorant of their several Offices otherwise than that they are *Organa Colatoria*, through which something is strain'd, and all that has been said of them besides by the most sagacious Men has been nothing but Conjectures, in which the best Anatomists could yet never agree . . .[15] There are no doubt certain Rules in Nature why a Horse comes to his full growth always in Six Years, and a Man hardly in One and Twenty. If we could undress Nature, and penetrate into the first Elements of her we might perhaps give reasons for those things but before we can do that I shall always laugh at the Ignorance and Vanity of those that pretend to it.[16]

How can this ignorance be dissipated? The proper method, Mandeville, tells us, is the one followed by the astronomers, who first 'observe diligently the *Phaenomena* of the Celestial Bodies, from thence afterwards they ascend into Theories exactly delineated after a Geometrical manner'.[17] By this means they are able to foretell the movements of the heavenly bodies with great accuracy. This is, Mandeville thinks, encouraging for physicians. A man ignorant of both astronomy and medicine who spent twenty years simply observing the sick and the stars 'would not believe the Knowledge that could be got by observing the different motions of the Celestial Bodies more capable of ever being reduced to an Art of Rules and Certainty, than that which might be acquired by likewise observing the various courses of Distempers incident in our Terrestrial ones'.[18]

Mandeville distinguishes here between 'rules' and 'hypotheses'. Like some modern statisticians, he seems suspicious of anything that goes beyond the quantification and analysis of the data and extrapolation from them. Astronomers, he tells us, 'have among them several Systems of the Heavens, as that of *Ptolomey*, *Copernicus*, *Tycho Brahe*, etc., that contradict and clash with one another',[19] yet they do not differ in their forecasts of eclipses and the like.

Phil. . . . from this Instance of Astronomy it is evident, that the same *Phaenomena* exactly answer to different Hypotheses, of which at best only one can be true.
Misom. But I think this is rather against you; for that all Astronomers of what Hypothesis soever agree in their Calculations shews that not to be mistaken it is sufficient to have one, that explains the *Phaenomena*.

---

[15] *Treatise*, 1st ed., 1711, pp. 103–4.   [16] Ibid., pp. 140–1.
[17] Ibid., p. 109.   [18] Ibid., p. 111.   [19] Ibid., p. 109.

Phil. So it is, as long as they don't reason from what they suppose, and then any one may serve; for from their not erring it is manifest that they conclude nothing but from their Observations by Rules as certain; whilst the Hypotheses only make a shew and are wholly insignificant.[20]

Consistently with this view, Mandeville makes fun of the controversies of scientists and philosophers, while at the same time giving an account of the history of science that is not entirely unlike Thomas Kuhn's in *The Structure of Scientific Revolutions*:

An Hypothesis when once it is establish'd a little time becomes like a Sovereign, and receives the same homage and respect from its Vassals, as if it was Truth it self: This continues till Experience or Envy discovers a flaw in it.

Yet unless it be a great Man indeed, that finds fault first, his discovery is only answered with contempt for a while: But when another Hypothesis is broach'd (which is commonly soon after) that not having the fault of the former, and being likewise well contriv'd, gets a considerable number of followers; Then you see all that fought under the banners of the old Hypothesis bristle up, and every Man of Note among them thinks himself personally injured, and in honour obliged to stand by it with his Life and Fortune. Now all Arts and Sciences are ransack'd, and whatever can be drawn from Wit, Eloquence, or Learning, is produced to maintain their own Leige Hypothesis, and destroy the upstart one, and the whole Party is alarm'd with as much concern as they are in a Man of War, when they have receiv'd a Shot under Water: In the mean time they that have listed themselves into the new Hypothesis are not idle, and thus both Parties enter into a perfect state of War; the better sort fighting with Arguments, the rest with personal Reflections. This Play is generally continued for a considerable time with a great deal of violence; and I have observ'd as much hatred and animosity between the *Aristotelians* and *Cartesians*, when I was at *Leiden*, as there is now in *London* between *High* Church and *Low*-Church.[21]

It is also consistent with it, however, that when Misomedon, momentarily won over to this pragmatist position, is reminded of an occasion when his son had the smallpox and was cured by a nurse with long experience of the disease, after a doctor had bungled the case, he gets this reply:

Phil. I should be loth to trust one with the Curing of Distempers no better qualified than this Nurse: What I said of Prognosticks, I meant

---

[20] Ibid., pp. 111–12.   [21] Ibid., pp. 114–15.

of Physicians, of whom we cannot suppose, but if they had made Judicious Observations as long as Nurse had made hers at random, they would in that time have likewise got a vast Experience of the *Juvantia* and *Laedentia* in that distemper; especially, if they had had the skill in the *Materia Medica*, that is required in the meanest Practitioners.[22]

When Misomedon suggests that his practice amounts to using medicines 'at random only because they have often done good', accuses him of saying that doctors 'must not rely upon anything, but what is within the reach of their outward Senses, and never make use of, or at least trust to their Reason', and asks him, how, in that case, a doctor differs from a good nurse, Philopirio answers:

... I would not make a step without Reason ... I would not have you think, that I speak of that lofty self-sufficient Reason that boldly trusts to its own Wings, and leaving Experience far behind mounts upon Air, and makes Conclusions in the Skies; what I make use of is plain and humble, not only built upon, but likewise surrounded with, and every way limited by Observation, from view of which it never cares to stir.[23]

At the same time Mandeville notices that it is often possible, as a result of repeated observations over a period of years, to arrive at conclusions without being able to give reasons for them: for instance one may be able to tell a copy of a van Dyck from an original without being able to state what criteria one applies;[24] or a quite unintelligent shepherd may, in the same way, be able to distinguish one sheep from another with perfect ease, where 'a Witty Man, proud of his Parts, that has always lived in the City'[25] will be quite at a loss, even if he spends two or three months in examining the flock. This would seem to support what Misomedon says about the nurse; but in general reason and knowledge are needed to guide observation and to detect, in the mass of data, the principle which will enable one to make predictions.

In fact, of course, the book contains a good many examples of reasoning about observed data, and about the way in which hypotheses may be tested by observation. To give just one, Willis's theory, that hypochondria is the result of some deficiency

---

[22] *Treatise*, 1st ed., 1711, p. 66.
[23] Ibid., pp. 118-19.
[24] Ibid., p. 53.
[25] Ibid., p. 68.

in the spleen, is criticized because it fits some of the facts, but not all of them:

> Then what will they say of all the Dogs that have had their Milts cut out; as *Diemerbrock, Etmullers* with Fifty more, and I myself have seen more than once, that Eat as voraciously, digested as well, and as far as I could see, were as sensible Dogs as their Neighbours? Does not one such an instance destroy their whole Fabrick? But not to insist upon this, and make it appear what Cobweb reasons they depend upon; let us mind the Observations themselves, and the Consequences they draw from them. The hinge of the whole turns upon the Spleen's not performing its Office in Children nor soft-headed People; because in them it looks Red, and not Livid, as it does in Men of sharp Sense. As to Children, I know their Observation is very true: But neither the Liver, the Kidneys, nor any of the other *Viscera*, nor the Muscles, the Flesh it self, are of so deep a colour in no Animals, when they are Young, as when they are come to their full growth: Would they conclude from this likewise, that they did not perform their Office? But that the same redness of Spleen is always to be found in slothful soft-headed People I doubt much: At least I don't believe that they have observ'd it often enough, to lay so much stress upon it: But, as I am not able to contradict them, I must allow whatever they can make of it. The next, I shall enquire into, is what we are to understand by the Spleen's but little performing its Office: In order to which we'll divide the Functions of it in two parts; the one, to receive the Dregs from the Blood, and the other to Volatilize them into a Ferment, to quicken and enliven the Blood. If the Spleen in those instances of its redness performs neither of the two Functions, then what becomes of the Dregs of the Blood? Which way does the Blood get rid of them? And where are they laid up during the Nonage of the Spleen? But if it receives the Dregs, and is only deficient in volatilizing them into a Ferment, and sending it away into the Blood, then it ought to be more livid in them than in adult and witty People; because it keeps all the Dregs: Besides, that, when the Spleen would be stuff'd with *Faeces*, and no more able to receive the Recrements of the Blood, which should be forced to flow back into the Neighbouring branches of the *Caeliack* Artery, etc., this would produce the same Distempers, which according to the Hypothesis and *Willis's* own words must follow in all Stoppages of the Spleen.[26]

The disastrous results of allowing one's hypotheses to dictate one's method of treatment are illustrated by Misomedon's

[26] Ibid., pp. 96-8.

experiences with the profession before he has the good luck to consult Philopirio.

Misomedon, it should be realized, is not merely a valetudinarian, suffering from an imaginary illness. The primary meaning of the word 'hypochondria' is, according to the *Oxford English Dictionary*, 'those parts of the human abdomen which lie immediately under the ribs and each side of the epigastric region; (b) the viscera situated in the hypochondria; the liver, gall-bladder, spleen, etc., formerly supposed to be the seat of melancholy and "vapours" '. The Dictionary also gives, as a further meaning: '2. A morbid state of mind, characterized by general depression, melancholy or low spirits, for which there is no real cause'. As Mandeville uses the term hypochondria, the disease seems to be thought of as a disorder of the hypochondria in sense 1, and to be a fairly specific complaint (though characterized by a wide variety of symptoms) with a definite physical cause, even though it might not be known. The Oxford Dictionary also records that Sir John Hill gave his treatise on 'the disorder commonly called the Hyp and Hypo', published in 1766, the title *Hypochondriasis*, which the Dictionary defines as 'a disease of the nervous system, generally accompanied by indigestion, but chiefly characterized by the patient's unfounded belief that he is suffering from some serious bodily disease'. That would seem to fit Misomedon's case fairly well.

Certainly he suffers from indigestion, in the form of heartburn, wind, and 'sowre Belches': these are his earliest symptoms. Later he has gnawing pains, a distended stomach, 'pricking and sometimes shooting pains in my Bowels' and 'strange torments in my Back and Belly', constipation, haemorrhoids, headaches and vertigo, a ringing in his ears and a mist before his eyes. Not all his symptoms are physical: 'strange roving thoughts would slide through my Brain, and wild as well as ridiculous Fancies stole upon me, and for a while employ'd my Imagination. I had often unaccountable apprehensions of things, which, tho' one moment I thought 'em absurd, I could hardly conquer the next with all my strength of Reason.'[27] He has nightmares, from which he wakes 'in fright, and often in cold Sweats'. And, although he knows it to be impossible, he develops an irrational fear that he has the pox.

While the symptoms are still relatively mild, he seeks advice.

[27] *Treatise*, 1st ed., 1711, pp. 23–4.

The first doctor he goes to, 'an eminent physician of great learning', believes that it is heat that enables the stomach to digest food, the spleen being 'to the Stomach as a Furnace to a Copper'. Misomedon's trouble is that somehow his liver has got heated instead of his stomach, which is cold. Fortunately a single remedy, bleeding, will rectify both conditions: 'the Fountain of heat, the Blood, of which my Liver had too much, would . . . be drawn from the Right side . . . and would procure heat to that side where the motion was made', the vein to be opened having, according to Galen, a peculiar effect on the spleen.[28] He is also to take a purge, containing violets and bugloss to cool the liver, and citron-peel, ginger, and fennel seeds to warm the stomach, and he is to spend two or three weeks drinking the waters at Epsom.

The next Day I sent for the Surgeon and Apothecary both and according to Prescription in Eight Days I was copiously Blooded twice, and Purged four times: It is true that by this time I had lost my Heart-burning, and sowreness I complained of in my Stomach; but instead of it I had a pain in it, which I had never felt before: I was as much troubled with Wind in my Bowels as ever, and so Weak and Faint that I could hardly crawl along.[29]

He drinks the Epsom waters, and is made even worse, with sharper pains, and 'a violent Looseness' which makes him 'so feeble and dispirited that I could keep up no longer, and was ready to swoon away'. A doctor at the spa only gives him another purge. Finally he is given relief by 'an honest Gentleman, that Lodged in the same House as I did', who makes him drink mulled claret, 'burnt with good store of Cinnamon, Cloves and Mace, and a pretty deal of Orange-Peel; whilst this was a-boiling he sent for some Syrup of Quinces to sweeten it, and when it was ready made me take half a Pint of it, with a very brown Toast well rubb'd with Nutmeg, and sup it off as hot as I was able.'[30] This remedy soon takes effect, and 'by the help of a wholesome and nourishing Diet, gentle Exercise, and the moderate use of the best Claret I could buy, I found myself perfectly well in a little time, tho' I never again recover'd that Strength and Vigour, which before the unmerciful Bleeding and Purging I had been possess'd of.'[31]

This experience leaves him 'as much afraid of Physick, as a Child of being whipt';[32] but some two years later, 'the Grumbling

[28] Ibid., p. 9. [29] Ibid., p. 11. [30] Ibid., p. 13.
[31] Ibid., pp. 13–14. [32] Ibid., p. 14.

in my Bowels' having returned, his wife persuades him to consult another doctor, 'one of the most Noted Physicians about Town.' This man, unlike the first, is a modern: he pooh-poohs the cold stomach and the hot liver: '*Subterfugia,* as he called them, *ignorantiae,* Figments, that never had any existence, but in the Brains of the Inventors; good for nothing, but to shew the small Knowledge they had in Anatomy: As to Galen himself ... he never had seen a Human Body open'd in his Life.'[33] He believes that digestion is not caused by heat, but by a 'Menstruum, or Ferment' in the stomach, which acts, 'not by any *Muscular* or other *Organick* Force, but an *Intestine* motion not unlike that of Yeast or Leaven in Dough'.[34] He prescribes emetics, to be followed by alkaline preparations 'to subdue the fix'd *Acid Salts*'. This treatment is effective at first, but the symptoms return as soon as Misomedon stops taking the medicines. After a while they cease to have any effect. Unable to do more, the doctor, 'tho' in less than a Twelve Month he had received above an Hundred *Guineas* in Fees of me; which in a *Chronick* Disease, where the same Remedies are for some time continued, and no constant Attendance is required, is pretty Considerable',[35] avoids Misomedon as much as he can, and finally makes an excuse to get rid of him.

And so it goes on, with Misomedon's ailments steadily getting worse, with new and more distressing symptoms constantly appearing, and none of the doctors he calls in able to do more than give him occasional Temporary relief, so that he decides that the art of medicine is a delusion. His first words to Philopirio are: 'I have sent for you, Doctor, to consult you about a Distemper, of which I am very well assured, I shall never be Cured'.[36] and he goes on: 'You think, perhaps, I'm a Mad-Man, to send for a Physician, when I know before-hand, that he can do me no good: Truly, Doctor, I am not far from it.'[37]

Philopirio himself is not without his hypotheses, but he entertains them tentatively, and with scepticism, and never allows them to dictate his treatment, which has been arrived at, we can only suppose, by cautious trial and error.

Phil. . . . let us first examine, what all along has been believ'd to be the cause of the *Hypochondriack* Passion: The generality of the Ancients

---

[33] *Treatise,* 1st ed., 1711, pp. 14–15.   [34] Ibid., p. 16.
[35] Ibid., pp. 17–18.   [36] Ibid., p. 1.   [37] Ibid., p. 2.

accused the Spleen, but no otherwise, than as it was the Office of their *Atra bilis*, or Melancholy; except *Diocles*, who would have it, that in this Distemper part of the *Ventricle* was inflamed: But as these Opinions are not much insisted upon, we'll spend no time about them.

Some of the Modern would lay all the fault upon the *Meseraick* Vessels, others again blame nothing but the empty space, that is under the Diaphragm between the Stomach and the Spleen; as the most proper Nursery, as well as Receptacle for the many Winds that always infest the *Hypochondriack* Patients. . . .[38]

What I think most suitable to the Observations I have made, and consequently most probable, is the Opinion of those that, absolving the Spleen, Meseraick Vessels, Bilious, and Pancreatick Juice, etc. throw all the fault upon the Stomach.

Misom. Now you surprise me again: For how can you approve of no Hypothesis, and yet think them in the right, that suppose the fault to be in the Stomach?

Phil. Let me explain my self: I may know one to be an ill Man, and yet have reason not to believe some Crimes that are laid to his charge: So here, by what I know from Observation, it is demonstrable to me, that the cause of Hypochondriack and Histerick Diseases is in the Stomach, and yet I am not satisfied with what is said about it by others, when they begin to particularize, tho' they are of the same Opinion as to the *Viscus* to be blamed.[39]

Philopirio's theory has to do with the animal spirits, the contemporary term for whatever modern physiologists are talking about when they speak of 'impulses' from the brain, except that they were thought of as 'exquisitely small Particles that are the *Internuncii* between them [soul and body] by the help of which they manifest themselves to each other'.[40] Philopirio paints a highly coloured picture of what may happen when we are trying to recall something:

. . . how nimbly those volatil Messengers of ours will beat through all the Paths, and hunt every Enclosure of the Organ set aside for thinking, in quest of the Images we want, and when we have forgot a Word or Sentence, which yet we are sure the great Treasury of Images received, our Memory, has once been charged with, we may almost feel how some of the Spirits flying through all the *Mazes* and *Meanders* rummage the whole substance of the Brain: whilst others secret themselves into the inmost recesses of it with so much eagerness and labour, that the difficulty they meet with some times makes us uneasie, and

---

[38] Ibid., p. 78.   [39] Ibid., pp. 81–2.   [40] Ibid., p. 125.

they often bewilder themselves in their search, till at last they light by chance on the Image that contains what they look'd for, or else dragging it, as it were, by piece-meals from the dark Caverns of oblivion, represent what they can find to our Imagination.[41]

This account, though deliberately fanciful, is not very different from the one suggested to the mind by those modern writers who, with the computer in mind, use the metaphor of scanning. The dialogue continues:

Misom. I hope you'll conclude nothing from this Volatile Oeconomy of the Brain, of your own making.
Phil. I don't intend it, and only hinted at the most exquisite Functions of the Spirits, that the nicety of the performance and the swiftness of the Execution might convince you of the transcendent subtilty of those airy velocious Agents, the chief and immediate Ministers of Thought; that officiating between the Soul and the grosser Spirits of the Senses have always access to her invisible self.[42]

There are, then, different kinds of animal spirits, of varying degrees of fineness: we must suppose the most ethereal of them to be concerned with thinking. Philopirio's (and presumably Mandeville's) hypothesis is that these finer spirits are also responsible for digestion, that, 'trickling down into the Stomach through the innumerable little Nerves, that discharge themselves there', they make up at least a large part of the 'Stomachic ferment, *Menstruum*, or what you please to call it'.[43] His evidence for this is that thinking seems to have a direct and immediate effect on the stomach: 'when we see, or hear others Discourse of things that are nasty, and we abhor, the very thinking on them shall make us nauseate, and cause some People to Vomit, that are of a delicate contexture';[44] and bad news will take away the appetite. Rather less obviously, the connection between stomach and brain is shown by the fact that people with abnormal cravings seem able to digest all sorts of weird food, even when their digestions are normally weak: a little of what we fancy does us good.[45] Mandeville adds that only the stomach and the genitals are so directly and dramatically affected by mere thoughts, 'as if Nature, by the extraordinary commerce she has contriv'd between the Soul, and those parts, would shew us that they are the most

[41] *Treatise*, 1st ed., 1711, pp. 130–1.   [42] Ibid., p. 131.
[43] Ibid., p. 123.   [44] Ibid., p. 131.   [45] Ibid., pp. 122–3.

noble of the whole Body; the latter being as necessary to continue the whole Species, as the first is to preserve every individual Person'.[46]

In the 1730 edition Mandeville makes the point that his argument does not depend on his conjectures about the animal spirits: 'I am convinced that there is such a Communication and Agreement, such an extraordinary Consensus between Brain and Stomach, without entring into any Hypothesis, what Instrument this is perform'd by.'[47]

One consequence of this consensus is that hypochondriacs are usually highly intelligent. If we invoke the hypothesis, we may suppose that the close thinking they indulge in exhausts the available supply of the finer animal spirits, so that there is not enough left for the stomach to perform its function adequately. A similar scarcity may be caused by excessive use of the other noble part of the body. If he had cared to, Mandeville might have appealed here to the authority of Bacon (not to mention Shakespeare's hundred and twenty-ninth sonnet). Bacon tells us: 'It hath been observed by the ancients that much use of Venus doth dim the sight: and yet eunuchs, which are unable to generate, are nevertheless also dim-sighted. The cause of dimness of sight in the former is, an expense of spirits; in the latter, the over-moisture of the brain; for the over-moisture of the brain doth thicken the spirits visual, and obstructeth their passages.'[48] For Mandeville, of course, it was not 'the visual spirits', the particles concerned in sight, that were expended by lust, but the finer ones needed for the brain and the stomach. But he shares Bacon's assumption that the thickness or coarseness of the animal spirits will impede their passage to and fro. That is why the finer ones are needed for thinking, though the coarser ones may be adequate for gross muscular movements.

Consequently exercise, since it wastes only the coarser spirits and leaves the finer ones unimpared, actually aids digestion.

Philopirio now explains the course of Misomedon's illness by referring back to his account of the story of his life. As a very young man he had been dissolute, but, marrying at twenty-five,

---

[46] Ibid., pp. 132–3.
[47] *Treatise*, 3rd ed., 1730, p. 162.
[48] Sir Francis Bacon, *Sylva Sylvarum*, VII. 693. In *Works*, ed. James Spedding, 1863, vol. 4, p. 468.

'was soon reclaim'd from my former Vices: Love and Pastime was all our Employment, from Morning till Night; we study'd nothing, but how to please and divert one another.'⁴⁹ Philopirio points out that lawful pleasures have the same physical effect as unlawful ones: the expense of spirit may occur without the waste of shame. Both these episodes in Misomedon's life, then, helped to lay the foundation for his illness. This disclosure inspires some edifying reflections:

Misom. I have long suspected that Cause which you now mention, and can but Smile at the Comical way we have of digging our own Graves. The Hectick Fire of Conjugal Love is without doubt no less consuming, tho' more slow than the more raging blasts of Ignominious Name, and the fond Passion, tho' it is pernicious to every Condition of Life, is yet most mischievous to the Married State, because in that it has a double bait, and the soothing our Thoughts with the Lawfulness of the act is no less inticing to destruction than the Pleasure it self. Oh! how sollicitous is prudent Nature to maintain her self in the Successive revolutions of every Species! how strangely are the most Rational Animals imposed upon to their own undoing by that *Hyaena*, Love, so as to believe it the only Sweet for which Life is valuable, notwithstanding the innumerable Calamities, Diseases and Deaths they see it has brought upon others? Is it comprehensible which way that Sagacious Creature Man should be guilty of so much Folly, as with the best and most Balsamick parts of his Arterial Blood daily to feed an insatiable Monster, and suffer it luxuriously to draw the Marrow from his Bones, and Vital Strength from every part less solid, till by its destructive breath he is quite enervated, and his Constitution devour'd? *Phil*. You speak with the Zeal and Wisdom of Fifty Five; but what Pity it is we should never be saving before our Stock is spent! ... There is a Season in which we cannot believe, that the Spirits, squander'd away in *Venereal* Pleasures, cannot be restor'd, and the Losses that were sustain'd are irretrievable.⁵⁰

For the young Misomedon the delights of the married state seemed likely to be spoiled by lack of money; but, just as he was down to his last thirty pounds, and in debt for about three hundred, a distant relative died, leaving him 'a Thousand a Year in Land, and a good Estate in Money. . . . I could not look without horror on the dismal prospect of Poverty and Want, to which I must in a very little time inevitably have been reduced, had not propitious Fortune, as it were by a Miracle, so unexpec-

⁴⁹ *Treatise*, 1st ed., 1711, p. 4. ⁵⁰ Ibid., pp. 144–5.

tedly snatch'd me from the frightful Precipice.'[51] The bequest included a well-stocked library, which led Misomedon to become 'a great lover of Reading, and by degrees fell to hard Study; but notwithstanding that I was very intent on my Books, I still remain'd, as I had always been, *rei Uxoriae addictissimus*, and divided my Hours *inter Venerem et Musas*.'[52] It is after this that his first symptoms appear, Venus and the Muses being the two great consumers of those finer animal spirits also required for digestion. Even his rescue from poverty is not as providential as it seemed.

Phil. ... Immoderate Griefs, Cares, Troubles and Disappointments are likewise often Concomitant Causes of their Disease; but most commonly in such, as either by Estate, Benefices or Employments have a sufficient Revenue to make themselves easie: Men that are already provided for, or else have a Livelyhood by their Callings amply secured, are never exempt from Sollicitudes, and the keeping not only of Riches, but even moderate Possessions is always attended with Care. Those that enjoy 'em are more at leisure to reflect, besides that their Wishes and Desires being larger, themselves are more likely to be offended at a great many passages of Life, than People of lower Fortunes, who have seldom higher Ends, than what they are continually employ'd about, the getting of their Daily Bread; which if they accomplish to satisfaction, they are commonly pleas'd and happy, because they think themselves so; if not, they labour under such a variety of Necessities, and are so diverted with their present Circumstances, that they have not time stedfastly to think of one thing, and consequently the vexations of the Mind have not so great an influence over them ... Give me leave to observe, that if you had been reduced to the Want that threatened you and forced to maintain your Family, either by Copying, Hackney-Writing, or some other miserable shift, where you must have work'd *de pane ad panem*, and always lived from Hand to Mouth, I am of Opinion, that your Distemper (if it had ever troubled you at all) would neither so soon, nor so severely have attack'd you.[53]

However, he was attacked; and the attack was made much worse by the treatment of 'your Learned *Galenist*', whose violent bleedings and evacuations, 'quite destroying the Tone of your Blood and Spirits compleated their ruine'.[54]

Misomedon raises an objection to the theory that thinking is one cause of the disease. He points out that everybody is thinking

[51] Ibid., p. 5.   [52] Ibid., p. 6.   [53] Ibid., pp. 150-1.   [54] Ibid., p. 146.

all the time: why, then, should some kinds of thought use up the animal spirits more quickly than others? Philopirio agrees that thinking never ceases, even in sleep; even our dreams 'depend immediately upon the Tone and Contexture of the Spirits'. But in sleep 'the Spirits, not administering any Images to the Soul from the outward Senses, are only wandring at leisure about the Images that are within'.[55] He goes on:

... as Thinking consists in a various Disposition of the Images received; so what we call Wit is nothing but *an aptitude of the Spirits by which they nimbly turn to, and dexterously dispose the Images that may serve our purpose*. From hence it follows, that if witty Men and Blockheads spend the same time in Thinking, the first must in all likelyhood waste the most Spirits: Nay, it is unreasonable to suppose, that the slow and heavy Thinking of a Drowsie Thick-Skull'd Fellow, should require as much Agility and Workmanship of the Spirits as the quick and sprightly Thoughts of a clear-headed, Ingenious Man; and to me it seems highly probable, that there is no more action or greater labour perform'd in the Brain of the first, when he is as broad awake as he can be, than there is in that of the latter, when he is half a Sleep.[56]

Why, then, asks Misomedon, are women subject to the same disorder in the slightly different form of hysteria? 'For studying and intense thinking are not to be alledged as a cause in Women, whom we know (at least for the generality of them) to be so little guilty of it; and yet the number of Hysterick Women far exceeds that of Hypochondriack Men. What is it that so much consumes the Spirits of Girls of Eighteen, Sixteen, nay, Fourteen and Younger?'[57]

Philopirio replies that there are two causes of a deficiency in animal spirits: they may be wasted by intellectual or other excesses, or there may simply never have been enough of them in the first place. The second is the cause of hysteria in young girls. In them the manufacture of the animal spirits has been affected by 'the depauperation of the blood' resulting from agues, greensickness, and the like, which are in turn caused by 'very gross Errors in Diet'.[58] With some dialectical acuteness, Misomedon asks whether this is not inconsistent with what Philopirio has said earlier about our being able to digest the food we fancy. The answer he is given is that there is a great difference between a

[55] *Treatise*, 1st ed., 1711, p. 160. [56] Ibid., pp. 164-5.
[57] Ibid., p. 166.   [58] Ibid., p. 167.

genuine craving and 'the fanciful hankering after Trash, generally observ'd in Green sick Girls; of whom it cannot be so properly said, that they long for what they eat, as that by degrees they have brought themselves to like what first was indifferent to them and they only tasted out of wantonness'.[59]

Apart from errors in diet, women are also disposed to the disorder by 'their idle Life, and want of Exercise'.[60] Moreover, the spirits may be defective in quality, as well as in quantity. Women's bodies are in general less robust than men's, though made of finer material:

Their immortal substance is without doubt the same with ours, and it is only the Body in which we differ: We are of a stronger, but they of a more Elegant composure, and Beauty is their attribute, as Strength is ours: Their frame tho' less firm is more delicate, and themselves more capable both of Pleasure and of Pain, tho' endued with less constancy of bearing the excess of either. This delicacy as well as imbecillity of the Spirits in Women is Conspicuous in all their actions, those of the Brain not excepted: They are unfit both for abstruse and elaborate Thoughts, all studies of Depth, Coherence, and Solidity that fatigue the Spirits, and require a steadiness and assiduity of thinking; but where the Advantages of Education and Knowledge are equal, they exceed the Men in Sprightliness of Fancy, quickness of Thought and off-hand Wit; as much as they out-do them in sweetness of Voice, and Volubility of Tongue.[61]

The 'tone and elasticity', then, of the animal spirits are weaker in women than in men, with the result that in women the spirits are more easily exhausted. It is when there are not enough of them, or not enough of an adequate quality for the brain to function properly, that women fall into fainting fits, or fits of other kinds. There are two types of hysteric: those who are in a chronic state of indigestion as well as being subject to swoons, fits, and the like, and those who are normally in good health, but who 'are thrown into Convulsive Fits' by 'some accident of Grief, Passion, Surprise, immoderate drinking, etc.'[62] All women are 'more or less liable to become Hystericks of the second Class',[63] and so are children. This is simply the result of the weakness ('imbecillity') of the spirits. In hysterics of the first class the spirits have, in addition, been wasted in some way, and this occurs much more easily

[59] Ibid., p. 168. [60] Ibid., p. 172. [61] Ibid., pp. 174-5.
[62] Ibid., pp. 175-6. [63] Ibid., p. 178.

in women than in men: 'One Hours intense Thinking wastes the spirits more in a Woman, than six in a Man.'[64]

Nothing is said about the other activity that wastes the spirits. Indeed, Mandeville seems to assume, perhaps inconsistently, that one cause of hysteria in young girls is sexual repression. When Philopirio prescribes exercises for Misomedon's hysteric seventeen-year-old daughter:

Misom. But might not Marriage be as effectual as all these Exercises?
Phil. Yes, but I never prescribe an uncertain Remedy, that may prove worse than the Disease.[65]

The modern, or post-Freud, reader may be tempted to read more into this than was meant: though, remembering what is said in *The Virgin Unmask'd* about the desires and behaviour of adolescent girls, it would not be surprising to find Mandeville attributing hysteria to the psychological effect of enforced chastity. From what follows, however, it seems that he has in mind some alleged physical benefit to be derived from intercourse:

I know everything that can be said of the *Venereal* Ferment, the power it has over all the Fluids, and the means that can most effectually raise it; yet from frequent Observation I can assure you, not only that the Three Exercises I mention'd are jointly of great Efficacy upon every part of the body as to enliven it, but likewise that the repeated motions of only the first, even as to the exalting of the Ferment I speak of (which perhaps seems incredible) are not much inferior to the *Amplexus Viriles* themselves. Without Marriage then you may depend upon it, these Exercises will assist and revive Nature, which in your Daughter has of late been fatigued and oppress'd with loads of Physick.[66]

The exercises referred to are swinging, horse-riding, and massage. Swinging is the one whose effects are said to rival those of manly embraces. No attempt is made to reconcile this with what has been said earlier. We are not told whether Polytheca's vapours, like her husband's hypochondria, are partly due to 'the Hectick Fire of Conjugal Love'. Philopirio prescribes for both Polytheca and her daughter, but does not say what caused their ailments, though he remarks that they have been aggravated by the vast quantities of physic they have swallowed.

Polytheca's entry, indeed, is made the occasion of a lengthy discussion of medicines and of the apothecaries who dispense

---
[64] *Treatise*, 1st ed., 1711, p. 177.   [65] Ibid., p. 237.   [66] Ibid., pp. 238–9.

them. This was a controversial topic: apothecaries were accused by physicians of prescribing medicines as well as merely dispensing them, and the College of Physicians took legal action to stop them. The case was, however, decided against the College by the House of Lords in 1703.

Misom. . . . What she has made use of lately I can't tell; for it is above six Months ago, that my Wife, has left the whole Care and Management of her [his daughter] to her Apothecary, who I suppose won't let her want Medicines: He is a famous Man among the Ladies, for making up Things very palatable, and a great lover of keeping up the Spirits. I never yet examin'd any liquid that came from his House, but it tasted of Wine or Brandy.
Polyth. I know these Things are chargeable, and wish with all my Heart, that neither your Daughter nor my self had any occasion to put you to so much expense.
Misom. I don't speak of the Charge; neither would I grudge any thing that is necessary for the meanest Servant I keep, much less for my Wife and Children, *Polytheca*; but I think it is an odd fancy that People must have half their Diet out of the Apothecaries Shop. Can Wine or Brandy become more Cordial by being call'd Alexipharmick, or receive any Sanction by being balderdash'd with two or three sorts of Simple-Waters, that are equally insipid, tho' not half so clear, as what you may have either from the Pomp or the Sky? Or do you think that a Candied Syrup of two Years standing, because it comes out of a Galley-Pot, that has a fine Label on the outside, tho' perhaps it is Mouldy within, and cover'd with Furr of an Inch thick, is more wholesome to sweeten any thing with than double Refin'd Sugar, that won't stand you in half a quarter of the Money?[67]

One of the complaints against apothecaries is that they overcharge. No other dealers, Misomedon tells us, 'get so much Money by laying out so little';[68] and he refers Polytheca to a book by 'an Eminent Physician, Dr. *Pit*, who for the good of the Publick has shewn the vast difference between the prime Cost, that Simples are bought at from the Druggists, and Herb-Women, and the extravagant rates, they are sold at by the Apothecaries, when they have disguis'd them in mixtures of specious Titles'.[69] This was Robert Pitt (1653–1713), who wrote three books on this subject between 1702 and 1705, partly to defend the action of the College of Physicians in establishing its own dispensary. Misomedon

[67] Ibid., pp. 208–10.   [68] Ibid., p. 228.   [69] Ibid., pp. 232–3.

probably refers to the first of the three, *The Craft and Frauds of Physick Exposed*.

Apart from overcharging, apothecaries are likely to persuade the patient to take more medicine than he needs:

Phil. . . . in the first place, I would for one Month prescribe a course of Exercise, and no Medicines at all.
Polyth. A Course of Exercise! and no Medicines at all!
Misom. Yes, my Dear, a course of Exercise and no Medicines at all. I think it is very good English; tho' I confess, such Language never came from an Apothecaries Mouth, or Physicians either, that ever was twice recommended by one, and therefore I ought not to think it strange, if you don't apprehend it so readily.
Polyth. You are very pleasant, *Misomedon*. But how came the Apothecaries in? Or must you have a fling at them right or wrong? Sure there are honest Men among them, as well as there is in all other Callings.
Misom. So there may be for ought I know, tho' no People of any other Calling lie under so great a temptation of being otherwise; for if an Apothecary's business be Selling of Medicines, and you commit a Patient to his management, it is plain to me that he is left to himself to sell him as many as his Conscience will allow of, and is this not leading him into a vast Temptation? Certainly the People that trust to their advice must be either Fools, or think that the Apothecaries are *Saints*. Pray tell me what Grocer, Druggist, Linnen or Woollen Draper, Mercer, Goldsmith or other Tradesman of the most reputable Employment you can name, would you put that Confidence in, that he should sell you as much of his Commodity as he thought you wanted? It is a Trust not to be reposed in Mortals. They have a whole Shop full of Medicines, of which a great many too are in danger of being spoil'd, and would you imagine they won't dispose of them, and vent as many as they can? Ought not everybody to promote his trade?[70]

When Polytheca points out that the same temptation must assail doctors who make up their own prescriptions (as Philopirio does), Misomedon says that doctors have less opportunity: they come only when called for, whereas an apothecary is 'always making a frivolous Errand to enquire after what is his only grievance, your Health'.[71]

I have known an Apothecary in an idle Afternoon go to a Person of Quality's, where they made use of him: There happen'd to be no body at home but Children and Servants, that from the highest to the lowest

---

[70] *Treatise*, 1st ed., 1711, pp. 212–14.   [71] Ibid., p. 215.

were all in perfect Health: If here he came for Business (you'll say) he was disappointed; but you are mistaken, the Courteous Gentleman with an engaging familiarity accosts every Servant in the House, and puts off a Purge to the Cook, a Vomit to the Butler, a Box of Pills to one of the Footmen, and a Pot of *Lucatellus* Balsam to old Nurse. The Children absolutely refusing to take any Physick at least inwardly, he coaxes the little Master into the use of a charming *Dentifrice*, and a sweet-scented *Collyrium* to rinse his mouth with after it, that shall preserve his Teeth, and make them look like Ivory, tho' he was to eat nothing but Sugar and Sweet-Meats all Day long; to pretty Miss he'll send a Lotion for her Hair, and a Paste for her Hands, that shall render the one so bright as Silver, and the other whiter than Snow, with a Beauty-wash for their Maid, that assisted in the persuading of them. The affable Gentleman has every bodies good word: The Children are pleas'd, the Servants commend him, my Lady is obliged to him; and Ten to One but the first opportunity of driving that way her Coach stops at his Door, and she thanks him for the care he took of her Family in her absence.

Tell me, pray, if a Fishmonger or Poulterer should go to a Customer's House after Dinner, whence the Master and Mistress were abroad, advise the Servants, the one to a fine Salmon, the other to a Dozen of Turkey-Poults, and send them home accordingly, Would you not think them very impudent Rascals?[72]

All this is put into Misomedon's mouth. Philopirio stays discreetly silent until Polytheca appeals to him, when he gives an evasive answer. Later he defends the apothecaries against one charge, that the special jargon in which prescriptions are written has been adopted 'to conceal the meanness of the Ingredients . . . from the People that are to pay dear for them'.[73] But this, of course, tells against doctors as well; moreover, Mandeville allows Misomedon to have the last word on this issue. Philopirio has said that many patients have an irrational prejudice against some medicines. Misomedon replies that this applies to only a few: 'I would not take it amiss that they should call Old Cheese *Palaetyrus*, and Dog's Turd *Cynocropus*, because a great many People have an aversion to both; but can you say the same of Bran, or Spring-water, that the one must be called *Leptopityron*, and the other *Hydropege* . . . ?'[74] After Polytheca has left (pleading a headache) Philopirio tells Misomedon that his criticisms have been too severe. On the other hand, he says that the medicines taken by

[72] Ibid., pp. 216–17.   [73] Ibid., p. 230.   [74] Ibid., p. 231.

Polytheca and her daughter have aggravated their condition, and his reason for being his own dispenser is, at least in part, that he is able to use cheap and simple ingredients apothecaries would not think it worth their while to stock.

Mandeville is rather devious here. Misomedon shows Philopirio, as a matter of interest, the prescriptions (or 'bills', as they are called) for those medicines that have been of benefit to him at various stages of his illness. These are printed in full (though in what Misomedon calls the 'Shorthand, and Heathen Characters' used by doctors and chemists). Mandeville must have realized that to give prescriptions in full in a semi-popular treatise intended for patients was to ensure that his readers would try them. Yet what he actually says about the taking of medicines is on the whole discouraging. He contrives to have Philopirio interrupted just as he is about to give his opinion of the prescriptions:

Phil. Most of the Bills you have read are very Judiciously Writ, and the chief Ingredients of them enter all the Prescriptions that are generally recommended in your Distemper, by the most Eminent physicians of *Europe*, but the intricacy of—
Misom. With your leave, *Philopirio*, we shall break off the Discourse we are upon for a quarter of an Hour. Here my Spouse is come to give you an account of the Hysterick Case I told you of.[75]

When Polytheca leaves, and the discussion is resumed, the prescriptions have been forgotten. Philopirio is obviously no great believer in drugs and other medicines, but he does not eschew them altogether: he prescribes an emetic (which he seems to prefer to a purgative) for Misomedon, and he does not rule out the possibility of an 'Internal Medicine' (or even bleeding and cupping) for his daughter, after 'her Body [has] been freed from the force of Physick for Three or four Weeks'.[76] His main emphasis, however, is on exercise and diet; presumably this is the new cure, 'after a manner never attempted yet', that Mandeville speaks of in the preface. Misomedon is to go for a ride on 'some gentle, but merry generous Horse' every morning and evening, and for a walk before going to bed. After each ride he is to 'make use of a warm Bath, with Emollient Roots and Herbs'.[77] His food is to be very plain, without sauces, and is to consist of just one dish at every meal; boiled stockfish is especially recommended.

[75] *Treatise*, 1st ed., 1711, pp. 195–6.   [76] Ibid., p. 243.   [77] Ibid., p. 244.

For his breakfast he may have 'a small Mess of Water-Gruel, Burgoe, Panado or Barley-Broth', with 'a Glass of some rich Wine, such as Malaga, *Madera*, or Sherry',[78] and he may repeat this after his ride and bath. Since he is to cut out supper altogether, one may suppose that his only other meal will be the single dish of boiled stockfish or whatever. 'Burgoe' is presumably burgoo, an oatmeal porridge, and 'Panado' panada, bread and water flavoured with sugar, currants and nutmeg. When Misomedon shows some reluctance to embark on this Spartan regime, Philopirio admonishes him:

Thousands, and Ten Thousands of Pounds are Yearly thrown away upon Apothecary Ware, in this City alone, to remove what might be more effectually cured by Diet. It is incredible what prodigious benefits may sometimes be received, especially in disorders of the Stomach, from Abstinence alone; and it is certain, that Millions of People are now in their Graves, who have Died of Distempers, as well Chronick as Acute, that at first of all one Night's Fasting might have prevented.[79]

For Polytheca, as well as abstinence from her present medicines, Philopirio prescribes cold baths, and the drinking of spa water; for the daughter, as we have seen, swinging, horse-riding, and massage. Every patient, he says, is different, and requires slightly different treatment, even though they are all suffering from the same disease. Especially in hypochondria and hysteria, the quirks and idiosyncrasies of each patient need to be taken into account and perhaps humoured, for these are 'Distempers ... in which the Fancy has so great a share, and the least trifle is of moment'.[80]

Not much is known about Mandeville's medical practice (nor indeed of his life in general) but there is some evidence that it was a successful one: a letter about a patient shows him to have been in a position to consult with Sir Hans Sloane, described by Kaye as 'perhaps the leading physician of the day'.[81] The modern reader of the *Treatise* gets the impression that Mandeville was a good doctor. His great virtue is his humility: he says several times that we are almost completely ignorant of the body's inner workings. He is prepared to speculate about the animal spirits and the like, but not to let his speculations dictate his treatment. For that he depends entirely on what he (and his father before him, who

---

[78] Ibid., pp. 249–50.   [79] Ibid., pp. 254–5.   [80] Ibid., p. 277.
[81] *Fable of the Bees*, ed. Kaye, vol. 1, p. xxvi, and frontispiece.

specialized in the same diseases) found to work. The scepticism, and perhaps the materialism which, in his writings, scandalized opponents like Berkeley and Law, were not out of place in his professional practice.

4
THE SOCIAL REFORMER

Two of Mandeville's publications are pamphlets written about specific social abuses, for which he prescribed clear and detailed remedies. With them may be classed (as a kind of mirror-image) the *Essay on Charity and Charity-Schools*, which is an attack on social reforms which he thought misguided. These three works will be considered in this chapter, but it would of course be a mistake to suppose that Mandeville's views on social reform can be found only in them. All Mandeville's writings are satirical, or at least critical: there is hardly a page which does not tell us something about what he thought wrong with society. It is not so easy to tell how, or indeed whether, he thought things could be set right. But something can be gleaned about his views on reform in general, as distinct from certain particular reforms.

I shall begin, however, with the proposals for particular reforms, of which the first was his plan for state-owned brothels. *A Modest Defence of Publick Stews, or An Essay upon Whoring* was published anonymously in 1724. The title-page says that it is 'Written by a LAYMAN', without telling us exactly what professional expertise the author is disclaiming: the preface is signed with the defiant, or at least flippant, pseudonym Phil-Porney. A second edition was called for in 1725, and four more by 1740; the French translation was reprinted as late as 1881. It seems safe to suppose that not all Mandeville's readers were disinterested enthusiasts for social improvement.

The pamphlet begins in Mandeville's best hard-hitting style, with a dedication to 'the Gentlemen of the Societies', further identified in an appendix as 'Societies for Promoting a Reformation of Manners'. 'Your Endeavours to suppress Lewdness', Mandeville tells them, 'have only serv'd to promote it.'[1] The reason is that they have been using the wrong remedies. Even marriage is an inadequate restraint, at least for men:

Marriage indeed, is just such a cure for Lewdness as a Surfeit is for Gluttony; it gives a Man's Fancy a Distaste to this particular Dish, but

---
[1] B. Mandeville, *A Modest Defence of Public Stews*, 2nd ed., 1725, p. iii.

leaves his Palate as Luxurious as ever; for this Reason we find so many marry'd Men, that, like Sampson's Foxes, only do more Mischief by having their Tails ty'd.[2]

What is certain is that prostitution cannot be wiped out by whipping or imprisoning prostitutes:

It is very possible, indeed, that leaving a Poor Girl Penny-less may put her in a Way of living Honestly, tho' the want of Money was the only Reason of her living otherwise; and the Stripping of her Naked may, for ought I know, contribute to her Modesty, and put her in a State of Innocence; but surely, Gentlemen, you must all know, that Flogging has a contrary Effect.[3]

The 1725 edition has an appendix which purports to be an answer on behalf of the societies. It merely lists the number of prosecutions brought by them in the year 1724: 1,951 for lewd and disorderly practices, 29 for keeping bawdy or disorderly houses, 600 for exercising their trades or ordinary callings on Sunday, 108 for profane swearing and cursing, 12 for drunkenness, and so on. It adds that the societies have distributed some 400,000 pious books. This, of course, merely reinforces Mandeville's point: prosecution, punishment, and exhortation have plainly had no effect.

Diagnosis must precede cure: Mandeville begins by listing the evil consequences of whoring, in order to see how they may be prevented. He finds several: disease, expense, abortion and infanticide, the deterioration of the race, the alienation of wives from their husbands, and the debauching of young women.

Most of these seem obvious enough, though Mandeville (pandering to his audience, or perhaps treating his argument as he treated his tea-pot) seems to exaggerate the second item:

... if once Men suffer their Minds to be led astray by this unruly Passion, no worldly consideration whatever will be able to stop it; and Wenching, as it is very expensive in itself, without the ordinary Charges of Physick or Children, often leads Men into a thousand other Vices to support its Extravagance: Besides, after the Mind has once got this extravagant Turn, there naturally follows a Neglect and Contempt of Business; and Whoring itself disposes the Mind to such a sort

---

[2] *A Modest Defence of Public Stews*, 2nd ed., 1725, pp. viii-ix.
[3] Ibid., p. ix.

of Indolence, as is quite inconsistent with Industry, the main support of any, especially a trading Nation.[4]

One suspects that somewhere about the middle of this passage Mandeville's tongue shot into his cheek. He is no doubt serious enough about disease and infanticide: he may be pandering to his audience again in what he says about the deterioration of the race. It seems that, though marriage is a doubtful cure for 'lewdness', lewdness is none the less inimical to marriage:

> How many thousand young Men in this Nation would turn their Thoughts towards Matrimony, if they were not constantly destroying that Passion, which is the only Foundation of it? And tho' most of them, sooner or later, find the Inconvenience of this irregular Life, and think fit to confine themselves to One, yet their Bodies are so much enervated, by the untimely or immoderate Increase of this Passion, together with the Relicks of Venereal cures, that they beget a most wretched, feeble, and sickly Offspring: We can attribute it to nothing else but this, that so many of our ancient Families of Nobles are of late extinct.[5]

These evil consequences, he goes on, are not necessarily the effects of whoring as such, but only of the way it is organized, or rather fails to be organized. They are the evils of private whoring, and may be avoided by the substitution of public whoring. This is no vague proposal: Mandeville has worked out all the details. London is to have one hundred brothels, each with twenty women, and country towns are to have a proportionate number. 'Each House must be allow'd a certain Quantity of all sorts of Liquor, Custom and Excise free; by which Means they will be enabled to accommodate Gentlemen handsomely, without the Imposition, so frequently met with in such Houses.' The twenty women are to be divided into four classes: eight charging half a crown, six charging a crown, and four charging half a guinea, while two 'are design'd for Persons of the first Rank, who can afford to pay a Guinea for the Elegancy of their Taste'. Each house will have an infirmary, with two physicians and four surgeons, as well as a matron, who will be generally in charge, and there are to be 'three Commissioners appointed to superintend the whole, to hear and redress complaints, and to see that each House punctually observes the Rules and Orders as shall be

[4] Ibid., p. 3. [5] Ibid., p. 4.

thought Necessary for the good Government of this Community'.[6] Mandeville knows what at least some of these rules will be: the women will be strictly supervised by the matron, their health will be carefully watched, drunkenness will be checked, and 'Musick or Revelling' will not be allowed 'in any Room, to the Disturbance of the rest'.[7]

How will this proposal avoid the evils Mandeville has listed? Disease, no doubt, would be at least much reduced. So perhaps would expense: even the fastidious gentleman who paid his guinea would no doubt have spent much more on a mistress, since this is a calling in which the so-called amateur often costs more than the professional. At first sight it does not seem likely that the other economic consequence Mandeville puts under the heading of expense, the growth of indolence and the decline of industry, would be much altered. He does suggest that at least time will be saved:

... if a Man should be overtaken with a sudden Gust of Lechery, it will be no Hindrance to him even in the greatest Hurry of Business, for a ready and willing Mistress will ease him in the twinkling of an Eye, and he may prosecute his Affairs with more Attention than ever, by having his Mind entirely freed and disengag'd from those troublesome Ideas which always accompany a wanton Disposition of the Body.[8]

Mandeville is speaking here of 'the Man of Business who leads a sober regular Life', but who, because of his very abstinence, is occasionally troubled with 'amorous Heats'; in fact, of the kind of man who is so preoccupied with making money that he regards any other emotion he may have as just a nuisance. With no public brothels available, such a man

must employ both his Time and Rhetorick, and perhaps too his Purse, in deluding some modest Girl, which, besides the Loss of Time in carrying on such an Intrigue, is apt to give the Head such an amorous Turn as is quite inconsistent with Business, and may probably lead a Man into After-Expenses, which at first he never dreamt of.[9]

Abortion and infanticide will be reduced because 'every profess'd Courtezan, that is legally licens'd, will have an Apartment allotted her in the Infirmary when she is ready to lie in, and will

---

[6] *A Modest Defence of Public Stews*, 2nd ed., 1725, p. 10.
[7] Ibid., p. 11.   [8] Ibid., p. 19.   [9] Ibid., p. 19.

be obliged to take care of her child'.[10] Moreover, many servant girls, who destroyed their babies only because they were afraid of unemployment and starvation, would prefer to enter the brothels instead when they saw 'the handsome Provision made for them' there.

As for the deterioration of the race, this results from excessive masturbation, disease, or excessive indulgence. Public brothels will make the first unnecessary, and prevent the second. They will also at least reduce the third, since 'a Man acting out of a general Principle of Love to the whole Sex, will be in no Danger of proceeding any farther than he is prompted by Nature, and the particular Disposition of his Body at that time.'[11]

What Mandeville is in fact relying on is the unlikelihood that any man will actually fall in love with any of the girls in the brothels. When Mandeville talks of 'private whoring', which he contrasts unfavourably with 'public whoring', he seems to mean two things, which he does not clearly distinguish: paid prostitution not subject to any control, and extramarital intrigues generally, whether with kept mistresses, other men's wives, young girls seduced for the purpose, or any other women outside the profession. It is the second kind that is likely to lead to neglect of business, enfeeblement through excess, and the disruption of marriages. The first kind of course has its dangers too: disease chiefly, and the promotion of robbery, drunkenness, and general disorderliness. Public whoring will make it possible to stamp out the first kind of private whoring by legal action: prosecution and punishment are only ineffective because, for the unfortunate women who are whipped or imprisoned, the only alternatives are prostitution or starvation. Public brothels would provide another alternative: '... for altho' a poor Itinerant Courtezan could not by any Means be persuaded to starve at the Instigation of a *Reforming* Constable, yet a little *Bridewell* Rhetorick, or the Terrors of a Transportation, will soon convince her that she may live more comfortably and honestly in a *Publick Stew*.'[12]

Legal action can hardly be taken against the second kind of private whoring, but Mandeville thinks that it will be discouraged if there is a safe, accessible, and moderately priced alternative available.

By this means the institution of marriage will be preserved.

[10] Ibid., p. 20. [11] Ibid., p. 24. [12] Ibid., p. 12.

Marriage, Mandeville tells us, 'is absolutely necessary, not only for the regular Propagation of the *Species*, and their careful Education, but likewise for preserving that Distinction of Rank among Mankind, which otherwise would be utterly lost and confounded by doubtful Successions'.[13] Yet it is a peculiarly vulnerable institution, likely to suffer if men are either too lustful, or not lustful enough:

This necessary Passion is, indeed, of such ticklish Nature, that either too much or too little of it is equally prejudicial, and the *Medium* is so hard to hit that we are apt to fall into one of the Extremes. We are naturally *furnish'd* with an extraordinary *Stock* of Love; and by the *Largeness* of the Provision, it looks as if Nature had made some Allowance for *Wear and Tear*. If young Men were to live entirely chaste and sober, without blunting the Edge of their Passions, the first Fit of Love would turn their brains Topsy-turvy, and we should have the Nation pester'd with Love Adventures and Feats of Chivalry: By the time a *Peer's* Son came to be Sixteen, he would be in danger of turning Knight-Errant, and might possibly take a Cobler's Daughter for his *Dulcinea*, and who knows but a sprightly young *Taylor* might turn an Orlando Furioso, and venture his Neck to carry off a Lady of Birth and Fortune. In short there are so many Instances every day of these ruinous disproportion'd Matches, notwithstanding our present Intemperance, that we may justly conclude, if the Nation was in a state of perfect Sobriety, no Man could answer for the Conduct of his Children.

It must, indeed, be confess'd, as Matters now stand, the Excess of Chastity is not so much to be fear'd, as the other Extreme of Lewdness, tho' there are Instances of both; and many Fathers now living would gladly have seen their Sons fifty times in a *Stew*, rather than seen them so unfortunately marryed. The other Extreme is equally or rather more dangerous, as it is more common; for most young Men give too great a Loose to their Passions, and either quite destroy their Inclinations to Matrimony, or make their Constitutions incapable of answering the Ends of that State.

To avoid these two dangerous Extremes we have erected the *Publick Stews*, which every considerate Man must allow to be that Golden Mean so much desir'd: For, in the first Place, we avoid the Inconvenience of too strict a Chastity. When a Man has gained some Experience by his Commerce in the *Stews*, he is able to form a pretty good comparative Judgment of what he may expect from the highest Gratifications of Love; he finds his Ideas of Beauty strangely alter'd after Enjoyment, and will not be hurry'd into an unsuitable Match by

---

[13] *A Modest Defence of Public Stews*, 2nd ed., 1725, p. 20.

those romantick chimerical Notions of Love, which possess the Minds of the inexperienced Youth, and make them fancy that Love alone can compleat the Happiness of a Marryed State. But this will be so readily granted, that I shan't insist upon it farther.

In the next Place, the *Publick Stews* will prevent the ill effects of excessive Lewdness, by Preserving Men's Constitutions so well, that although they may defer Matrimony some time for their specific Advantage, yet they will have a sufficient Stock of Desire left to persuade them, one time or another, to quit the Gaiety of a Single Life: And when they do marry, they will be able to answer all the Ends and Purposes of that State as well, and rather better, than if they had lived perfectly chaste.[14]

All this, it will be noticed, applies to men. What about women? Will they, too, be saved from chimerical notions of romantic love and so make wiser marriages if they avoid an excessive premarital chastity? Mandeville's arguments would seem to apply equally to them; yet in fact he takes it for granted that it is important for women to preserve their virginity until marriage, and to be faithful to their husbands thereafter. He does not, indeed, believe that sexual desire is weaker in women than in men, or that an unchaste woman is somehow corrupt and unnatural. On the contrary, he explains, with much anatomical detail, why this cannot be the case. If desire were not fairly easily excited, neither men nor women could perform their normal sexual function. But the moral Mandeville draws is that female chastity is peculiarly vulnerable, and needs special pains to preserve it:

If a Woman is handsome, she has more Tryals to undergo; if homely and for that Reason seldom attack'd, the Novelty of the Address makes the greater Impression: If she is married, it is odds but there's a Failure at home, and habitual Pleasures are not easily forgone, especially when they may be enjoy'd with Safety: If a Maid, her unexperienc'd Virgin-Heart is capable of any Impression: If she is rich, Ease and Luxury make the Blood run mad; and Love, if high-dieted, is ungovernable: If poor, she will be easier bribed, when Love and Avarice jointly must be gratified.

In short, to sum up all, there is in the Passion of Love a certain fatal *Crisis*, to which all Women-kind are capable of being wrought up: The Difference of Virtue consisting only in this, that it is very hard to work a virtuous Woman up to this *Crisis*, and requires a very unlucky

---

[14] Ibid., pp. 21–2.

Concurrence of Circumstances: Whereas a Woman without a good Stock of Virtue, must have an unaccountable Series of good Fortune if she escapes. But, Virtuous or not Virtuous, when this Passion is once rais'd to the *critical* Height, it is absolutely irresistible.[15]

Why is it so important that chastity should be preserved? Mandeville does say, in one place, that 'the Minds of Women are corrupted by the Loss of Chastity'[16] but he immediately adds the qualification: 'or rather by the Reproach they suffer upon that Loss'. Later he says that unchaste women

are commonly guilty of almost the whole catalogue of immoral Actions: The Reason is evident; They are utterly abandon'd by their Parents, and thereby reduc'd to the last Degree of Shifting Poverty; if their Lewdness cannot supply their Wants, they must have Recourse to Methods more criminal, such as *Lying, Cheating, open Theft*, etc. Not that these are the necessary concomitants of Lewdness, or have the least Relation to it as *lewd Men of Honour* can testify; but the Treatment such Women meet with in the World is the Occasion of it.[17]

It is, then, just a social fact that women are expected to remain chaste, and suffer if they do not. Mandeville accepts this as a datum, without asking whether or not it ought to be the case, and goes on to ask how female chastity can be preserved. This leads him to propound 'the following Syllogysm': 'The only way to preserve Female Chastity, is to prevent the Men from laying Siege to it: But this Project of the *Publick Stews* is the only Way to prevent Mens laying Siege to it: Therefore the Project is the only Way to preserve Female Chastity.'[18]

Obviously, however, not all female chastity can be preserved by this method. The women in the brothels are to be sacrificed for the sake of the rest. Mandeville makes this clear by means of a number of similes:

If Reason fails to convince, let us profit by Example: Observe the Policy of a Modern Butcher, persecuted with a Swarm of Carnivorous Flies; when all his Engines and Fly-flaps have prov'd ineffectual to defend his Stall against the Greedy Assiduity of those Carnal Insects, he very Judiciously cuts off a Fragment already blown, which serves to hang up for a Cure; and thus, by sacrificing a Small Part, already Tainted, and not worth Keeping, he wisely secures the Safety of the Rest.[19]

---

[15] *A Modest Defence of Public Stews*, 2nd edn., 1725, pp. 37–8.
[16] Ibid., p. 7.   [17] Ibid., p. 13.   [18] Ibid., p. 37.   [19] Ibid., p. x.

That this is hard on the women who are sacrificed, Mandeville does not deny. Their numbers, he says, must be kept as low as possible, and he even considers the possibility of preserving the honour of Englishwomen entirely by importing foreigners:

But since the Necessity of debauching a certain Number of young Women, is entirely owing to the Necessity of supplying the *Publick Stews*: a question may very reasonably arise, whether this Project might not be vastly improv'd . . . by an Act for *encouraging the Importation of foreign Women*? This, I must confess, deserves a serious Debate: For, besides the Honour of our Females, which would be preserv'd by such an Act, it might bring this farther Advantage; That whereas most of our estated Youth spend a great Part of their Time and Fortunes in travelling Abroad, for no other End, as it seems by most of them, but to be inform'd in the *French* and *Italian* Gallantry; they would then have an Opportunity of satisfying their Curiosity in foreign Amours, without stirring out of *London*.[20]

Mandeville defends his proposal with utilitarian arguments: he says, for example, that if a quarantine ship sinks and some of the crew, known to be infected, struggle ashore half-drowned, it will be a just act for the Government to order them to be shot, as the only way of preventing the contagion from spreading. That he should have argued in this way is interesting, and will need to be considered when we come to examine his moral philosophy; but his strongest argument here is simply that his proposal would not increase the numbers of these women, and that the women themselves would be rather better treated than before. There can be little doubt that Mandeville's proposals would have been an enormous improvement on what actually went on in eighteenth-century London. One need only read Boswell's London journal, written fifty years later, to be convinced of that.

What one might take exception to is not so much the proposals themselves as some of the assumptions that seem to underlie Mandeville's arguments for them: his acceptance of the double standard in sexual morality (even though he rejects the mythology about female sexuality often used to justify it); his continual suggestion that a love affair is merely the appeasement of a troublesome physical appetite, which had better be quenched as quickly as possible before it begins to interfere with the serious things in life. But discussion of these attitudes would raise the

[20] Ibid., p. 48.

larger question of Mandeville's views on the reform of society in general, which we have postponed until his specific proposals have been dealt with. Let us pass on, then, to his next pamphlet, the *Enquiry into the Causes of the Frequent Executions at Tyburn*.

This was, in a way, a piece of topical journalism. It first appeared as a series of letters in the *British Journal* between February and May, 1725, a time when the activities of Jonathan Wild were attracting a good deal of attention. Wild was arrested not long after the series began.

Jonathan Wild, the original of Gay's Peachum and the occasion of Fielding's satire, *Jonathan Wild the Great*, was, according to his most recent biographer,[21] the spiritual father of Al Capone, living as he did in a world, the London of the 1720s, not unlike Chicago two centuries later. According to the indictment presented to the court when he was eventually brought to trial,[22] he 'formed a Kind of Corporation of Thieves of which he was the Head or Director'; he 'divided the Town and Country into so many Districts, and appointed district Gangs for each, who regularly accounted with him for their Robberies'. He also had 'a particular Sett to steal at Churches in Time of Divine Service: And likewise other moving Detachments to attend at Court, on Birth-days, Balls, etc., and at both Houses of Parliament, Circuits and Country Fairs'. Many of his employees were convicts who had been transported and had illegally returned to England before their time was up. They were liable to be hanged if caught, which meant that Wild had a perfect hold on them. The indictment goes on to say that he had 'several Warehouses for receiving and concealing stolen Goods; and also a Ship for carrying off Jewels, Watches, and other valuable Goods, to Holland, where he had a superannuated Thief for his Factor' and that 'he kept in Pay several Artists to make Alterations, and transform Watches, Seals, Snuffboxes, Rings, and other valuable Things, that they might not be known.'

This was organized crime on a large scale: probably larger than ever before and most times since. But Wild was not notorious merely for that. In crime stories the Master Criminal goes to great pains to hide his identity. Wild took equal pains to make

[21] G. Howson, *Thief-taker General: the Rise and Fall of Jonathan Wild*, London, Hutchinson, 1970, p. 7.
[22] Quoted in Howson, pp. 238-9.

himself known: he advertised extensively in the newspapers of the day. In Wild's early days, before his gang was fully organized, the advertisements were for lost property, offering a reward 'and no questions asked'. They were in fact inviting the thieves to dispose of the booty through Wild rather than some other receiver. What Wild did with it, often though not always, was to return it to the owner, for a fee. It was well known that if you were robbed, the best thing to do was to seek out Jonathan Wild at his office, Mandeville tells us how the system worked:

As soon as any Thing is missing, suspected to be stolen, the first Course we steer is directly to the Office of Mr. *Jonathan Wild*. If what we want is a trinket, either enamel'd, or otherwise curiously wrought; if there is Painting about it; if it be a particular Ring, the Gift of a Friend; or any Thing which we esteem above the real Value, and offer more for it than Mr. *Thief* can make of it we are look'd upon as good Chaps, and welcome to redeem it. But if it be plain Gold or Silver, we shall hardly see it again, unless we pay the Worth of it. Some Years ago, it is true, a Man might, for half a Piece, have fetch'd back a Snuff-Box that weigh'd twenty or thirty shillings: But this was in the Infancy of the Establishment. Now they are grown wiser and calculate exactly what such a Thing will melt down for: To offer less is thought unreasonable, and unless Mr. *Thief-catcher* stands your Friend indeed, if you have it, you will seldom save anything but the Fashion. If in this Place you can hear no Tidings of your Goods, it is counted a Sign that they are in the Hands of irregular Practitioners, that steal without Permission of the Board.[23]

Wild pretended, of course, that he had nothing to do with the actual thefts, and was able to recover the goods only because of his prowess as a detective. But it is clear that, by the time Mandeville came to write his pamphlet, the pretence had worn very thin. As Mandeville points out in the preface, an Act had been passed in 1718 which made it a felony to take 'Money or Reward directly or indirectly, under Pretence or upon account of helping any Person or Persons to any stolen Goods or Chattels . . . unless such Person doth apprehend, or cause to be apprehended, such Felon to be brought to his Trial for the same, and give Evidence against him'.[24] This was aimed directly at Wild, and was indeed nicknamed 'the Jonathan Wild Act'; it was under it that he was eventually charged.

[23] *Enquiry into the Causes of the Frequent Executions at Tyburn*, 1725, pp. 3-4.
[24] Ibid., p. [viii].

By the time Mandeville wrote Wild had eliminated a good many of the 'irregular practitioners' who did not operate under his control. He did this by informing against them (impeaching or 'peaching' them). This was also his method of getting rid of his own men when they became troublesome to him in any way. This was Wild's other great source of fame: he proclaimed himself 'Thief-taker General of Great Britain and Ireland', and on one occasion petitioned the Aldermen of the City of London for recognition of his services. At his trial he had a pamphlet distributed to jurymen and others containing a list of the criminals he had brought to justice, and thence to the gallows or transportation: it contained seventy-five names. Moreover, Mr. Howson tells us, it was not complete. Mandeville comments that the executioner was to the thief-taker as the butcher to the grazier: 'of the Cattle in either Sense, few are killed by the one that were never cherished by the other.'[25]

One reason then for the high incidence of crime and the consequent frequency of executions is the readiness with which owners of stolen property connive at Wild's schemes. Mandeville deploys all his irony against them. (He is speaking of advertisements offering a reward for the return of stolen goods.)

> ... a Panegyrist on the present Times might justly say of them, That in no Performances the true Spirit of Christianity was so conspicuous as in these: That they were not only free from Calumny and ill Language, but likewise so void of Reproach that speaking to a Thief we never called him so in those charitable Addresses: that in them the very Catalogues of Injuries receiv'd, were penn'd with as little Heat, or Resentment, as ever Tradesmen shew'd in a Bill of Parcels directed to his best Customer: That here we are so far from hating our Enemy, that we proffer him a Recompence for his Trouble, if he will condescend to let us have our own again; and leaving all Revenge to God, to shew that we are willing to forgive and forget, we consult, in the most effectual Manner, the Safety of a Person that deserves hanging for the Wrong he has done us.[26]

Apart from the condoning of felony by its victims, a further cause of crime is the way criminals are treated once they are caught. Mandeville's vivid descriptions of Newgate and of the processions to Tyburn have already been quoted. The point he is

[25] *Enquiry into the Causes of the Frequent Executions at Tyburn*, 1725, p. 16.
[26] Ibid., p. 4.

making is that the whole atmosphere is of riot, hysteria, bravado, and, on execution day itself, of carnival. In Newgate: 'They eat and drink what they can purchase, every Body has Admittance to them, and they are debarr'd from nothing but going out.'[27] A really notorious criminal could hold a kind of court in prison, with his admirers flocking to see him: Howson records that visitors to Jack Sheppard's cell were charged three shillings and sixpence each, the equivalent of about £3 50p in modern money, by the turnkeys.[28]

The whole purpose of a public execution, Mandeville points out, is 'the Terror we would have it strike in others of the same loose Principles'.[29] This purpose is defeated by the thoughtlessness of the spectators, who applaud the bravery of the condemned men, and encourage them to go swaggering to their deaths, so that public executions 'are exemplary in the wrong Way, and encourage where they should deter'.[30] Mandeville accordingly gives a little disquisition on courage:

... the original Reason why Courage is generally esteemed, is, because it is taken for granted, that both the Principle we act from, and the End we labour for in conquering our Fears, are praise-worthy, and have a visible Tendency, either to the Good of others, or our own spiritual Felicity. Nothing, therefore, is more unjust, than that we should continue our Esteem for Valour when it degenerates, and both the Motive Men set out with, and the Scope they aim at, are palpably destructive ... What perverse and miserable Judges are we then, that applaud a Person's Intrepidity in fighting a Duel, when in the Act itself, we see him wilfully violate the Laws of God and Man? But should human Honour here break in upon me, and my Reasoning, how right soever, be overpower'd by the irresistible Clamour of the fashionable World, what can be said for the senseless Intimidity of a vulgar Rogue, who not only professes an utter Disregard to Honour and Conscience, but has likewise, at his first Setting out, as a Preliminary to his Business, disclaim'd all Pretensions to common Honesty? Why should we delight in the Intrepidity, tho' it was real, of a Villain in his Impiety? Why should Christians be pleased to see a great Sinner give up his Ghost impenitent; or imagine that he dies bravely, because he bids Defiance to Heaven, and boldly plunges himself into an Abyss of eternal Misery? Yet nothing is more common amongst us:

---

[27] Ibid., p. 17. [28] Howson, op. cit., p. 221.
[29] *Enquiry into the Causes of the Frequent Executions at Tyburn*, p. 36.
[30] Ibid., p. 37.

And the further a Man is removed from Repentance, nay, the more void he seems to be of all Religion, and the less Concern he discovers for Futurity, the more he's admired by our sprightly People: Whereas, he who shews but the least Sorrow for his Sins, or, by his Tears, or Dismality of Gestures, lets us know that he is under Apprehensions of the divine Wrath, is a weak silly Creature, not worth looking at: And he only, in the Opinion of many, dies like a Man, who, in reality, goes off most like a Brute.[31]

Having thus appealed to Christians Mandeville suggests, interestingly enough, that some of his readers may not be Christians. He warns them against supposing that the criminal is indifferent to death because he does not believe in an afterlife in which he will be punished:

The Enthusiasm of Atheists has other Symptoms; deplorable as it is, the Appearance of it is more sedate, and they make some Pretences to Reasoning; But what Probability is there, that a poor Rascal, who was brought up in Ignorance, and perhaps cannot read, one who never troubled his Head with thinking, much less with thinking on abstruse Matters, and Metaphysicks, should so far lose himself in the Mazes of Philosophy, as to become a speculative Atheist?[32]

The apparent courage, he concludes, is not even genuine, but is usually due partly to the fear of being thought a coward, and, predominantly to drink:

Tho' before setting out, the Prisoners took care to swallow what they could, to be drunk, and stifle their Fear; yet the Courage that strong Liquors can give wears off, and the Way they have to go being considerable, they are in Danger of recovering and, without repeating the Dose, Sobriety would often overtake them: For this Reason they must drink as they go; and the Cart stops for that Purpose three or four, and sometimes half a dozen Times, or more, before they come to their Journey's End.[33]

Having explained why crimes are common, and executions frequent, Mandeville goes on to suggest remedies. First he proposes something more like a modern prison, though certainly a grim one: instead of the riotous assemblies at Newgate, there is to be solitary confinement in small, dimly lit cells. There would be no irons. After a day in which they would be allowed to say

[31] *Enquiry into the Causes of the Frequent Executions at Tyburn*, pp. 31–2.
[32] Ibid., pp. 33–4.   [33] Ibid., p. 23.

goodbye to friends and relations, prisoners would have three days by themselves, 'to make their Peace with Heaven, and prepare themselves for Death', seeing no one but 'a sober Keeper' and a clergyman, who is to be a man of some public reputation, and not a full-time prison chaplain.

In most Employments Use makes Perfectness, but here it incapacitates: and was a Man, even of the greatest Prudence and Watchfulness over himself, always to converse with Rogues, and do nothing else but instruct and attend Malefactors in their last Hours, the very Habit he would contract from it, would spoil him for that Purpose: and it is impossible, but constant Practice would, in a little Time, wear out, or at least take off the greatest part of that Earnestness and Concern, which ought to be inseparable from the Charge I speak of.[34]

During all this time the prisoner is to have nothing but bread and water.

... what I have in View by this low Diet chiefly regards the eternal Welfare of those unhappy People, as it would be instrumental to an early Repentance. When, free from Fumes of Food, and all intoxicating Comforts, the serious Thoughts of a Criminal shall be obliged to dwell upon his wretched Self, and behold the Prospect of a future State so near, so certainly to come, the loosest and most abandon'd will be brought to Reason. Death being unavoidable, and nothing upon Earth to save him, Self-defence will make him turn his Eyes elsewhere: His continued Abstinence will help to clear his Understanding; then searching after Truth, he will be soon convinced of the Folly and Weakness of those Arguments, by which he has been used to harden his Conscience, keep out Remorse, and fortify his Steadiness in Guilt.[35]

If Mandeville is not sincere here, one is inclined to say, he must have been a cruel hypocrite. Yet is it likely that he, as a doctor, really believed that men thought more clearly on a starvation diet? Why did he not just prescribe plain wholesome food, with no intoxicants? In the *Origin of Honour*, he makes Horatio say: 'The mechanical Effect, which Fasting can have upon the Spirits, is to lower, flatten and depress them.'[36] Perhaps that is the real reason he wants the condemned man fed on bread and water: so that 'the Paleness of his Countenance, and the Shaking of every Limb'[37] should really strike terror into the beholders.

[34] Ibid., pp. 39-40. [35] Ibid., pp. 40-1.
[36] *Enquiry into the Origin of Honour*, 1732, p. 205 (Fourth Dialogue).
[37] *Enquiry into the Causes of the Frequent Executions at Tyburn*, p. 41.

Mandeville goes on, however, to a quite nauseating piece of pious rhetoric. 'It is more than probable', he suggests, that many of the felons, their minds clarified by bread and water, 'would become good Christians, and make exemplary ends'.

What a visible Alteration would it not make in them, when they should perceive their Spirits, that the Moment before were overwhelm'd with Grief, or fill'd with black Despair, cherish'd and enlighten'd by the powerful Beams of heavenly Grace and Clemency: Transported with the Prospect of approaching Bliss they then would wish to die, and rejoice that they should be made Examples to frighten Evildoers from their Ways ...

Sometimes they would deter the Wicked and in the same Breath solicite Heaven for their Conversion: At others, reasoning from the Changes they had experienced within, they would combat Impiety with Vehemence, and conjure unbelievers no longer to doubt of an everlasting Futurity: They would paint to them, in the strongest Colours, the Horrors they had felt from an accusing Conscience, and the Abyss of Misery they had been plunged in, whilst yet labouring under the dire Reflection on eternal Vengeance; And thus, mixing fervent Prayers with strenuous Exhortation, they would employ the few Moments, that were left them, in Exercises intirely spiritual and holy.[38]

It is hard to know what to make of this. Perhaps the passage is the best evidence for the genuineness of Mandeville's professed Christianity: for if he is not sincere here, if he is merely seizing the opportunity to parody an evangelical tract, he is not only being callous but is also defeating the purpose of the pamphlet, which is certainly mainly serious. Yet it may be noted that the chapter ends with the assertion that 'such Executions would be of vast use to compass Happiness, both here and hereafter'; and, he goes on significantly, 'should we regard the first only, it would be no exaggeration to assert that one of them would be more serviceable to the Peace and Security of this immense City, than a thousand of those that are now so frequent among us.'[39] It is almost certainly the here rather than the hereafter that really concerns Mandeville: perhaps all he really means is that public executions should be quiet, sober, and awe-inspiring, and throws in the fantasy of the evangelist on the gallows either as an argument to appeal to his more pious readers or as a piece of burlesque he was unable to repress.

[38] *Enquiry into the Causes of the Frequent Executions at Tyburn*, pp. 44-5.
[39] Ibid., p. 46.

Another proposal of Mandeville's is that at each execution a certain number of bodies, not fewer than six, should be delivered to the surgeons for dissection. No felon would know whether or not his body would be one of these. He probably advocated this simply because he was, as a doctor, concerned about the advancement of medicine; but he may also have intended to increase the severity of the punishment. For, odd though it seems, the criminals of the day seem to have been almost more afraid of dissection than of death itself. In his description of the executions Mandeville tells us how the surgeons often had to fight the mob for the corpses. 'They have suffer'd the Law (cries the Rabble) and shall have no other Barbarities put upon them: We know what you are, and will not leave them before we see them buried'.[40] And Howson relates that John Applebee, the publisher, who employed Defoe, among others, and who had bought the rights to Jack Sheppard's dying speech, was believed to have agreed, as part of the bargain, to provide Sheppard with a coffin and a funeral so that his body would not be taken for dissection. The mob, however, believed that the hearse and four Applebee provided belonged to the surgeons, and smashed it to matchwood.[41]

In a final chapter Mandeville considers transportation, which, he notes, 'for some Years last past, on many Occasions, has been substituted, and inflicted in the room of capital Punishment'.[42] This is, he says, 'just and commendable', but unfortunately transportation has not proved an effective deterrent.

But our subtle Criminals have found out Means hitherto to render it ineffectual: Some have made their Escape in the Voyage itself; others, condemn'd to this Punishment, never have been put on board; several have reach'd the Plantations, but been return'd again by the first Shipping, and great Numbers have been come back before half their Time was expir'd. Those that are forced to stay, do very little Service themselves, and spoil the other Slaves, teaching the *Africans* more Villainy and Mischief than ever they could have learn'd without the Examples and Instructions of such *Europeans*.[43]

Mandeville's proposal is that, instead of being sent to the West Indies, transported felons should be exchanged for British sailors

---

[40] Ibid., p. 26. [41] Howson, op. cit., p. 221.
[42] *Enquiry into the Causes of the Frequent Executions at Tyburn*, pp. 46–7.
[43] Ibid., p. 47.

captured and enslaved in Morocco, Tunis, Algiers, and 'other Places on the Coast of *Barbary*'.

Should it be objected, that such abandon'd People would turn Mahometans, and our selves become accessary to their eternal Ruin, I would ask what Surety we had for those that were there already. Amongst our Seafaring Men, the Practice of Piety is very scarce: Abundance of them lead very bad Lives, who yet, as to the Love of their Country, and the *Meum and Tuum*, are very honest Fellows. There are not many that are well grounded in the Principles of their Religion, or would be capable of maintaining it against an Adversary of the least Ability; and we are not certain, that under great Temptations, they would remain stedfast to the Christian Faith. The Danger then of Apostacy being the same in both, we must be manifestly the Gainers, when we change lazy cowardly Thieves, and incorrigible Rogues for brave laborious and useful People.[44]

The tone here is very different from that of the preceding chapter in which he looks forward to the conversion of criminals on the gallows and may be another reason for doubting the sincerity of that passage.

Mandeville goes on to consider the objection that slavery would be an unduly severe punishment. He points out that it would be no worse than hanging, and that imprisonment with hard labour is in fact slavery under another name. Moreover, the more severe the life of these slaves, the more urgent it is that something should be done to redeem the innocent sailors whose lot it now is. The felons themselves might in time be exchanged for further felons, so their punishment need not be perpetual.

In both the Tyburn pamphlet and the *Modest Defence*, Mandeville's starting-point is that the measures being taken to get rid of acknowledged evils were notoriously ineffective. Prostitutes could not be deterred by punishment if they had no other means of earning a living; public executions would not deter the criminally inclined when they were so conducted that the victims were regarded as public heroes. In each case he goes on to ask what measures would be effective. Prostitution itself could not, he thought, be stopped, but its worst evils might be prevented. Hanging might be expected to deter if the bravado and braggadocio surrounding Tyburn were eliminated. Mandeville wants to substitute 'public whoring' for 'private', and he toys with the

[44] *Enquiry into the Causes of the Frequent Executions at Tyburn*, pp. 48–9.

idea of substituting private executions for public ones ('If no Remedy can be found for these Evils, it would better that Malefactors should be put to Death in private'),[45] though in the end he settles for other measures.

Both these pamphlets mention charity schools. The alleged reply which Mandeville prints at the end of the *Modest Defence* contains the following paragraph as part of the eulogy of the activities of the Societies for the Reformation of Manners:

Those therefore that have a just Zeal for the Honour of God and Religion, who desire to prevent the spreading of the Leprosy of Sin; who are unwilling to have their Children, and other Relations, or their Friends and Servants, corrupted by ill Examples and wicked Allurements: Those that sincerely wish well to those excellent and hopeful Nurseries of Piety and good Manners, the CHARITY-SCHOOLS: and would be heartily grieved to see the Christian Instruction and pious Education that Children receive therein miscarry through prevailing open Temptations to Wickedness, and a general Contempt of Religion: Those, lastly who have any due Love to their Country, and would prevent a National Guilt, and thereby keep off National Judgements, cannot possibly, one would think, but heartily approve and assist this useful Design for Suppressing Prophaneness and Immorality.[46]

In the first paragraph of the Tyburn pamphlet, Mandeville says:

Many good Projects have been thought of to cure this Evil, by sapping the Foundation of it: A Society has been set up to reform our Manners; and neither Workhouses, nor Discipline on small Crimes, have been wanting: An Act has been made against prophane Cursing and Swearing; and many Charity Schools have been erected. But the Event has not answer'd hitherto the good Design of those Endeavours.[47]

Charity schools, then, seem to be firmly associated in Mandeville's mind with the wowserism of the Societies for the Reformation of Manners, and to typify pious smugness, self-righteousness, and stupidity. The year before the *Modest Defence* appeared, Mandeville had published *An Essay on Charity and Charity-Schools*, as part of the new material in the 1723 edition of *The Fable of the Bees*. The first part of this essay discusses charity,

[45] Ibid., p. 36. [46] *A Modest Defence of Public Stews*, pp. 63-4.
[47] *Enquiry into the Causes of the Frequent Executions at Tyburn*, p. 1.

its motives and counterfeits, and will need to be considered in a later chapter. Most of the essay, however, is taken up with what Mandeville calls 'that kind of Distraction the Nation has labour'd under for some time, the Enthusiastick Passion for Charity-Schools.'[48]

Charity schools, begun apparently in Wales, seem to have spread throughout England largely as a result of the foundation of the Society for Promoting Christian Knowledge (still in existence as a publisher) in 1698. Its aim was 'to set up catechetical schools for the education of poor children in reading, writing, and more especially in the principles of the Christian religion'. In 1704 there were 54 such schools in London, and 35 in 'the country' (presumably anywhere in England that was not London). By 1718 the numbers had grown to 74 and 274 respectively, with a total enrolment of 28,610 children, of which about a quarter were girls.[49]

Why did Mandeville object to the education of the poor? One of his objections seems to have been to the hypocrisy of those who promoted the schools.

Would both Parties agree to pull off the Masque, we should soon discover that whatever they pretend to, they aim at nothing so much in Charity-Schools, as to strengthen their Party, and that the great Sticklers for the Church, by Educating Children in the Principles of Religion, mean inspiring them with a Superlative Veneration for the Clergy of the Church of *England*, and a strong Aversion and immortal Animosity against all that dissent from it.[50]

There may have been some truth in this. In 1685 Thomas Tenison, later Archbishop of Canterbury and at that time Vicar of St. Martin's-in-the-Fields, observed that 'a crafty Jesuit' had erected a free school in the suburbs of London. He promptly built his own free school in Castle Street, 'for the educating of divers poor boys in his parish in opposition to that of the Jesuit'. In 1697, as Archbishop, he endowed this school with £1,000 of his own money and another £500 left him for charitable uses.[51]

Again Mandeville objects that the claims made for the schools

---

[48] *Fable of the Bees*, ed. Kaye, vol. 1, p. 268.
[49] See *Cyclopedia of Education*, ed. Paul Monroe, New York, 1911, vol. 1, pp. 574-7.
[50] *Fable of the Bees*, ed. Kaye, vol. 1, p. 309.
[51] See *Cyclopedia of Education*, loc. cit.

were simply false. As he indicates in the Tyburn pamphlet, charity schools were regarded as a means of preventing crime:

How perverse must be the Judgment of those, who would not rather see Children decently dress'd, with clean Linen at least once a Week, that in an orderly Manner follow their Master to Church, than in every open place meet with a Company of Black-guards without Shirts or any thing whole about them, that insensible of their Misery are continually increasing it with Oaths and Imprecations. 'Can any one doubt but these are the great Nursery of Thieves and Pick-pockets? What numbers of Felons and other Criminals have we Tried and Convicted every Sessions.' This will be prevented by Charity-Schools, and when the Children of the Poor receive a better Education, the Society will in a few Years reap the better of it, and the Nation will be clear'd of so many Miscreants as now this great City and all the Country about it are fill'd with. This is the general Cry, and he that speaks the least Word against it, an Uncharitable Hard-hearted and Inhuman, if not a Wicked, Profane, and Atheistical Wretch . . .[52]

But this, Mandeville argues, is a quite mistaken notion of the causes of crime. The chief cause is, not 'the want of Reading and Writing', but the offender's knowledge that he has a good chance of escaping punishment.

To be Stupid and Ignorant is seldom the Character of a Thief. Robberies on the Highway and other bold Crimes are generally perpetrated by Rogues of Spirit and Genius, and Villains of any Fame are commonly subtle cunning Fellows, that are well vers'd in the Method of Trials, and acquainted with every Quirk in the Law that can be of use to them . . .[53]

It is also a mistake, Mandeville suggests, to suppose that religion is promoted by knowledge.

As to Religion, the most knowing and Polite Part of a Nation have everywhere the least of it. Craft has a greater Hand in making Rogues than Stupidity, and Vice in general is no where more predominant than where Arts and Sciences flourish. Ignorance is, to a Proverb, counted to be the Mother of Devotion and it is certain that we shall find Innocence and Honesty no where more general than among the most illiterate, the poor silly Country People.[54]

This is no doubt more an attack on religion than on learning; and more than either, perhaps, on the inconsistencies of the

[52] *Fable of the Bees*, ed. Kaye, vol. 1, pp. 268–9.
[53] Ibid., pp. 272–3. [54] Ibid., p. 269.

pious supporters of the schools. But Mandeville's main objection is one that is likely to antagonize the modern reader. He is against the education of the poor, simply as such. 'All the Comforts of Life', he says, arise ultimately from 'the Labour of the Poor'. It is essential, then, that the class of poor labourers shall be numerous and its members not encouraged to rise above their station:

The Proportion of the Society is spoil'd and the Bulk of the Nation, which should every where consist of Labouring Poor, that are unacquainted with every thing but their Work, is too little for the other Parts. In all Business where downright Labour is shun'd or over-paid, there is plenty of People. To one Merchant you have ten Bookkeepers or at least Pretenders; and every where in the Country the Farmer wants Hands. Ask for a Footman that for some Time has been in Gentlemen's Families, and you'll get a Dozen that are all Butlers. You may have Chamber-maids by the Score, but you can't get a Cook under extravagant Wages.

No Body will do the dirty slavish Work, that can help it. I don't discommend them; but all these things shew that the People of the meanest Rank know too much to be serviceable to us. Servants require more than Masters and Mistresses can afford, and what madness is it to encourage them in this, by industriously increasing at our Cost that Knowledge which they will be sure to make us pay for over again.[55]

Mandeville then gives us a diatribe against the dishonesty and laziness of servants, and goes on to tell us, in tones of horror, that some servants had reached such a 'height of Insolence' as to form a kind of trade union, 'and made Laws by which they oblige themselves not to serve for less than such a Sum, nor carry Burdens or any Bundle or Parcel above a certain Weight, not exceeding Two or Three Pounds, with other Regulations directly opposite to the Interest of those they Serve'.[56] These things, he concedes, are not 'altogether owing to Charity-Schools', but they are 'Accessary, or at least they are more likely to Create and Increase than to lessen or redress these Complaints'.[57]

Education, then, should be reserved for the children of those who can afford to pay for it:

If every Body's Children are well taught, who by their own Industry can educate them at our Universities, there will be Men of Learning

---

[55] *Fable of the Bees*, ed. Kaye, vol. 1, p. 302.
[56] Ibid., p. 305.   [57] Ibid., pp. 306–7.

enough to supply this Nation and such another; and Reading, Writing or Arithmetick would never be wanting in the Business that requires them, tho' none were to learn them but such whose Parents could be at the Charge of it.[58]

So long as there is abundance of hard work to be done the more cheerfully it is done the better. Let us not, then, make the poor discontented. Moreover, it is better for their children 'to wear out their Clothes by useful Labour, and blacken them with Country Dirt for something, instead of tearing them off their Backs at play, and dawbing them with Ink for nothing'.[59] It is necessary for there to be 'a certain Portion of Ignorance in a well-order'd Society'. Russia, it is true, has 'too few Knowing Men', but Great Britain has too many.[60]

The modern reader is very likely to conclude that Mandeville was a callous reactionary, complacent about the existing structure of society, blind to the suffering it caused, and impatient of any attempts to improve it. Even the two reforming pamphlets, it might be said, only serve to demonstrate his resistance to change and his suspicion of the unfamiliar. Mandeville, was after all, a foreigner in England, and the reforms he advocated would have had the effect of making England more like his native Holland. This is true at any rate of the proposal for public brothels: Remark H of the *Fable* gives an account of the 'houses' of Amsterdam, tolerated by 'the Wise Rulers of that well-order'd City'.[61] Probably it is also true of his proposal for penal reform: John Howard tells us that in Holland there were very few executions, and that this was due to 'the awful solemnity of executions, which are performed in presence of the magistrates, with great order and seriousness, and great effect on the spectators'.[62] He was writing about what he found in 1776; but it is quite likely that conditions were not very different fifty years before.

Moreover, it might be added, the reforms Mandeville advocates are intended, not to remove the basic injustices of eighteenth-century society, but if anything to perpetuate and strengthen them. The strategy is always the same: the oppressed classes are to be sacrificed to the rest. Poor women are to be debauched so that the women of the middle classes may preserve their virtue:

---
[58] Ibid., p. 298.   [59] Ibid., p. 318.   [60] Ibid., p. 322.
[61] Ibid., p. 96 (Remark H).
[62] John Howard, *The State of the Prisons*, 1777. Everyman ed., 1929, p. 47.

Mandeville is cruel and coarse enough to compare the daughters of the poor to the tainted meat the butcher gives to the flies in order to save his choicer flesh. The middle-class women themselves, though better off than the poor women who suffer for them, are in their turn sacrificed to the men: Mandeville accepts the double standard, though he realizes that it has no biological justification. When desperation drives the poor to crime, they are not only to be hanged, but deprived of everything that might make hanging a little less unendurable; although Mandeville admits that they 'are put to Death for Trifles',[63] and that 'the Punishment is greater than the Laws, framed by God himself for the *Jewish* Commonwealth, inflicted; or what natural Justice, proportioning the Punishment to the Crime, seems to require.'[64] The essay on charity schools only makes explicit the social outlook that underlies the two pamphlets.

This raises the question we have so far postponed, of Mandeville's attitude to reform in general as distinct from a few specific reforms. Is it true that he was complacent about the basic social structure, and concerned only to make a few superficial adjustments? There is certainly a strong case for saying so. Many of Mandeville's arguments have since become the standard clichés of dyed-in-the-wool conservatives: that prostitution is necessary to save respectable women from sexual assaults; that education (or higher wages) will 'spoil' the working classes and only make them dissatisfied with their allotted station in life; that people who have been brought up in poverty get used to it and do not regard it as a hardship;[65] that wealth does not make for happiness and peasants are on the whole happier than kings.[66]

Sometimes indeed he goes so far that the reader suspects that his tongue is in his cheek. For example:

... whatever is necessary to Salvation and requisite for Poor Labouring People to know concerning Religion, that Children learn at School, may fully as well either by Preaching or Catechizing be taught at Church, from which or some other Place of Worship I would not have the meanest of a Parish that is able to walk to it be absent on *Sundays*. It is the Sabbath, the most useful Day in seven, that is set apart for

---

[63] *Enquiry into the Causes of the Frequent Executions at Tyburn*, p. 1.
[64] Ibid., p. 36.
[65] *Fable of the Bees*, ed. Kaye, vol. 1, p. 311 (*Essay on Charity and Charity-Schools*).
[66] Ibid., pp. 315–16.

THE SOCIAL REFORMER

Divine Service and Religious Exercise as well as resting from Bodily Labour, and it is a Duty incumbent on all Magistrates to take particular Care of that Day. The Poor more especially and their Children should be made to go to Church on it both in the Fore and Afternoon, because they have no Time on any other. By Precept and Example they ought to be encouraged and used to it from their very Infancy; the wilful Neglect of it ought to be counted Scandalous, and if downright Compulsion to what I urge might seem too Harsh and perhaps Impracticable all Diversions at least ought strictly to be prohibited, and the Poor hindered from every Amusement Abroad that might allure or draw them from it.[67]

Here one's suspicions are strengthened by Mandeville's attitude to the sabbatarianism of the Societies for the Reformation of Manners. He took a mischievous pleasure in embarrassing his pious opponents by using their own arguments against them, often parodying their style as well. The 'answer' attached to the *Modest Defence* should be warning enough against taking everything Mandeville writes at face value.

We can hardly suppose, however, that Mandeville's whole attack on charity schools was an elaborate spoof, or that he was not at least mainly serious in advancing the arguments we have been considering. Yet it is hard to believe that he was simply a reactionary even by twentieth-century standards, which are not of course the standards of his own time. Certainly he attacks many established institutions: the church and the army for example. This hardly looks like complacency about existing social arrangements. There is, as we have seen, evidence in *The Virgin Unmask'd* that Mandeville sympathized with such feminism as existed in his day. And, if Mandeville was reactionary and complacent, how did he come to write these verses on military honour, which appear in one of his contributions to the *Female Tatler*?

> Far from the throng'd Luxurious Town
> Lives an Inchantress of Renown
> Call'd HONOUR, who by secret Charms
> Pulls Swains from yielding Virgin's Arms
> . . . .
> The silly Sweethearts she bewitches
> Admire the Rods for their own Breeches
> Many (is't not a Thousand Pities

---
[67] Ibid., p. 307.

> A Lover's Brain so void of Wit is?)
> Their Limbs shot off imagine Charms
> Where Sleeves hang dandling without Arms
> Others, t'a Leg of Flesh and Bone,
> Prefer a sorry Wooden One
> . . . .
> In Bloody Fields she sits as Gay
> As other Ladies at a Play
> Whilst the wild Sparks on which she Doats
> Are cutting one another's Throats.
> And when these Wild Folks for their Sins
> Have all the Bones broke in their Skins
> Of her Esteem the only Token
> Is t'have Certificates they're broken
> Which in grave Lines are cut on Stone
> And in some Church or Chappel shewn
> To People that neglecting Pray'r
> Have Time to mind who's bury'd there;
> Till some half witted Fellow comes
> To Copy what is writ on Tombs
> And then, to their Immortal Glory
> Forsooth, they're said to live in Story,
> A Recompense which, to a Wonder,
> Must please a Man that's cut asunder!
> . . . .
> But then, they say, the ill-natur'd Jade,
> For all her Sparks, is still a Maid;
> Because none e'er lay in her Bed,
> Unless they first were knock'd o' the Head.[68]

These verses are, it is true, attributed to Artesia, and form part of a controversy between her and her sister Lucinda about the military enthusiasm of their uncle, who forces all his sons to go into the army. One need not, then, suppose they represent Mandeville's own views. But there is evidence from the *Free Thoughts* and the *Origin of Honour* that they do. In any case, if Mandeville were a Colonel Blimp, he would not have written these verses at all.

As we have seen, Mandeville did not accept the usual comforting fictions by which complacency about society was sustained. He did not believe, for example, that women had different desires from men, were automatically corrupted by the loss of

[68] *Female Tatler*, no. 77, 30 Dec. 1709 to 2 Jan. 1710.

virginity (as distinct from society's attitude to that loss), or were intellectually inferior to men. He admitted that 'God has not debarr'd them [the poor children] from Natural Parts and Genius more than the Rich.'[69] He realized that many of the crimes for which capital punishment was inflicted were trifling, and that the penalty was contrary to natural justice. He realized, too, that 'Poverty itself is a strong Temptation to Thieving.'[70]

The exposure of comforting fictions, indeed, is Mandeville's most constant purpose. He continually protests against hypocrisy, self-deception, the refusal to face unpalatable facts. The theme of *The Grumbling Hive* is that the basis of society is actually quite different from what it is complacently supposed to be. What annoys him about the Societies for the Reformation of Manners is that they congratulate themselves on having rectified evils which, if anything, they have made worse.

This is also his complaint against the charity schools. The plain fact, whether men liked it or not, was that 'the comforts of life depended upon the labouring poor'. The system would not work unless large numbers of men and women lived out their lives in poverty. That being so, teaching them to read and write would not help much: it would do little but make them dissatisfied. I have quoted the sentence in which Mandeville admits that the children of the poor have as much native capacity as rich children. He goes on: 'But I cannot think that this [denying them education] is harder, than it is that they should not have Money as long as they have the same Inclinations to spend as others.'[71] It is their poverty that is the basic fact: since that cannot be remedied, the system being as it is, the efforts of the charitable will do more harm than good. To suppose otherwise is to delude oneself.

He would probably have said much the same about the treatment of women. Mandeville does not try to justify the double standard; but the fact was that the institution of marriage was built upon it, and a good many other social arrangements upon the institution of marriage. If marriage was to be preserved, given the existing attitudes, then women had better avoid extramarital love altogether. It was clear that men would not be willing to do that, but at least they had better see to it that their emotions were

[69] *Fable of the Bees*, ed. Kaye, vol. 1, p. 310 (*Essay on Charity and Charity-Schools*).
[70] *Enquiry into the Causes of the Frequent Executions at Tyburn*, p. 36.
[71] *Fable of the Bees*, ed. Kaye, vol. 1, p. 310 (*Essay on Charity and Charity-Schools*).

not seriously engaged outside marriage. Mandeville does not, I think, regard this as an ideal state of affairs, but it was the one most likely to make existing institutions work. And any radical change in existing institutions (as distinct from superficial amendments, like the establishment of public brothels) would be too far-reaching to be undertaken lightly, or, indeed, to have much chance of success.

Mandeville is, in short, arguing, as a Marxist might, that attempted reforms, undertaken without any real understanding of the structure of society, will not do what they are intended to do. He is also like a Marxist in that he insists that merely inveighing against an evil is not enough: one must understand its origin and, as a result, come to see what alone will be effective in stopping it. Duelling, for example, cannot be stopped by laws against it, since the duellist already risks death: Louis XIV took the only effective measure when he set up Courts of Honour as a substitute, to soothe the vanity of those who thought themselves affronted.[72]

Mandeville is, however, unlike Marx in that he does not look forward to any eventual transformation of society. Minor reforms may be made, if one understands the causes of men's behaviour and applies that knowledge. Having noted that the measures being taken against crime and prostitution were plainly not working, Mandeville set himself to see what measures might be effective. But most social evils are, he is convinced, too deeprooted in human nature for there to be any obvious remedy, perhaps for there to be any remedy at all. He does not really have the reforming temperament: he is more interested in diagnosis than cure. In the *Origin of Honour* he complains that moralists are like mole-catchers:

The Moralists have endeavour'd to rout Vice, and clear the Heart of all hurtful Appetites and Inclinations: We are beholden to them for this in the same Manner as we are to Those who destroy Vermin, and clear the Countries of all noxious Creatures. But may not a Naturalist dissect Moles, try Experiments upon them, and enquire into the Nature of their Handicraft, without Offence to the Mole-catchers, whose Business is only to kill them as fast as they can?[73]

His point, as he makes clear a little further on, is that '... the Passions are counted to be Weaknesses, and commonly call'd

---

[72] See *An Enquiry into the Origin of Honour*, 1732, pp. 65–75 (Second Dialogue).
[73] Ibid., p. 5 (First Dialogue).

Frailties; whereas they are the very Powers that govern the whole Machine; and, whether they are perceived or not, determine or rather create the Will that immediately precedes every deliberate Action.'[74]

Mandeville's aim, in short, is to understand human nature, not to change it. Of course, he also wants to say that the efforts to change it (or the behaviour resulting from it) will be fruitless unless it is first understood. But it is understanding that he is chiefly interested in. He will be satisfied if he can get rid of all the cant that surrounds the subject, and see what man and his society are really like. He is content simply to record the facts, even though he records them sardonically. One need not suppose, however, that he was complacent about what he saw.

[74] Ibid., p. 6 (First Dialogue).

5
THE PSYCHOLOGIST

In the seventeenth and eighteenth centuries, many people aspired to be 'the Newton of the moral sciences', long before Hume: some of them, like Hobbes and Spinoza, also antedated Newton. What they wanted to do was to explain all human behaviour in terms of a few simple principles, preferably mechanistic ones. For Hobbes the basic mechanism is desire, which is ultimately biological: essentially a reaching out towards (appetite for) some things in the environment, and a shrinking away from (aversion to) others. We may suppose very simple organisms to be endowed with just these basic responses: the sea anemone opens its tentacles to receive some of the things that come near to it, and closes them tight against others. In man, with his ability to reason, desires may be gratified by indirect and devious means, and new desires may spring up as a result of association with the original, innate ones. None the less, this simple basic mechanism gives us the key to his whole complex emotional life. Hobbes explains all the emotions as a combination of an appetite or aversion plus a belief about a matter of fact. Fear, for example, is an aversion, plus the belief that the object of the aversion will harm one; anger is an aversion plus the belief that harm may be avoided by resistance; hope is an appetite plus the belief that one will attain its object; and so on.

There seems no reason why the desires Hobbes speaks of should not be altruistic ones. At least the acquired ones might be: Hobbes's account of the social contract might, indeed, very well serve to explain how such desires come to be acquired. Hobbes did not, of course, believe that innate desires were altruistic: he strongly attacked the view that man is a social animal by nature.

We know [says Shaftesbury] that every Creature has a private Good and Interest of his own; which Nature has compel'd him to seek, by all the Advantages afforded him, within the Compass of his Make. We know that there is in reality a right and a wrong State of every Creature; and that his right one is by Nature forwarded, and by Himself affectionately sought. There being therefore in every Creature a certain *Interest* or *Good*; there must be also a certain END, to which every thing in his Constitution must *naturally* refer.[1]

This is, or is at least influenced by, the thesis of natural law ethics: that nature impels each individual to strive, consciously or otherwise, to attain the state appropriate for members of his species. Man's peculiarity, as an animal, is that he is rational; so that the appropriate state for him is the fully rational life, which is identified, by a swift and usually unexamined transition, with the morally good life. Man's nature, that is to say, impels him to be virtuous. Hobbes tries to demythologize the natural law theory: he asks what nature actually does impel men to aim at. If we trust to observation, rather than to the definition of man as a rational animal, it would seem that he aims at such goals as food, comfort, sexual gratification, and, above all, at self-preservation. The ability to reason may indeed lead him to discover that in order to attain these goals he needs the co-operation of other men, and that he will not get it unless he and they agree on certain rules of behaviour: so that it is true enough that he is impelled to morality, but only by this round-about route.

Shaftesbury is much closer to the traditional natural law theory; but he distinguishes between 'interest' (the state of the individual by Nature forwarded and by himself affectionately sought) and 'virtue'. Virtue consists in aiming at public rather than private interest: at the good of 'the whole system' of which every individual, and even every species, is a mere part; at the very least, at the good of the species of which the individual is a member.

Shaftesbury could hardly deny that, at least for some individuals of some species, public and private good conflict. In arguing that each species of animal contributes to the well-being of the whole '*Animal-Order* or *Oeconomy*, according to which the Animal Affairs are regulated and dispos'd',[2] he gives this illustration:

For instance; To the Existence of the Spider, that of the Fly is absolutely necessary. The heedless Flight, weak Frame and tender Body of this latter Insect, fits and determines him as much *a Prey* as the rough Make, Watchfulness and Cunning of the former, fits him for Rapine, and the ensnaring part. The Web and Wing are suted to each other. And in the Structure of each of these Animals, there is as apparent and

---

[1] Shaftesbury, *Characteristics*, 1714, vol. 2, p. 15.   [2] Ibid., p. 19.

perfect a relation to the other, as in our own Bodys there is a relation of Limbs and Organs; or, as in the Branches or Leaves of a Tree, we see a relation of each to the other, and all, in common, to *one* Root and Trunk.[3]

The private good of the fly, one can only suppose, is in opposition to the good of the system, which demands that he be eaten. Man is, however, in a happier position. Shaftesbury sets out to prove that for him virtue and interest coincide, and much more directly than on the Hobbist view.

Affections or passions, Shaftesbury tells us, may be divided into three classes: those which tend to public good, and which he rather tendentiously calls the natural affections; those which tend to private good, or the self-affections; and those which tend to neither, and are called unnatural affections. In the first class are all 'such as are founded in Love, Complacency, Good-will and in a Sympathy with the Kind or Species'.[4] The members of the second class ('the Affections which relate to the private System, and constitute whatever we call *Interestedness* or *Self-Love*') are: 'Love of Life; Resentment of Injury; Pleasure, or Appetite towards Nourishment and the Means of Generation, Interest, or Desire of those Conveniences by which we are well provided for, and maintained; Emulation, or love of Praise and Honour; Indolence, or Love of Ease and Rest'.[5] When carried to excess, these become respectively cowardice, revengefulness, luxury, avarice, vanity and ambition, and sloth. Examples of the third class are disinterested malice, sadism, envy, misanthropy, and sexual perversions.

Shaftesbury then argues that the natural affections are the chief source of happiness to the individual who has them, that the self-affections cause misery when carried to excess, and that 'to have the unnatural affections is to be miserable in the highest degree'.

It is obvious that in all this Shaftesbury is using 'self-interest' in two senses: the narrower sense in which it refers to private good as distinct from public good, and a wider sense in which it refers to the happiness of the individual. In gratifying the natural affections the individual is, after all, satisfying his desires no less than when he gratifies the self-affections. If it is true that they are the major source of happiness, then it is in his interest to give free

---

[3] Shaftesbury, *Characteristics*, 1714, vol. 2, pp. 18–19.
[4] Ibid., p. 99.   [5] Ibid., pp. 139–40.

rein to the public affections, and to curb the private ones. It is to his interest, that is to say, to neglect 'whatever we call Interestedness or Self-Love'.

Bishop Butler, who was much influenced by Shaftesbury, seizes on this point and develops it. He insists that 'cool self-love', the calculating pursuit of one's own greatest happiness, is to be sharply distinguished from the gratification of desire, or 'the passions', as such. It follows that the thesis that all actions spring from self-interest is either trivial or false. If it means that all actions are prompted by some desire or other, it is true but trivial; if it means that all actions result from the calculated pursuit of one's own greatest happiness, it is false. In neither case does it imply that genuinely disinterested desires cannot exist.

It is against this background that Mandeville proceeds to his own Newtonizing. Hume was to remark later that the attempts to reduce all apparently disinterested emotions and actions to self-interest were of two very different kinds: one 'utterly incompatible with all virtue or moral sentiment' which could 'proceed from nothing but the most depraved disposition', and one quite harmless 'to morality and practice', which 'proceeded entirely from that love of *simplicity* which has been the source of much false reasoning in philosophy'. According to the first view, all benevolence was consciously hypocritical: 'friendship a cheat, public spirit a farce, fidelity a snare to procure trust and confidence'. According to the second, disinterested friendship was genuine enough, but had its origin in self-love. One man's self-love was 'so directed as to give him a concern for others, and render him serviceable to society'; another's led him to regard nothing but his own gratifications and enjoyment. The difference between the two was still real and important.[6] Hume puts Hobbes in the second, or harmless, class, and there is little doubt that Mandeville belongs there too, though much of the outcry against him (as against Hobbes) came from assigning him to the first.

Characteristically, Mandeville makes great fun of Shaftesbury. *The Fable of the Bees*, Part 2, begins with a declaration by Cleomenes that he has renounced his former Mandevillian errors and is now a convert to 'the lovely System of Lord *Shaftsbury*'. Henceforth he will put the best possible construction on all men's

[6] David Hume, *Enquiry concerning the Principles of Morals*, 1751, Appendix II.

motives and suppose them to be influenced only by benevolence and public spirit.

Cleomenes: ... What I desire your Attention to is my Reformation, which you seem in doubt of, and the great Change that is wrought in me. The Religion of most Kings and other high Potentates, I formerly had but a slender Opinion of, but now I measure their Piety by what they say of it themselves to their Subjects.
Horatio: That's very kindly done.
Cleo.: By thinking meanly of things, I once had strange blundering Notions concerning Foreign Wars: I thought that many of them arose from trifling Causes, magnify'd by Politicians for their own Ends; that the most ruinous Misunderstandings between States and Kingdoms might spring from the hidden Malice, Folly or Caprice of one Man; that many of them had been owing to the private quarrels, Piques, Resentments, and the Haughtiness of the chief Ministers of the respective Nations, that were the Sufferers; and that what is call'd Personal Hatred between Princes seldom was more at first, than either an open or secret Animosity which the two great Favorites of those Courts had against one another: But now I have learned to derive these things from higher Causes. I am reconciled likewise to the Luxury of the Voluptuous, which I used to be offended at, because now I am convinc'd that the Money of most rich Men is laid out with the social Design of promoting Arts and Sciences, and that in the most expensive Undertakings their principal Aim is the Employment of the Poor.
Hor.: These are Lengths indeed.
Cleo.: I have a strong Aversion to Satyr, and detest it every whit as much as you do: The most instructive Writings to understand the World, and penetrate into the Heart of Man, I take to be Addresses, Epitaphs, and above all the Preambles to Patents, of which I am making a large Collection.
Hor.: A very useful Undertaking![7]

Cleomenes goes on to give further examples of his charitableness:

As for instance, If we see an industrious poor Woman, who has pinch'd her Belly, and gone in Rags for a considerable time to save forty Shillings, part with her Money to put out her Son at six Years of Age to a Chimney-sweeper; to judge of her charitably according to the System of the Social Virtues we must imagine, That tho' she never paid for the sweeping of a Chimney in her Life, she knows by Experience that for want of this necessary Cleanliness the Broth has been often spoyl'd, and many a Chimney has been set o' Fire, and therefore

---

[7] *Fable of the Bees*, ed. Kaye, vol. 2, pp. 42–3 (First Dialogue).

to do good in her Generation, as far as she is able, she gives up her All, both Offspring and Estate, to assist in preventing the several Mischiefs that are often occasion'd by great Quantities of Soot disregarded; and, free from Selfishness, sacrifices her only Son to the most wretched Employment for the Publick Welfare.
Hor.: You don't vy I see with Lord *Shaftsbury*, for Loftiness of Subjects.[8]

Cleomenes replies that he can apply the same method in judging men higher in the social scale.

Let the Enemies to the Social System behold the venerable Counsellor, now grown eminent for his Wealth, that at his great Age continues sweltering at the Bar to plead the doubtful Cause, and regardless of his Dinner shortens his own Life in endeavouring to secure the Possessions of others. How conspicuous is the Benevolence of the Physician to his Kind, who from Morning till Night visiting the Sick, keeps several Sets of Horses to be more serviceable to many, and still grudges himself the time for the necessary Functions of Life! In the same manner the indefatigable Clergyman, who with his Ministry supplies a very large Parish already, sollicites with Zeal to be as useful and beneficent to another, tho' fifty of his Order yet unemploy'd offer their Service for the same Purpose.[9]

All this is, of course, rather unfair to Shaftesbury, who does not deny that men often act from selfish motives. His main thesis is the very different one that men are happier when they subordinate the 'self-affections' to the benevolent ones. At the same time, Shaftesbury does claim that benevolent impulses play a larger part in human conduct than is usually supposed, and that many apparently selfish motives are derived from them. Some of his arguments in support of this claim are certainly open to question. For example, he puts the pleasure of solving a mathematical problem among the 'natural' or 'public' affections, partly because he would otherwise have to label it 'unnatural', and so a source of misery and corruption:

And tho' the reflected Joy or Pleasure, which arises from the notice of this Pleasure once perceiv'd, may be interpreted a *Self-Passion* or *interested Regard*: yet the original Satisfaction can be no other than what results from the Love of Truth, Proportion, Order, and Symmetry, in the Things without. If this be the Case, the Passion ought in reality

---

[8] Ibid., pp. 43–4 (First Dialogue). [9] Ibid., pp. 47–8 (First Dialogue).

to be rank'd with *natural Affection*. For having no Object within the compass of the private System; it must either be esteem'd superfluous and *unnatural* (as having no Tendency towards the Advantage or Good of anything in Nature) or it must be judg'd to be, what it truly is, a natural Joy in the Contemplation of those *Numbers*, that *Harmony*, *Proportion*, and *Concord*, which supports the universal Nature, and is essential in the Constitution and Form of every particular Species, or Order of Beings.[10]

Again, Shaftesbury tells us that the pleasures of the body depend on 'social and natural affection'. His reason is that we need company if we are to enjoy them fully.

The very Notion of *a Debauch* (which is a Sally into whatever can be imagin'd of Pleasure and Voluptuousness) carries with it a plain reference to Society, or Fellowship. It may be call'd a *Surfeit*, or *Excess of Eating and Drinking*, but hardly a *Debauch* of that kind, when the Excess is committed separately, out of all Society, or Fellowship. And one who abuses himself in this way, is often call'd a *Sot*, but never a *Debauchee*. The Courtezans, and even the commonest of Women, who live by Prostitution, know very well how necessary it is that every-one whom they entertain with their Beauty, shou'd believe there are Satisfactions reciprocal; and that Pleasures are no less *given* than *receiv'd*. And were this Imagination to be wholly taken away, there wou'd be hardly any of the grosser sort of Mankind, who wou'd not perceive their remaining Pleasure to be of slender Estimation.[11]

Cleomenes refers to this argument when Horatio protests that his lawyer, his physician, and his clergyman are plainly not disinterested, and concerned only for the public good:

From Mens preferring Company to Solitude, his Lordship pretends to prove the Love and Natural Affection we have for our own species: If this was examin'd into with the same Strictness as you have done every Thing I have said on behalf of the three Faculties, I believe that the Solidity of the Consequences would be pretty equal in both.[12]

Shaftesbury's argument is not negligible: the fact that pleasures are increased when shared does suggest that men are not wholly engrossed in their own physical sensations. Hobbes's contention that men meet 'only for gain or for glory' (glorying in their own superiority) can hardly stand examination. Yet Mandeville is right in saying that Shaftesbury goes beyond the evidence.

[10] Shaftesbury, *Characteristics*, 1714, vol. 2, pp. 104–5.   [11] Ibid., pp. 127–8.
[12] *Fable of the Bees*, ed. Kaye, vol. 2, p. 51 (First Dialogue).

Pleasure in the company of others can hardly be identified with disinterested benevolence. If Hobbes over-simplifies in one direction, so does Shaftesbury in the other.

Shaftesbury's assumptions are teleological. He takes it for granted that men's natural impulses must be *for* something: must be implanted in them for some purpose. If no purpose can be found, the impulse is 'unnatural'. The purpose may be the welfare of the individual, or of the species, or of 'the system' made up of many species. The food-seeking impulse, for example, tends to the survival, and so to the good, of the individual, and the mating impulse to the survival of the species. Shaftesbury's point is that far more of our impulses, or 'affections', than we realize are directed to the public rather than the private good. This is of course what one might expect if 'Nature' is some kind of directing intelligence, concerned to make everything in the universe fit together, so that they all make up a single smoothly functioning 'System'. Shaftesbury gives his dialogue 'The Moralists' the subtitle 'A Rhapsody' (perhaps in order to disarm ridicule—the test of truth). It was this topic that he rhapsodized about. Mandeville, of course, was not disarmed:

Cleo.: When in a Starry Night with Amazement we behold the Glory of the Firmament, nothing is more obvious than that the whole, the beautiful *All*, must be the Workmanship of one great Architect of Power and Wisdom stupendious; and it is as evident, that every thing in the Universe is a constituent Part of one entire Fabrick.
Hor.: Would you make a Jest of this too?[13]

To say that an impulse tends to the public (or the private) good is not, however, to say that the Agent need have the public or private good in mind. To eat because one feels hungry is different from eating, perhaps on doctor's orders, to keep one's strength up, and the young man in the grip of the mating instinct cares very little about the perpetuation of the species. Shaftesbury moves too readily from a human tendency connected, sometimes very obliquely, to the public good (as a taste for mathematics is, for example) to disinterested benevolence.

Moreover, Shaftesbury insists that nothing is 'properly either Goodness or Illness in a Creature, except what is from *natural Temper*; A good creature is such a one as by the natural Temper or

[13] Ibid., p. 44 (First Dialogue).

Bent of his Affections is carry'd *primarily and immediately*, and not *secondarily and accidentally*, to Good, and against Ill.'[14] A little earlier, he says that 'if . . . a Creature be accidentally induc'd to do Good (as he might be upon the same terms induc'd to do ILL) he is no more a good Creature for this Good he executes, than a Man is the more an honest or good Man either for pleading a just Cause, or fighting in a good one, for the sake merely of his Fee or Stipend.'[15]

This, coupled with his claim that the 'natural affections' play a predominant part in human motivation, does lend some colour to Mandeville's accusations. Mandeville attacked Shaftesbury so vehemently because he saw him as typifying what he most detested: the refusal to look facts in the face, to see society as it really was. Early in the second Part of *The Fable of the Bees*, he introduces a third character, Fulvia, for the express purpose, he tells us in the Preface, of enabling him 'to say some things on Painting and Operas'. This is not the digression it seems. The discussion with Fulvia turns on realism in art. Horatio, as a representative of fashionable taste, and Cleomenes, in his assumed character as a convert to Shaftesbury, admire those works of art in which nature is prettified, and sordid realities kept out of sight, or in the background.

Cleo.: Look upon that *Dutch* Piece of the Nativity: what charming Colouring there is!. what a fine Pencil, and how just are the Out-Lines for a Piece so curiously finish'd! But what a Fool the Fellow was to draw Hay and Straw and Cattle, and a Rack as well as a Manger; it is a Wonder he did not put the *Bambino* in the Manger.
Ful.: The *Bambino*? That is the Child, to suppose; why it should be in the Manger; should it not? Does not the History tell us, that the Child was laid in the Manger? I have no Skill in Painting, but I can see whether things are drawn to the Life or not: sure nothing can be more like the Head of an Ox than that there. A Picture then pleases me best when the Art in such a Manner deceives my Eye, that without making any Allowances, I can imagine I see the Things in reality which the Painter has endeavour'd to represent. I have always thought it an admirable Piece; sure nothing in the World can be more like Nature.
Cleo.: Like Nature! So much the worse: Indeed, cousin, it is easily seen that you have no Skill in Painting. It is not Nature, but agreeable Nature, *la belle Nature*, that is to be represented; all Things that are abject, low, pitiful and mean, are carefully to be avoided, and kept out

---

[14] Shaftesbury, *Characteristics*, 1714, vol. 2, p. 26.   [15] Ibid., p. 24.

of Sight; because to Men of the true Taste they are as offensive as Things that are shocking, and really nasty.
Ful.: At that rate, the Virgin *Mary's* Condition, and our Saviour's Birth are never to be painted.
Cleo.: That's your Mistake; the Subject it self is noble: Let us go but in the next Room and I'll show you the Difference.—Look upon that Picture, which is the same History. There's fine Architecture, there's a Colonnade; can any thing be thought of more Magnificent? How skilfully is that Ass removed, and how little you see of the Ox; pray mind the Obscurity they are both placed in: It hangs in a strong Light, or else one might look ten times upon the Picture without observing them: Behold these Pillars of the *Corinthian* Order, how lofty they are, and what an Effect they have, what noble space, what an *Area* here is! How nobly every thing concurs to express the majestick Grandeur of the Subject, and strikes the Soul with Awe and Admiration at the same time!
Ful.: Pray Cousin, has good Sense ever any Share in the Judgment which your Men of true Taste form about Pictures?
Hor.: Madam!
Ful.: I beg pardon, Sir, if I have offended: but to me it seems strange to hear such Commendation given to a Painter, for turning the Stable of a Country Inn into a Palace of extraordinary Magnificence: This is a great deal worse than *Swift's* Metamorphosis of *Philemon* and *Baucis*; for there some Shew of Resemblance is kept in the Changes.
Hor.: In a Country Stable, Madam, there is nothing but Filth and Nastiness, or vile abject Things not fit to be seen, at least not capable of entertaining Persons of Quality.[16]

Horatio agrees with what Cleomenes says, but is puzzled that Cleomenes should say it: 'What he said about Painting is very true, whether he spoke it in Jest or in Earnest; but he Talks so diametrically opposite to the Opinion which he is known every where to defend of late, that I don't know what to make of him.'[17]

Mandeville's point is, of course, that Cleomenes, in pretending to be a disciple of Shaftesbury, must also pretend to believe that, as he puts it, 'a Master cannot commit a more unpardonable Fault, than sticking to, or being influenc'd by Truth, where it interferes with what is agreeable.'[18] There is some support for this in Shaftesbury's writings on aesthetics:

The mere Face-Painter [he says], like the mere Historian, copies what he sees, and minutely traces every Feature, and odd Mark. 'Tis other-

---

[16] *Fable of the Bees*, ed. Kaye, vol. 2, pp. 32–4 (First Dialogue).
[17] Ibid., p. 41 (First Dialogue).   [18] Ibid., p. 32 (First Dialogue).

wise with the Men of Invention and Design. 'Tis from the *many* Objects of Nature, and not from *a particular one*, that those Genius's form the Idea of their Work. Thus the best Artists are said to have been indefatigable in studying the best Statues; as esteeming them a better Rule, than the perfectest Human Bodys would afford.[19]

Shaftesbury is not here saying that the ox and the ass, the filth and the nastiness, should be kept out of sight, or at least away from persons of quality: he is making the Aristotelian point that the artist reveals the universal in the particular. To prefer statues to actual human bodies may be, however, to suggest that nature is best when tidied up and prettified. And Mandeville, who is more concerned with Shaftesbury's psychology than his aesthetic, is sure that his portrait of man, and of society, is very much prettified and idealized. It is significant that Cleomenes brings in the chimney-sweep's mother, and that Horatio, the real follower of Shaftesbury, protests. ('You don't vy I see with Lord *Shaftsbury* for Loftiness of Subjects.') Mandeville did not forget that 'all the Comforts of Life arise from the Labour of the Poor' with all that that implied. It meant, among other things, that the poor woman had somehow to be induced to sacrifice her six-year-old, and she could not be expected to do that out of disinterested zeal for the public good. The interplay of motives which kept society going was much more sordid than Shaftesbury supposed: there was a good deal of filth and nastiness to be kept out of the sight of persons of quality.

Mandeville sets out, then, in opposition to Shaftesbury, to show that all motives have their origin in self-interest. But he took Butler's point about the difference between particular desires and cool self-love. Impressed as he was by the folly of mankind, Mandeville was far from saying that every action sprang from a far-sighted calculation of the agent's greatest happiness in the long run: the convicts swaggering to Tyburn, or the soldiers hobbling home from the wars, were sufficient refutation of that. But he does not, either, merely advance the trivial thesis that every action springs from some desire or other. One of the things he is saying is that Shaftesbury's 'self-affections' are sufficient to explain behaviour: the 'public' or 'natural' affections, so far as they exist at all, arise out of the self-affections.

[19] Shaftesbury, *Characteristics*, 1714, vol. 1, pp. 144–5.

But that is not all. Particular desires exist side by side, and often conflict: one will hardly explain behaviour unless one explains by what principle the agent chooses between them. Butler pointed out that cool self-love functions as such as principle. So does Shaftesbury's 'moral sense', or Butler's 'conscience'. Both Shaftesbury and Butler wanted to maintain that it was possible to control and direct the passions without making self-love either the only human motive or the supreme one. Their position was complicated because they also wanted to say that men were on the whole happier when they were virtuous, so that self-love, if only it was cool enough, gave the same practical directions as conscience. This argument, however, presupposed that men had other sources of happiness besides the 'self-affections'.

Mandeville needed a regulating principle or tendency in order to explain how men chose between conflicting desires and how, as a result of applying it, the 'public affections' came into existence. He found it in one of Shaftesbury's 'self-affections': 'Emulation, or Love of Praise and Honour', which, when immoderate, became Vanity and Ambition.

By the end of the first dialogue of Part 2 of the *Fable*, Cleomenes has succeeded in shaking Horatio's faith in Shaftesbury. In the second dialogue, he sets out to show that 'Pride or Vain-glory' is sufficient to account for all the virtues.

Cleo.: The true Object of Pride or Vain-glory is the Opinion of others; and the most superlative Wish which a Man possess'd, and entirely fill'd with it can make is, that he may be well thought of, applauded, and admired by the whole World, not only in the present, but all future Ages. This Passion is generally exploded, but it is incredible, how many strange and widely different Miracles are and may be perform'd by the force of it; as Persons differ in Circumstances and Inclinations. In the first place, there is no Danger so great, but by the help of his Pride a Man may slight and confront it; nor any manner of Death so terrible, but with the same Assistance, he may court, and if he has a firm Constitution, undergo it with Alacrity. In the second, there are no good Offices or Duties, either to others or ourselves, that *Cicero* has spoke of, nor any Instances of Benevolence, Humanity, or other Social Virtue, that Lord *Shaftsbury* has hinted at, but a Man of good Sense and Knowledge may learn to practise them from no better Principle than Vain-glory, if it be strong enough to subdue and keep under all other Passions, that may thwart and interfere with his Design.[20]

Mandeville (or Cleomenes) is at pains to point out that he is not saying that these virtues always do result from pride, but only that they might do so. Nor is he accusing men of conscious hypocrisy: they themselves are unaware of their own underlying motivation.

Later, in the third dialogue, Cleomenes suggests that there is a more fundamental disposition underlying pride:

Cleo.: That Self-love was given to all Animals, at least the most perfect, for Self-Preservation, is not disputed; but as no Creature can love what it dislikes, it is necessary, moreover, that every one should have a real liking to its own Being, superior to what they have to any other. I am of Opinion, begging Pardon for the Novelty, that if this Liking was not always permanent, the Love, which all Creatures have for themselves, could not be so unalterable as we see it is.
Hor.: What Reason have you to suppose this Liking, which Creatures have for themselves, to be distinct from Self-love; since the one plainly comprehends the other?
Cleo.: I will endeavour to explain myself better. I fancy that to encrease the Care in Creatures to preserve themselves, Nature has given them an Instinct, by which every Individual values itself above its real Worth; this in us, I mean in Man, seems to be accompany'd with a Diffidence, arising from a Consciousness, or at least an Apprehension, that we do overvalue ourselves; It is this that makes us so fond of the Approbation, Liking and Assent of others; because they strengthen and confirm us in the good Opinion we have of ourselves.[21]

That self-liking is distinct from self-love, Cleomenes argues, is shown by the fact that men sometimes commit suicide. The assumption here is the teleological one that self-love has as its purpose self-preservation. There seems no reason why we should not regard self-love as the urge, not merely to go on living, but to have a certain quality of life. The man who commits suicide because he is suffering from an incurable disease and sees no prospect before him but continual and gradually increasing pain, is after all acting from self-love. But Mandeville's point may be vindicated if we think of the man who commits suicide to avoid disgrace. No doubt he is acting from self-love too, in the wide

---

[20] *Fable of the Bees*, ed. Kaye, vol. 2, pp. 64–5 (Second Dialogue).
[21] Ibid., pp. 129–30 (Third Dialogue).

sense in which that means the gratification of any (or perhaps of the strongest) desire. But in that sense to say that someone acts from self-love is only trivially true. To avoid this triviality, we need to distinguish desires for physical satisfaction from the more spiritual desires for, say, revenge or applause. That these can be stronger than physical desires is certainly a fact that needs explaining: it is to explain it that Mandeville introduces the concept of self-liking.

In the *Origin of Honour*, which consists of another set of dialogues between the same two men, Horatio accuses Cleomenes of coining terms unnecessarily, and says that self-liking is merely pride. Cleomenes replies that pride is merely one effect of self-liking, and that there are others. He also says that there is need of emotively neutral terms to refer to the passions: they have been christened by moralists whose primary purpose has been persuasion rather than accurate description. Eventually Horatio is convinced, and indeed obligingly summarizes Cleomenes' position:

Hor.: I now understand perfectly well what you mean by Self-liking. You are of Opinion, that we are all born with a Passion manifestly distinct from Self-love; that, when it is moderate and well regulated, excites in us the Love of Praise, and a Desire to be applauded and thought well of by others, and stirs us up to good Actions: but that the same Passion, when it is excessive, or ill turn'd, whatever it excites in our Selves, gives Offence to others, renders us odious, and is call'd Pride. As there is no Word or Expression that comprehends all the different Effects of this same Cause, this Passion you have made one, *viz.* Self-liking, by which you mean the Passion in general, the whole Extent of it, whether it produces laudable Actions, and gains us Applause, or such as we are blamed for and draw upon us the ill Will of others.

Cleo.: You are extremely right; this was my design in coining the Word Self-liking.[22]

Mandeville is careful to distinguish self-liking from self-love; but he does not, of course, deny the existence of self-love in its Hobbist guise of the urge for self-preservation; and that this brings with it related instincts.

It is evident, that the Necessaries of Life stand not every where ready dish'd up before all Creatures; therefore they have Instincts, that

---

[22] *Enquiry into the Origin of Honour*, 1732, pp. 6–7 (First Dialogue).

prompt them to look out for those Necessaries, and teach them how to come at them. The Zeal and Alacrity to gratify their Appetites is always proportion'd to the Strength and the Degree of Force with which those Instincts work upon every Creature: But considering the Disposition of things upon Earth, and the multiplicity of Animals, that have all their own Wants to supply, it must be obvious that these Attempts of Creatures, to obey the different Calls of Nature, will be often oppos'd and frustrated; and that, in many Animals, they would seldom meet with Success; if every Individual was not endued with a Passion that summoning all his Strength, inspired him with a transporting Eagerness to overcome the Obstacles that hinder him in his great Work of Self-Preservation. The Passion I describe is call'd Anger. How a Creature possess'd of this Passion and Self-liking, when he sees others enjoy what he wants, should be affected with Envy, can likewise be no Mystery. After Labour, the most savage and industrious Creature seeks Rest: Hence we learn that all of them are furnish'd, more or less, with a Love of Ease; Exerting their Strength tires them; and the loss of Spirits, Experience teaches us, is best repair'd by Food and Sleep. We see that Creatures, who in their way of living must meet with the greatest Opposition, have the greatest share of Anger, and are born with offensive Arms. If this Anger was to employ a Creature always, without Consideration of the Danger he exposed himself to, he would soon be destroy'd: For this Reason they are all endued with Fear; and the Lion himself turns Tail, if the Hunters are arm'd, and too numerous.[23]

The urge for self-preservation, anger, envy, love of ease, and fear are, then, basic instincts besides self-liking, and much behaviour of men, as well as animals, can be explained without going beyond these instincts. It is self-liking, however, to which we must look to explain those human peculiarities that had misled Shaftesbury into postulating his 'natural', or 'public', affections.

There is a paradox here, not unlike the one Hobbes encounters in explaining such behaviour in terms of self-love. Self-love, if unchecked by reason, can only lead to the war of each against all, to a life that is nasty and brutish and short, which is of course the last thing self-love wants. Self-love itself then can prompt us to curb its own manifestations: to consider others, as well as ourselves, to aim at a compromise between our own interests and the interests of others, simply on the principle that half a loaf is better than no bread.

[23] *Fable of the Bees*, ed. Kaye, vol. 2, p. 176 (Fourth Dialogue).

In much the same way, self-liking (or pride), if unchecked, would lead us to be arrogant and contemptuous of others. But what we want is, after all, the approval of others; and to be arrogant and contemptuous is not the way to gain the approval of a creature whose ruling passion is pride. This enables Cleomenes to meet Horatio's objection:

I don't believe there ever was a Nation, that were not Savages, in which the Youth of both Sexes were not expressly taught never to be Proud or Haughty: Did you ever know a School, a Tutor or a Parent that did not continually inculcate to those under their Care to be civil and obliging; nay does not the word *Mannerly* itself import as much?[24]

Although he had not then elaborated the distinction between self-love and self-liking, Mandeville had already argued in Remark C of Part 1 of the *Fable* that 'all good Manners consist in flattering the Pride of others, and concealing our own.'[25]

A Man that asks considerable Favours of one who is a Stranger to him, without consideration, is called Impudent, because he shews openly his Selfishness without having any regard to the Selfishness of the other. We may see in it likewise the Reason why a Man ought to speak of his Wife and Children, and every thing that is dear to him, as sparingly as possible, and hardly ever of himself, especially in Commendation of them. A well-bred Man may be desirous, and even greedy after Praise and the Esteem of others, but to be prais'd to his Face offends his Modesty: the Reason is this; all Human Creatures, before they are yet polish'd, receive an extraordinary Pleasure in hearing themselves prais'd: this we are all conscious of, and therefore when we see a Man openly enjoy and feast on this Delight, in which we have no share, it rouses our Selfishness, and immediately we begin to Envy and Hate him. For this reason the well-bred Man conceals his Joy, and utterly denies that he feels any, and by this means consulting and soothing our Selfishness, he averts that Envy and Hatred, which otherwise he would have justly to fear . . .
The Man of Manners picks not the best but rather takes the worst out of the Dish, and gets of every thing, unless it be forc'd upon him, always the most indifferent Share. By this Civility the Best remains for others, which being a Compliment to all that are present, every Body is pleas'd with it: The more they love themselves, the more they are forc'd to approve of his Behaviour, and Gratitude stepping in, they are oblig'd almost whether they will or not, to think favourably of

---

[24] Ibid., p. 66 (Second Dialogue).   [25] Ibid., p. 108 (Third Dialogue).

him. After this manner it is that the well-bred Man insinuates himself in the esteem of all the Companies he comes in, and if he gets nothing else by it, the Pleasure he receives in reflecting on the Applause which he knows is secretly given him, is to a Proud Man more than an Equivalent for his former Self-denial, and over-pays to Self-love with Interest, the loss it sustain'd in his Complaisance to others.[26]

Horatio tells Cleomenes that he had found this passage horrifying, but was reluctantly compelled to recognize its truth. 'I'd give a hundred Guineas, with all my Heart, that I did not know it. I can't endure to see so much of my own Nakedness.'[27] Eventually, however, he becomes reconciled to this harsh truth, and once again, like an obedient pupil, gives back to Cleomenes a neat summary of his own argument:

Hor.: I understand you, I believe. Everybody, in this undisciplin'd State, being affected with the high Value he has for himself, and displaying the most natural Symptoms, which you have describ'd, they would all be offended at the barefac'd Pride of their Neighbours: and it is impossible, that this should continue long among rational Creatures, but the repeated Experience of the Uneasiness they received from such Behaviour, would make some of them reflect on the Cause of it; which, in tract of time, would make them find out, that their own barefaced Pride must be as offensive to others, as that of others is to themselves.
Cleo.: What you say is certainly the Philosophical Reason of the Alterations, that are made in the Behaviour of Men, by their being civiliz'd: but all this is done without reflection, and Men by degrees, and great Length of Time, fall as it were into these Things spontaneously.[28]

Eventually, he goes on to say, 'some of them grow impudent enough, not only to deny the high Value they have for themselves, but likewise to pretend that they have greater Value for others, than they have for themselves.'[29] Horatio has now become so apt a pupil that the remark only makes him smile, and he caps it by asking: 'When you talk of Flattery and Impudence what do you think of the first Man that had the Face to tell his Equal, that he was his humble Servant?'[30]

The modern reader is not likely to find any of this as revelatory

[26] *Fable of the Bees*, ed. Kaye, vol. 1, pp. 77–8 (Remark C).
[27] Ibid., vol. 2, p. 108 (Third Dialogue).
[28] Ibid., pp. 138–9 (Third Dialogue).
[29] Ibid., pp. 145 and 150 (Third Dialogue).
[30] Ibid., p. 150 (Third Dialogue).

(or as shocking) as Horatio does. Good manners, good breeding, urbanity, or politeness were, however, of crucial importance to Mandeville, because they were among the more obvious attributes of the Man of Honour. And, as Mandeville continually insists, it is the Man of Honour, and not the Christian saint, who is the real contemporary ideal. If he could be shown to be moved chiefly by self-liking, and the code of Honour itself derived from it, no further refutation of Shaftesbury would be necessary: certainly not to convince Horatio, and the fashionable world he represented. At the beginning Horatio takes the intuitionist line about the code of Honour that Mandeville's other opponents took about morality.

Cleo.: If Men of Honour would act consistently, they ought all to be *Roman* Catholicks.
Hor.: Why, pray?
Cleo.: Because they prefer oral Tradition to all written Laws: For no body can tell, when, in what King's or Emperor's Reign, in what Country, or by what Authority these Laws of Honour were first enacted: It is very strange they should be of such Force.
Hor.: They are wrote and engraved in every one's Breast that is a Man of Honour: there is no denying of it, you are conscious of it your self, every body feels it within.[31]

In the *Origin of Honour* Cleomenes suggests that the principles of the Man of Honour, so far from being self-evident, are of comparatively recent invention:

Cleo.: . . . Hitherto I have spoken of Honour in its first literal Sense, in which it is a Technic Word in the Art of Civility, and signifies a Means which Men by Conversing together have found out to please and gratify one another on Account of a palpable Passion in our Nature, that has no Name, and which therefore I call Self-liking. In this Sense I believe the Word Honour, both as a Verb and a Noun, to be as Ancient as the oldest Language. But there is another Meaning besides, belonging to the same Sound; and Honour signifies likewise a Principle of Courage, Virtue and Fidelity, which some Men are said to act from, and to be aw'd by, as others are by Religion. In this latter Sense, it is much more modern, and I don't believe to be met with a Thousand years ago in any Language.
Hor.: How! Is it but within these Thousand Years that there have been Men of Bravery and Virtue? Have not the *Greeks* and *Romans* had

---
[31] Ibid., p. 83 (Second Dialogue).

great Numbers of them? Were not the *Horatii* and *Curiatii* Men of Honour?

Cleo.: They were never call'd so. All Ages and most Countries have produc'd Men of Virtue and Bravery; but this I do not enquire into now: What I assert to be modern is the Phrase, the Term of Art; it is that which the Ancients knew Nothing of; nor can you with Ten Words, in either *Greek* or *Latin*, express the entire Idea which is annex'd to the Word Honour when it signifies a Principle. To be a Man of Honour, it is not sufficient that he who assumes that Title is brave in War, and dares to fight against the Enemies of his Country; but he must likewise be ready to engage in private Quarrels, tho' the Laws of God and his Country forbid it. He must bear no Affront without resenting it, nor refuse a Challenge, if it be sent to him in a proper Manner by a Man of Honour. I make no Doubt, but the Signification of the Word Honour is entirely Gothick, and sprung up in some of the most ignorant Ages of Christianity. It seems to have been an Invention to Influence Men, whom Religion had no Power over.[32]

In the *Fable*, Part 2, Cleomenes sketches his 'character' of a Gentleman (the 'set piece' I have already alluded to in Chapter 2) as a preliminary to demonstrating that all his noble qualities may be accounted for as due to pride, or 'self-liking'. Apart from urbanity and polished manners, physical courage is perhaps the most characteristic of these. Cleomenes persuades Horatio that courage is not simply an innate quality by asking him to reflect on his own experience. He has fought a duel, and would have thought it shameful to show fear of his adversary; but in a storm at sea, and again when dangerously ill with smallpox, he was frankly afraid of death, and showed it:

Hor.: . . . A Gentleman is not required to shew his Bravery, but where his Honour is concern'd; and if he dares to fight for his King, his Friend, his Mistress, and every thing where his Reputation is engaged, you shall think of him what you please for the rest. Besides that in Sickness and other Dangers, as well as Afflictions, where the Hand of God is plainly to be seen, Courage and Intrepidity are Impious as well as Impertinent. Undauntedness in Chastisements is a Kind of Rebellion: It is waging War with Heaven, which none but Atheists and Free-Thinkers would be guilty of; it is only they that can glory in Impertinence, and talk of dying hard.[33]

---

[32] *Enquiry into the Origin of Honour*, 1732, pp. 14–15 (First Dialogue).
[33] *Fable of the Bees*, ed. Kaye, vol. 2, pp. 86–7 (Second Dialogue).

He accepts Cleomenes' arguments against duelling but says that it is impossible for a gentleman to avoid fighting when the occasion arises:

Entirely to quit the World, and at once to renounce the Conversation of all Persons that are valuable in it, is a terrible Thing to resolve upon. Would you become a Town and Table-talk? could you submit to be the Jest and Scorn of Publick-Houses, Stage Coaches, and Market-Places? Is not this the certain Fate of a Man, who should refuse to fight, or bear an Affront without Resentment? Be just, *Cleomenes*: is it to be avoided? Must he not be made a common Laughing-stock, be pointed at in the Streets, and serve for Diversion to the very Children, to Link-boys and Hackney-Coachmen? Is it a Thought to be born with Patience?[34]

It is now easy for Cleomenes to point out that his courage is not natural, but artificial: his fear of death is overcome only by his greater fear of public disgrace. Why is this fear greater? Because of the predominance, in human nature, of pride or self-liking. The instinctive passions, such as fear of pain and love of ease, can be conquered only by the stronger instinct of self-liking.

What men pride themselves on depends entirely on what is expected of them. Horatio does not mind showing fear at sea, but sailors do: their professional honour is at stake there, as his gentleman's honour is when it comes to duelling. There are hardly any limits to what men may learn to be ashamed of: 'The same Passion, that makes the well-bred Man and prudent Officer value and secretly admire themselves for the Honour and Fidelity they display, may make the Rake and Scoundrel brag of their Vices and boast of their Impudence.'[35] That of course, though Mandeville does not make the point here, was why public executions, as currently conducted, did not have the intended effect: the whole mystique surrounding Tyburn built up a kind of rogues' honour, which led them to defy death as readily as the gentleman fighting a duel. The appeal to honour, it is clear, is a very powerful means of social control. Some of the things it can lead men to do are a fitting subject for satire, as Artesia's verses on 'Grinning Honour' bring out. But honour is also the means by which men can be made useful to one another. In its wider sense, 'the Word Honour, whether it is used as a Noun or a Verb, is

[34] *Fable of the Bees*, vol. 2, p. 88 (Second Dialogue).
[35] Ibid., p. 90 (Second Dialogue).

always a Compliment we make to Those who act, have or are what we approve of; it is a Term of Art to express our Concurrence with others, our Agreement with them in their Sentiments concerning the Esteem and Value they have for themselves.'[36] Since men will do almost anything to win this approval, everything depends on what qualities or actions are thought worthy of honour. And this, as we have seen, varies from community to community, and from sub-group to sub-group within a given community.

Once this is understood, it is possible for Mandeville (or Cleomenes) to explain the social dispositions in man on which Shaftesbury had laid so much stress.

Hor.: But is there in the Mind of Man a natural Affection, that prompts him to love his Species, beyond what other Animals have for theirs; or are we born with Hatred and Aversion, that makes us Wolves and Bears to one another?
Cleo.: I believe neither. From what appears to us in human Affairs, and the Works of Nature, we have more Reason to imagine that the Desire as well as the Aptness of Man to associate, do not proceed from his Love to others, than we have to believe that a mutual Affection of the Planets to one another, superior to what they feel to Stars more remote, is not the true Cause why they keep always moving together in the same solar System.
Hor.: You don't believe that the Stars have any Love for one another, I am sure: Then why, *more Reason?*
Cleo.: Because there are no *Phaenomena* plainly to contradict this Love of the Planets; and we meet with Thousands every Day to convince us, that Man centers everything in himself, and neither loves nor hates but for his own Sake. Every Individual is a little World by itself, and all Creatures, as far as their Understanding and Abilities will let them, endeavour to make that Self happy: This in all of them is the continual Labour, and seems to be the whole Design of Life. Hence it follows, that in the Choice of Things Men must be determin'd by the Perception they have of Happiness; and no Person can commit or set about an Action, which at that then present time seems not to be the best to him.[37]

Men born into society, he adds, are certainly desirous of it, but this can be explained by their love of ease and security. Whatever may be true of primitive man, civilized man is certainly

---

[36] *Enquiry into the Origin of Honour*, 1732, pp. 8–9 (First Dialogue).
[37] *Fable of the Bees*, ed. Kaye, vol. 2, p. 178 (Fourth Dialogue).

in 'a necessitous and helpless Condition': 'a Lady, who never stuck a Pin in herself, and is dress'd and undress'd from Head to Foot like a jointed Baby, by her Woman and the Assistance of another Maid or two, is a more helpless Creature than *Doll* the Dairy-maid, who all the Winter long dresses herself in the Dark, in less time than the other bestows in placing of her Patches.'[38] Man is not instinctively social, like a bee, but he is fit for society in precisely the sense that grapes are fit to make wine: he has qualities which will make him sociable if someone chooses to make use of them. These qualities are fear, which makes him governable, and understanding, which makes him realize the advantages of co-operation. In *A Search into the Nature of Society* Mandeville puts it a little differently: '. . . . the Sociableness of Man arises only from these Two things, *viz*. The multiplicity of his Desires, and the continual Opposition he meets with in his Endeavours to gratify them.'[39]

Men become social beings, Mandeville says, as a result of living in society: he anticipates Rousseau in complaining that writers attribute to primitive man qualities that could only be acquired in society. Cleomenes reads a passage from Sir William Temple's *Essay on the Original of Government* which moves Horatio to comment: 'This Man is no Savage, or untaught Creature; he is fit to be a Justice of Peace.'[40]

How then did society originate? The first motive, Cleomenes suggests, was the need to band together against wild animals, the second was the need to band together against other men. The first assemblies would be 'unsettled and precarious': 'their unruly Passions, and the Discords occasion'd by them, would never suffer them to be happy; their mutual Contentions would be continually spoiling their Improvements, destroying their Inventions, and frustrating their Designs.'[41]

The Hobbesian 'state of nature', in fact, is an early stage of society. Horatio suggests that the expedient of the social contract might occur to men as a means of avoiding this state of mutual hostility, and the constant fear and suspicion resulting from it. Cleomenes replies that 'among such ill-bred and uncultivated

---

[38] Ibid., p. 181 (Fourth Dialogue).
[39] Ibid., vol. 1, p. 344 (*Search into the Nature of Society*).
[40] Ibid., vol. 2, p. 192 (Fourth Dialogue).
[41] Ibid., p. 267 (Sixth Dialogue).

People, no Man would keep a Contract longer than that Interest lasted, which made him submit to it'.[42] There is, in fact, need of laws against violence and trickery, and of penalties to enforce them. This expedient will, however, work very imperfectly before there are written records. 'The third and last Step to Society is the Invention of Letters.'[43]

All this is very like Hobbes. Men are not naturally fit for society, but they may be made so: they must be broken in, as horses are. Even then, there will always be a certain tension between man's instinctual nature and his socially acquired habits:

Cleo.: . . . Vice proceeds from the same Origin in Men, as it does in Horses; the Desire of uncontroul'd Liberty, and Impatience of Restraint, are not more visible in the one, than they are in the other; and a Man is then call'd vicious, when, breaking the Curb of Precepts and Prohibitions, he wildly follows the unbridled Appetites of his untaught or ill-managed Nature. The Complaints against this Nature of ours, are every where the same: Man would have every thing he likes, without considering, whether he has any Right to it or not; and he would do everything he has a mind to do, without regard to the Consequence it would be of to others; at the same time that he dislikes every Body, that, acting from the same Principle, have in all their Behaviour not a special Regard to him.
Hor.: That is, in short, Man naturally will not do, as he would be done by.
Cleo.: That's true; and for this, there is another Reason in his Nature: All Men are partial in their judgments, when they compare themselves to others; no two Equals think so well of each other as both do of themselves . . .[44]

Self-love, then, and self-liking, the two main ingredients of human nature, both militate against the taming of man so that he shall be fit for society. Yet it is by means of them that this socializing process becomes possible. As we have seen, self-liking may be played off against self-love: even the fear of death may be cast out by the greater fear of being laughed at. No man will genuinely value his neighbour as highly as he does himself; but, in order to gain that neighbour's esteem, he may easily be persuaded to behave as if he did.

But the civilizing process goes further than the mere cultivation

---

[42] *Fable of the Bees*, ed. Kaye, Vol. 2, pp. 267-8 (Sixth Dialogue).
[43] Ibid., p. 269 (Sixth Dialogue).   [44] Ibid., pp. 270-1 (Sixth Dialogue).

of politeness. One of the natural qualities that make man fit for society, in the sense that grapes are fit for wine, is understanding. Hobbes had put all the stress on this: as a rational animal, man is capable of realizing that his best chance of serving his own interest (getting the half-loaf that is better than no bread) is to settle for the compromise between interests that society makes possible. Reason, Hobbes saw, was not quite enough: it needed to be reinforced by the fear of punishment. Mandeville does not think that this is quite enough, either: further reinforcement is necessary. Self-liking must be called in as well as fear. In the *Enquiry into the Origin of Moral Virtue* he had conjectured how, at some early stage of social development, this might have been done:

The Chief Thing, therefore, which Lawgivers and other wise Men, that have laboured for the Establishment of Society, have endeavour'd, has been to make the People they were to govern, believe that it was more beneficial for every Body to conquer than indulge his Appetites and much better to mind the Publick than what seem'd his private Interest. As this has always been a very difficult Task, so no Wit or Eloquence has been left untried to compass it; and the Moralists and Philosophers of all Ages employed their utmost Skill to prove the Truth of so useful an Assertion. But whether Mankind would have ever believed it or not, it is not likely that any Body could have persuaded them to disapprove of their natural Inclinations or prefer the good of others to their own, if at the same time he had not shew'd them an Equivalent to be enjoy'd as a Reward for that Violence, which by so doing they of necessity must commit upon themselves. Those who have undertaken to civilize Mankind were not ignorant of this; but being unable to give so many real Rewards as would satisfy all Persons for every individual Action, they were forc'd to contrive an imaginary one, that as a general Equivalent for the trouble of Self-denial should serve on all Occasions, and without costing any thing either to themselves or others, be yet a most acceptable Recompense to the Receivers . . .[45]

Consequently they 'began to instruct men in the Notions of Honour and Shame':

To introduce, moreover, an Emulation amongst Men, they divided the whole Species into two Classes, vastly differing from one another: The one consisted of abject, low-minded People, that always hunting

---

[45] Ibid., vol. 1, p. 42 (*Enquiry into the Origin of Moral Virtue*).

after immediate Enjoyment, were wholly incapable of Self-denial and without regard to the good of others, had no higher aim than their private Advantage; such as being enslaved by Voluptuousness, yielded without Resistance to every gross desire, and made no use of their Rational Faculties but to heighten their Sensual Pleasure. These vile grov'ling Wretches, they said, were the Dross of their Kind, and having only the Shape of Men, differ'd from Brutes in nothing but their outward Figure. But the other Class was made up of lofty high-spirited Creatures, that free from sordid Selfishness esteem'd the Improvements of the Mind to be their fairest Possessions; and setting a true value upon themselves, took no Delight but in embellishing that Part in which their Excellency consisted; such as, despising whatever they had in common with irrational Creatures, opposed by the Help of Reason their most violent Inclinations; and making a continual War with themselves to promote the Peace of others, aim'd at no less than the Publick Welfare and the Conquest of their own Passion . . . These they call'd the true Representatives of their sublime Species, exceeding in worth the first Class by more degrees than that it self was superior to the Beasts of the Field.[46]

'This', Mandeville tells us, 'was (or at least might have been) the manner after which Savage Man was broke.'[47] And he goes on to say, in a sentence which became notorious, that 'Moral Virtues are the Political Offspring which Flattery begot upon Pride.'[48] It is on these conjectures about prehistory that his reputation as a moral nihilist largely rests. Whether the charge is justified or not will be considered when we come to discuss his moral philosophy: at the moment we are concerned with his account of human psychology. If man is really as Mandeville describes him, would it be possible for any flatterer, however artful, to persuade him to take pride in self-denial? Why should he, unless he saw some intrinsic good in self-denial, which is just what Mandeville, *ex hypothesi*, denies? Mandeville's assumption here seems to be that men can pride themselves on anything at all. All that is necessary is that other men should esteem them for it, and they will soon come to esteem themselves on that account.

In *The Origin of Honour*, however, Cleomenes says: 'you can make no Multitudes believe contrary to what they feel, or what contradicts a Passion inherent in their nature . . . on the other

---

[46] *Fable of the Bees*, vol. 1. pp. 43–4 (*Origin of Moral Virtue*).
[47] Ibid., p. 46 (*Origin of Moral Virtue*).
[48] Ibid., p. 51 (*Origin of Moral Virtue*).

[hand], if you humour the Passion, and allow it to be just, you may regulate it as you please', and Horatio, the docile pupil, responds: 'It is not in the Power, then, you think, of Politicians to contradict the Passions, or deny the Existence of them, but that, when once they have allow'd them to be just and natural, they may guide Men in the Indulgence of them, as they please.'[49] The particular passion that prompts this reflection is the superstitious fear of an invisible cause, which Cleomenes says 'is as real in our Nature as the Fear of Death'.[50] Consequently 'the most subtle Unbelievers among Politicians have been forced, for their own Quiet, to counterfeit their Attachment to Religion, when they would a Thousand Times rather have done without it.'[51] This is interesting, since it rouses a suspicion that Mandeville, in professing his own attachment to religion, may have been playing the politician; but it is not clear whether or not it places bounds on the power of self-liking. The fear of death, after all, did not merely have to be manipulated, and channelled in a particular direction: the devotees of Honour could be persuaded to disregard it altogether. This passage may, however, suggest that Mandeville was beginning to doubt whether mere flattery would be enough to lead men to practise self-denial for its own sake.

At any rate, in the *Origin of Honour* he seems inclined to play down the efficacy of virtue.

Hor.: The Upshot is I find, that Honour is of the same Origin with Virtue.
Cleo.: But the Invention of Honour, as a Principle, is of a much later Date; and I look upon it as the greater Atchievement by far. It was an Improvement in the Art of Flattery, by which the Excellency of our Species is raised to such a Height that it becomes the Object of our own Adoration, and Man is taught in good Earnest to worship himself.
Hor.: But granting you, that both Virtue and Honour are of Human Contrivance, why do you look upon the Invention of the One to be a greater Atchievement than that of the other?
Cleo.: Because the One is more skilfully adapted to our inward Make. Men are better paid for their Adherence to Honour, than they are for their Adherence to Virtue: The First requires less self-denial, and the Rewards they receive for that Little are not imaginary but real and palpable. But Experience confirms what I say: The Invention of

---

[49] *Enquiry into the Origin of Honour*, 1732, p. 28 (First Dialogue).
[50] Ibid., p. 25 (First Dialogue).
[51] Ibid., 1732 p. 28 (First Dialogue).

Honour has been far more beneficial to the Civil Society than that of Virtue, and much better answer'd the End for which they were invented. For ever since the Notion of Honour has been receiv'd among Christians, there have always been, in the same Number of People, Twenty Men of real Honour, to One of real Virtue. The Reason is obvious. The Persuasions to Virtue make no Allowances, nor have any Allurements that are clashing with the Principle of it; whereas the Men of Pleasure, the Passionate and the Malicious, may all in their Turns meet with Opportunities of indulging their darling Appetites without trespassing against the Principle of Honour. . . . Do but consider the Instinct of Sovereignty that all Men are born with, and you'll find, that in the closest Attachment to the Principle of Honour there are Enjoyments that are ravishing to Human Nature. A virtuous man expects no Acknowledgement from others; and if they won't believe him to be virtuous, his Business is not to force them to it; but a Man of Honour has the Liberty openly to proclaim himself to be such, and call to an Account Every body who dares to doubt of it . . . The Enjoyments that arise from being virtuous are of that Nicety, that every ordinary Capacity cannot relish them: As, without Doubt, there is a noble Pleasure in forgiving of Injuries, to Speculative Men that have refin'd Notions of Virtue; but it is more Natural to resent them; and in revenging one's self, there is a Pleasure which the meanest Understanding is capable of tasting.[52]

So far, then, we have seen how, according to Mandeville, self-liking is sufficient to account for bravery, and for man's ability to attain some social harmony, however imperfect. Are there other qualities left to be explained? Horatio raises the point that a woman's honour, unlike a man's, consists in chastity, which must surely require genuine self-denial. Especially, he adds,

in handsome clever Women that seem to be made for Love, as you and I have seen a great many in the Nunneries in *Flanders*. Self-liking or Pride have Nothing to do there; for the more powerfully that Passion operates in either Men or Women, the less Inclination they'll shew to be mew'd up in a Cloyster, where they can have none but their own Sex to converse with.[53]

Cleomenes answers that only two forces are strong enough to keep men or women celibate: religion (which requires supernatural aid) and the fear of shame. The first is, he thinks, rare,

---

[52] *Enquiry into the Origin of Honour*, pp. 43–4 (First Dialogue).
[53] Ibid., p. 54 (Second Dialogue).

even in the religious houses: certainly the nuns' superiors do not trust this motive very much; they keep their charges locked up and barred, and men are not allowed near them. Fear of shame is much more effective:

> But there are Thousands of vain Women, whom no Thoughts of Futurity ever made any Impression upon, that lead single Lives by Choice, and are at the same Time careful of their Honour to the greatest Nicety, in the Midst of Temptations, gay sprightly Women, of amorous Complexions, that can deny a passionate, deserving Lover, whose Person they approve of and admire, when they are alone with him in the dark; and all this from no better Principle than the Fear of Shame, which has its Foundation in Self-liking, and is so manifestly derived from that and no other Passion.[54]

How successful has Mandeville been in maintaining his thesis? Remembering Hume's distinction between the two kinds of self-interest theory, perhaps one should ask first exactly what that thesis is. Is Mandeville denying the existence of any genuinely disinterested feeling, any love or benevolence that is not actively self-seeking? Or is he merely saying that, while such feelings do exist, they are not innate in man but result from education and conditioning? The innate disposition which makes such conditioning possible is self-liking.

When Horatio accuses Mandeville of asserting that virtue does not exist, Cleomenes denies the charge:

> *Cleo.*: Indeed, *Horatio*, this is a stronger Argument against the Social System, and more injurious to it, than anything that has been said by the Author whom you have exclaim'd against with so much Bitterness.
> *Hor.*: I deny that. I don't conclude from the Selfishness in some, that there is no Virtue in others.
> *Cleo.*: Nor he neither, and you very much wrong him if you assert that he ever did.[55]

This is in the first of the dialogues that make up Part 2 of the *Fable*: Cleomenes repeats the claim in the last dialogue:

> *Hor.*: Why don't you speak more openly and say that there is no Virtue or Probity in the World? for all the drift of your Discourse is tending to prove that.
> *Cleo.*: I have amply declared myself upon this Subject already in a

---

[54] Ibid., p. 58 (Second Dialogue).
[55] *Fable of the Bees*, ed. Kaye, vol. 2, p. 50 (First Dialogue).

former Conversation; and I wonder you will lay again to my Charge what I once absolutely denied: I never thought that there were no virtuous or religious Men; what I differ with in the Flatterers of our Species, is about the Numbers, which they contend for; and I am persuaded that you yourself, in reality, don't believe that there are so many virtuous Men as you imagine you do.[56]

This may, however, be misleading. Mandeville always insists that there is no virtue without self-denial, and sneers at Shaftesbury for maintaining the contrary. It might seem to follow from this (and Mandeville seems to imply it, often enough) that apparently virtuous behaviour is not genuinely so if it has its origin in a 'passion' and is merely a disguised form of self-liking. The self has not been denied: vanity has been pandered to. The moral virtues whose origin is described in *An Enquiry into the Origin of Moral Virtue* are not, on this view, really virtues at all. True virtue occurs only when human nature has been transcended altogether, and that is possible only with divine assistance. When Mandeville says that he does not deny that virtue sometimes occurs, he may merely mean to acknowledge that a few saints may, with God's help, rise above human limitations. He says more than once that he is talking about 'Men in Nature' and not 'Devout Christians, who alone are to be excepted here, being preternaturally assisted by the Divine Grace'.[57] He always insists that Devout Christians are extremely rare, even in the religious houses. Whether he is sincere in this or not, it is obviously a useful ploy, since it enables him to dispose of any counter-examples that may be brought against him without abandoning the thesis that human nature, as such, is completely selfish.

It would follow that, in showing that an alleged virtue arises from self-liking, and has been brought into existence by the skilful contrivances of wise men who know how to flatter their fellows into being useful to mankind, he is showing that it is not truly a virtue at all.

On the other hand, Mandeville also says, through his mouthpiece, Cleomenes: 'My Business is to demonstrate to you, that the good Qualities Men compliment our Nature and the whole Species with are the Result of Art and Education.'[58] He does not,

---

[56] *Fable of the Bees*, ed Kaye, vol. 2. p. 336 (Sixth Dialogue).
[57] Ibid., vol. 1, p. 166 (Remark O). See also p. 40 (*Origin of Moral Virtue*) and *Origin of Honour* (Second Dialogue), p. 56.
[58] Ibid., vol. 2, p. 306 (Sixth Dialogue).

in this passage, deny that they are genuinely good qualities. When he says, in the *Origin of Honour*, that Honour is more reliable than Virtue as a means of controlling human behaviour, his point is that Honour does less violence to human nature. It would seem, then, that even the virtue begotten by flattery upon pride does demand genuine self-denial. The 'noble Pleasure in forgiving Injuries' is, no doubt, derived from self-liking and is a subtle form of vanity, but there is nothing hypocritical about it: it does demand genuine forgiveness. What the virtuous man has been taught to pride himself on is, indeed, self-denial: refusing to gratify those passions which he shares with the lower animals and which, accordingly, he has been led to believe, are ignoble. Self has, of course, not been wholly denied: self-liking is gratified, though less obviously and perhaps less satisfyingly than by means of Honour. But perhaps there is enough self-denial for the artificial virtue engendered by skilful politicians without preternatural assistance to count nevertheless as genuine virtue. On this view, when Mandeville says that he does not deny that virtue occurs, but merely insists on its rarity, he may be simply saying that men do sometimes, but not often, allow their vanity to take the form of repressing those passions they share with the brutes.

Whichever view we take, the point at issue would seem to be what is to count as virtue. Perhaps there is a more pertinent question: is Horatio right when he accuses Mandeville of saying that 'the Words Honesty, Benevolence, and Humanity, and even Charity' are 'empty sounds only'?[59]

What would make them empty sounds? If they are disguised forms of vanity, or, in Mandeville's later, less tendentious terminology, of self-liking? Is there any reason to suppose that the benevolence is any less genuine because of that? Presented less paradoxically and provocatively than he himself chose to present it, Mandeville's thesis might be put like this: Man does not naturally have the qualities that make for harmonious living together in society, but it is possible for him to acquire them. What makes it possible is his appetite for esteem, and his readiness to esteem himself on whatever qualities he is taught to value. There are, however, many traits in his nature which are inimical to social harmony: civilization is precarious, and needs constant vigilance if it is to be maintained. The mere realization that

[59] Ibid., p. 30.

virtuous behaviour makes for the public good will not be enough to prevent backsliding: he constantly needs fresh inspiration; he needs to reflect on his own nobility, and his superiority to mere animals. Even this, indeed, may not be enough: which is why Honour, with its more direct appeal to vanity, is more efficacious.

This account of virtue would seem to put Mandeville firmly in Hume's second class of self-interest theorists: among those who were harmless, like Hobbes. It is true that he himself constantly talks as if, in explaining virtue, he has explained it away. Virtue properly so called, he seems to imply, does not exist. But if a man prides himself on his concern for others, does this mean that he has no genuine concern for others, but only pride? This seems clearly different from saying that he would never have developed a concern for others, if he had not had a capacity for pride.

So far we have been trying to see what Mandeville's thesis actually is. There is of course a different question, which we may now consider: is it true?

The difficulty here is to know what precisely would count as a refutation. It is a common criticism of self-interest theories in general that they turn out to be mere tautologies. Whatever you do voluntarily, the argument runs, you do because you desire to do it; therefore what you aim at is always the gratification of your own desires; therefore disinterested desires do not exist. Once the thesis is stated as barely as this, it is clear that this is true only in a special sense of 'disinterested'. Nothing has been said that would cast doubt on perfectly genuine benevolence, or that would make it impossible to desire the happiness of others.

There are times when Mandeville seems to be resorting to precisely this argument. Consider what he says, in the *Essay on Charity and Charity-Schools*, about Pity. The virtue of charity, he tells us,

is often counterfeited by a Passion of ours, call'd *Pity* or *Compassion*, which consists in a Fellow-feeling and condolence for the Misfortunes and Calamities of others: all Mankind are more or less affected with it; but the weakest Minds generally the most. It is raised in us, when the Sufferings and Misery of other Creatures make so forcible an Impression upon us, as to make us uneasy. It comes in either at the Eye or Ear, or both; and the nearer and more violently the Object of Compassion strikes those Senses, the greater Disturbance it causes in us, often to such a Degree as to occasion great Pain and Anxiety.

He goes on to give a grisly example, portrayed with his usual vividness of phrase; if anyone saw a large, wild, half-starved sow attacking and eating an infant, he would certainly feel great distress.

What Tortures would it give the Soul beyond Expression! Let me see the most shining Virtue the Moralists have to boast of so manifest either to the Person possess'd of it, or those who behold his Actions: Let me see Courage, or the Love of One's Country so apparent without any Mixture, clear'd and distinct, the first from Pride and Anger, the other from the Love of Glory, and every Shadow of Self-Interest, as this Pity would be clear'd and distinct from all other Passions.[60]

At first sight, this would seem to be a damaging admission for Mandeville, especially as he represents pity as a natural, untaught emotion owing nothing to the manipulations of crafty politicians. It would seem, then, that self-love and self-liking are not, after all, the sole original human dispositions: that there is a quite spontaneous tendency to be upset by the sufferings of others. Isn't this just what Shaftesbury claimed, and Mandeville denied? Yet in fact Mandeville exhibits pity triumphantly, as proof that genuine charity does not exist. He goes on:

There would be no need of Virtue or Self-Denial to be moved at such a Scene; and not only a Man of Humanity, of good Morals and Commiseration, but likewise an Highwayman, an House-Breaker, or a Murderer could feel Anxieties on such an Occasion; how calamitous soever a Man's Circumstances might be, he would forget his Misfortunes for the time, and the most troublesome Passion would give way to Pity, and not one of the Species has a Heart so obdurate or engaged that it would not ake at such a Sight, as no Language has an Epithet to fit it.[61]

Pity, then, does not involve self-denial. Why not, since it is directed solely to relieving the miseries of others, and is unmixed with any ulterior motive? The answer seems to be that it is a 'Passion'. That is to say, it is a desire of ours that the infant should not suffer, and in indulging it we are merely gratifying our own desire, and so being self-indulgent. This is precisely the classic argument for self-interest (or psychological hedonism) which has been dismissed some paragraphs back as empty.

---

[60] *Fable of the Bees*, ed. Kaye, vol. 1, pp. 255–6 (*Essay on Charity*).
[61] Ibid., p. 256 (*Essay on Charity*).

I think that Mandeville is relying, at least in part, on this argument; but he has others which cannot be dismissed so easily. He might, for example, deny that pity is directed to relieving the sufferings of others: it is, he might say, a mere reaction, a physical uneasiness. The desire it gives rise to is merely to get rid of that uneasiness, by any means that may present itself. Relieving the suffering is one possible means; another is to remove ourselves from the troubling sights and sounds. We do not like to see a beggar's sores; but we may not really care about the beggar, if only he would keep them decently covered. We can read about distant disasters and be quite unmoved, though they would distress us if we had to witness them.

This argument, however, cuts both ways: it might be taken to show that we remain unmoved only when, through lack of imagination, we do not fully realize the extent of the suffering. In any case, Mandeville does not maintain that we would always be satisfied to get rid of the sight of suffering, without relieving it. He does not, that is to say, altogether deny that we have a genuinely disinterested distaste for the suffering of others. His only reason for saying that pity is not a virtue seems to be that it does not involve the renunciation of all the passions, because it is itself one.

Pity, he concedes, both here and in the *Enquiry into the Origin of Moral Virtue* 'is the most amiable of all our Passions'.[62] He adds that it is none the less

> as much a Frailty of our Nature, as Anger, Pride or Fear ... it is an Impulse of Nature, that consults neither the publick Interest nor our own Reason, it may produce Evil as well as Good. It has help'd to destroy the Honour of Virgins, and corrupted the Integrity of Judges; and whoever acts from it as a Principle, what good soever he may bring to the Society, has nothing to boast of but that he has indulged a Passion that has happened to be beneficial to the Publick.[63]

That is in the *Origin of Moral Virtue*; in the *Essay on Charity* he adds that pity may prevent parents 'from managing their Children as their rational Love to them would require, and themselves could wish it'.[64]

---

[62] *Fable of the Bees*, ed. Kaye, vol. 1, pp. 260 (*Essay on Charity*) and 56 (*Origin of Moral Virtue*).
[63] Ibid., p. 56 (*Origin of Moral Virtue*).
[64] Ibid., p. 260 (*Essay on Charity*).

The point here seems to be that pity, as the impulse to relieve a particular piece of suffering that happens to be before our eyes, needs to be supplemented and controlled by reflection on the probable further consequences, both to the sufferer and to others, of trying to relieve it. As Shaftesbury and Hutcheson pointed out, this might be regarded as a more extensive pity, or benevolence, being called in to correct a partial and limited one. But they were concerned with the controversy about whether feeling or reason is the source of morality. Whatever view one takes about that, or about the need to control pity, there seems no reason to suppose that it is not genuinely disinterested, in the usual sense of that word. When Mandeville says: 'There is no Merit in saving an innocent Babe ready to drop into the Fire: The Action is neither good nor bad, and what Benefit soever the Infant received, we only obliged ourselves; for to have seen it fall, and not strove to hinder it, would have caused a Pain, which Self-preservation compell'd us to prevent',[65] he is clearly falling back on the psychological hedonist's argument: Whatever I do deliberately must give me gratification else I would not do it; so I act only to gratify myself.

Mandeville is not, however, only making the empty claim that all actions spring from some desire or other, and are to that extent self-indulgent, even if the desire is solely for the happiness of another and if I thwart a good many other desires of mine in order to gratify this one. He also makes what appears to be a more significant claim: that such human behaviour as is not due to self-love in its more obvious and disreputable forms can be explained as resulting not just from some desire or other, but from the specific desire for praise or esteem that Mandeville called self-liking.

Is this claim, too, an empty one? There is a case for saying that it is. At first sight, indeed, Mandeville seems to be saying something that would, if true, add considerably to our knowledge of human nature. It seems to be an empirical statement capable of refutation. For, if our less disreputable actions are done only for the sake of prestige, then presumably no one will do such actions if he knows that they will never be heard of, or that they will only bring him infamy. In fact, however, many men have done unselfish things which they did not expect to be bruited abroad, and

[65] Ibid., p. 56 (*Origin of Moral Virtue*).

others have done things they believed to be right which, they knew, their fellows disapproved of and would blame them for. It would seem, then, that Mandeville's thesis can be easily disproved.

But now a parallel with the other kind of self-interest theory begins to show itself. The thesis that no actions are disinterested also seems at first sight empirical, and refutable: one need only produce examples of disinterested actions. But then it turns out that the word 'interested' is being extended in meaning to cover all actions motivated by desire, and so all voluntary actions: so that the apparently bold and interesting (though false) assertion that no actions are disinterested turns into the tautology that all voluntary actions are voluntary. Similarly it soon appears that, when Mandeville talks about the desire for esteem and the fear of dishonour, he means more than simply standing well with one's fellows:

Cleo.: . . . It was not the Contrivance of one Man, nor would it have been the Business of a few Years, to establish a Notion, by which a rational Creature is kept in Awe for Fear of it Self, and an Idol is set up that shall be its own Worshipper.
Hor.: But I deny, that in the Fear of Shame we are afraid of our Selves. What we fear, is the Judgment of others, and the ill Opinion they will justly have of us.
Cleo.: Examine this thoroughly, and you'll find, that when we covet Glory, or dread Infamy, it is not the good or bad Opinion of others that affects us with Joy or Sorrow, Pleasure or Pain; but it is the Notion we form of that Opinion of theirs, and must proceed from the Regard and Value we have for it. If it was otherwise, the most Shameless Fellow would suffer as much in his Mind from publick Disgrace and Infamy, as a Man that values his Reputation. Therefore it is the Notion we have of Things, our own Thought and Something within our Selves, that creates the Fear of Shame: For if I have a Reason, why I forbear to do a Thing to Day, which it is impossible should be known before to Morrow, I must be with-held by Something that exists already; for Nothing can act upon me the Day before it has its Being.[66]

This has less than Mandeville's usual lucidity. What exists already, presumably, is what Mandeville's contemporaries might have called an 'idea': my imagining of the scornful comments others will make when my behaviour becomes known. It does not follow that what I fear is 'something in myself' if that is taken

[66] *Enquiry into the Origin of Honour*, pp. 41–2 (First Dialogue).

to mean that I fear my own opinion rather than theirs. But perhaps all Mandeville means is that the imagined comments which influence me will be different from the real ones, and different in ways that reflect my opinions of those who are to utter them. The assertion that I will not be influenced by these critics unless I value their opinions may be meant as a further and separate point.

In any case, however shaky Mandeville's argument may be here, his main point is clear enough. The Man of Honour, he declares, worships himself: why else should he swear 'upon my Honour'? This is 'a Kind of Swearing by himself, as others do by God'.[67] What the Man of Honour does, in fact, is to set up a kind of ideal self in his imagination: when his own conduct is at variance with this ideal, he feels shame; when the conduct of others is at variance with it (lacking in the respect the ideal would be bound to call forth), he feels affronted and demands satisfaction. The Man of Honour's ideal self is a jealous God, and a peculiarly prickly one, who is not above demanding human sacrifice; but each of us has his own ideal self, also demanding in its own way.

It appears, then, that the esteem and approval self-liking bids us seek is our own esteem and our own approval. This may seem different from what Mandeville started out by saying: that each of us has an instinctive tendency to overvalue himself, and that, subconsciously suspecting this, we are anxious that others should confirm our high opinion of ourselves. This tendency, Mandeville now tells us, is modified in two ways. First, it is internalized: we form the habit of admonishing ourselves: 'What would so-and-so say if he saw you doing that?' But, secondly and more importantly, we reflect that the opinion of others is not always worth having. What counts is the approval of those who have the same high standards as ourselves. Which means that it is ultimately our own standards, our own approval, that we appeal to.

This modification enables Mandeville to meet the argument that men sometimes do unselfish things in secret, or in defiance of public opinion:

But such Men, as without complying with any Weakness of their own, can part from what they value themselves and, from no other Motive but their Love to Goodness, perform a worthy Action in Silence:

---

[67] Ibid., p. 87 (Second Dialogue).

Such Men, I confess, have acquir'd more refin'd Notions of Virtue than those I have hitherto spoke of; yet even in these (with which the World has yet never swarm'd) we may discover no small Symptoms of Pride, and the humblest Man alive must confess, that the Reward of a Virtuous Action, which is the Satisfaction that ensues upon it, consists in a certain Pleasure he procures to himself by Contemplating on his own Worth: Which Pleasure, together with the Occasion of it, are as certain Signs of Pride, as looking Pale and Trembling at any imminent Danger, are the Symptoms of Fear.[68]

It is interesting to compare Mandeville with his opponents, Shaftesbury and Hutcheson. According to Hutcheson (who is elaborating views which in Shaftesbury are less explicit) all desires have, ultimately, one of just two objectives: our own interest or the interest of others, private good or the public good. This gives us the two important dispositions of self-love and benevolence. But there is a third disposition as well, the Moral Sense, which is a tendency, not to desire things of a certain kind, but to approve or disapprove of those desires. The Moral Sense acts as a judge or referee between self-love and benevolence, when they conflict. But it is a singularly partial judge, with one sole *ratio decidendi*: it invariably approves of subordinating self-love to benevolence.

Mandeville of course is sceptical of benevolence as an innate tendency to aim at the public good as such. And he would not want to ennoble the disposition to approve and disapprove with so tendentious a title as the Moral Sense. Since it influences action, moreover, it cannot be a merely contemplative or aesthetic disposition: it, too, must be a desire of some kind. In Mandeville's scheme there are not three dispositions but two: self-love and the appetite for approval (self-liking). That is all that is innate, part of 'original human nature'. Hutcheson was to say, and Shaftesbury had already indicated, that there is an innate disposition to approve of subordinating self-love to the public good; but, considering all the other things men can be brought to approve, it is clear to Mandeville that this is not innate but acquired, at the instance of 'skilful politicians'. What is innate is a desire to be approved, rather than to approve; though, as we have seen, the one rapidly develops into the other. The appetite for approval becomes an appetite for self-approval.

[68] *Fable of the Bees*, ed. Kaye, vol. 1, p. 57 (*Origin of Moral Virtue*).

This move, as we have seen, enables Mandeville to meet the obvious objections. But does his thesis now become empty, in the way that the more usual self-interest thesis is empty? According to that thesis, any action caused by desire (any voluntary action) aims at the gratification of desire, and so at self-gratification. Hence all actions are selfish. But of course they are not selfish in the ordinary sense of the word; so that all the argument succeeds in doing is to deprive the thesis that no actions are disinterested of all the implications that made it interesting.

Is something like this also true of Mandeville's thesis? According to it, we either approve or disapprove of our own actions. If we disapprove, but do them none the less, our motive must clearly be self-love (in its usual, disreputable sense). If we approve of them, then it must be self-approval we are aiming at. Hence all actions arise from self-love or self-liking. The weakness here is obviously in the assertion that it is self-approval we are aiming at, just as the weakness in the other argument lies in the assertion that we aim at self-gratification, as if that were the name of a special kind of sensuous thrill (often also called 'pleasure') and not just a way of saying that we do what we choose to do. Similarly Mandeville seems to think of self-approval as a smug glow of self-righteousness; whereas all that he is entitled to say is that we do what, on reflection, we think it right to do (except, of course, on those numerous occasions when we are led by temptation into doing what we think wrong). Which is surely a quite unexciting conclusion.

That is the obvious philosophical gambit to deploy against Mandeville, in his role as a Newton of the moral sciences; and he is certainly vulnerable to it. Yet it would be a mistake to suppose that that disposes completely of Mandeville's analysis of human nature. The grand comprehensive Newtonizing thesis fails, like most such theses, to stand critical examination; but in trying to establish it he makes less sweeping assertions, which may be worth thinking about. Consider, for example, his analysis of the Man of Honour. To us the defects of that eighteenth-century ideal are obvious enough, and we readily agree that vanity and arrogance were his ruling passions. But it was far from obvious to contemporaries like Horatio. No doubt the ideal was beginning to break down, as the attempts to outlaw duelling suggest, or, at a different level, the popularity of the many imitations of

Don Quixote. But it was still strong enough. In *L'Esprit des lois* (published sixteen years after the *Origin of Honour*) Montesquieu, arguing that each type of state has its distinctive 'spirit', which animates its citizens and keeps society more or less harmonious, finds the spirit of Monarchy (of which England and France were prime examples) in Honour, the pride in one's social rank and the determination to do what befits it. The spirit of Democracy (of which a prime example was ancient Sparta) was, it is true, Virtue, by which Montesquieu meant selfless public spirit; but it was generally conceded that democracy was impracticable just because the demands it made on human nature were too great. When Mandeville argued that society was held together by a peculiar mixture of vanity and snobbishness, he was not merely being perverse.

Again, consider the opening sentence of the *Essay on Charity*: 'Charity is that Virtue by which part of that sincere Love we have for our selves is transferr'd pure and unmix'd to others, not tied to us by the Bonds of Friendship or Consanguinity and even meer Strangers, whom we have no obligation to, nor hope or expect any thing from.' One can hardly help being struck by the aptness of the phrase: 'that sincere Love we have for our selves'. No one doubts that *that* love exists: we do not feel we have to account for actions that benefit ourselves (was there perhaps some ulterior motive of benevolence?) in the way we may possibly wonder about actions done to benefit others. Mandeville may well be right in saying that charity, when it is defined as rigorously as that, does not exist. Perhaps we never do regard others with quite the whole-hearted devotion we have for ourselves, unless simple fellow feeling is reinforced by parental affection, or friendship, or the like. Of course Mandeville makes things easy for himself by the rigour of his definition: why should friendship and the rest be ruled out? One need not accept the contention that they are disguised forms of self-interest. To say that we never love complete strangers quite as we love ourselves is not to say anything very startling: it certainly does not establish that there is no charity, in the ordinary sense of the word. But the fact that it is not startling does suggest that Mandeville is not being merely cynical when he insists, against Shaftesbury, that selfishness is a primary fact of human nature and that the claim that we are social animals at least needs qualification.

No doubt Mandeville exaggerates the amount of self-deception in human behaviour; but self-deception does exist and is (almost by definition) peculiarly difficult to detect. To expose it is, consequently, to do us a service, though one we are unlikely to be grateful for. There undoubtedly are people like Emilia, the pious ex-prostitute described in *Free Thoughts on Religion*, who 'flatters her self with having perform'd every christian duty' and 'knows not to this hour, that envy and vanity are her darling vices'.[69] Perhaps we are all, at least some of the time, more like Emilia than we like to think. Mandeville's strength lies in his skill at pointing out such possibilities to us, and in illustrating them with vividly sketched and shrewdly observed examples.

Apart altogether from his grand thesis, Mandeville makes a good many incidental remarks that show considerable psychological and sociological acumen. Kaye points out[70] that he is a pioneer in his account of the origin of language, which could, he thought, have come about only by a long, slow, and stumbling evolutionary process. This may seem to contrast with the rather crude account of the development of morality in the *Enquiry into the Origin of Moral Virtue*, where he seems to suppose that morality was invented at one stroke by 'those that have undertaken to civilize mankind'.[71] This is corrected, however, in *The Origin of Honour*:

Hor.: But, how are you sure, that this was the Work of Moralists and Politicians, as you seem to insinuate?
Cleo.: I give those Names promiscuously to All that having studied Human Nature, have endeavour'd to civilize Men, and render them more and more tractable, either for the Ease of Governours and Magistrates, or else for the Temporal Happiness of Society in general. I think of all Inventions of this Sort, the same which [I] told you of Politeness, that they are the joint Labour of Many. Human Wisdom is the Child of Time. It was not the Contribution of one Man, nor could it have been the Business of a few Years, to establish a Notion, by which a rational Creature is kept in Awe for Fear of it Self, and an Idol is set up, that shall be its own Worshiper.[72]

Whether because he was ahead of his time or because his time was not so far behind ours as we like to think, the modern reader

---

[69] *Free Thoughts on Religion*, 2nd ed., 1729, p. 35. And see p. 45 *supra*.
[70] *Fable of the Bees*, ed. Kaye, vol. 2, p. 288n. (Sixth Dialogue).
[71] Ibid., vol. 1, p. 42 (*Origin of Moral Virtue*).
[72] *Enquiry into the Origin of Honour*, p. 41 (First Dialogue).

continually finds passages in Mandeville that would not surprise him in a twentieth-century work on psychology. An instance is the discussion between Lucinda and Arabella in the *Female Tatler* about why women usually hate their daughters-in-law but not their sons-in-law. Arabella suggests that they like their sons-in-law because they identify themselves, in their imagination, with their daughters. The dislike of daughters-in-law she puts down to resentment at losing authority in their own homes. Lucinda agrees about the first but not the second, suggesting that there is a deeper reason. The mothers-in-law 'grudge them the Enjoyment of their Sons, because it so much resembles what they were possess'd of themselves, and thought a Crime in others to pretend to'. They cannot brook that 'strange Women . . . should rob them of that Intimacy and Affection which they think that they have so clearly deserved'.[73] The discussion is ended by 'an elderly gentlewoman', who says that the explanation is simply that daughters-in-law deserve the low opinion their husband's mothers form of them.

And here is a passage that might have come from John Bowlby:

Natural Affection prompts all Mothers to take Care of the Offspring they dare own; so far as to feed and keep them from Harm, while they are helpless: but where People are poor, and the Women have no Leisure to indulge themselves in the various Expressions of their Fondness for their Infants, which fondling of them ever encreases, they are often very remiss in tending and playing with them; and the more healthy and quiet such Children are, the more they are neglected. This want of pratling to, and stirring up the Spirits in Babes, is often the principal Cause of an invincible Stupidity, as well as Ignorance, when they are grown up; and we often ascribe to natural Incapacity, what is altogether owing to the Neglect of this early Instruction.[74]

The point is also made earlier in the same dialogue, where Cleomenes insists, against the common-sense objections of Horatio, that the first months of infancy are of great importance in a child's development:

Cleo.: . . . Therefore the more an Infant, in Health, is talk'd to, and jumbl'd about, the better it is for it, at least for the first two Years; and for its Attendance in this early Education, to the wisest Matron

---

[73] *Female Tatler*, no. 76, 28–30 Dec. 1709.
[74] *Fable of the Bees*, ed. Kaye, vol. 2, p. 189 (Fourth Dialogue).

in the World, I would prefer an active young Wench, whose Tongue never stands still, that should run about, and never cease diverting and playing with it, whilst it was awake; and where People can afford it, two or three of them, to relieve one another when they are tired, are better than one.

Hor.: Then you think Children reap great Benefit from the nonsensical Chat of Nurses?

Cleo.: It is of inestimable Use to them, and teaches them to think, as well as speak, much sooner and better, than with equal aptitude of Parts they would do without. The Business is to make them exert those Faculties, and keep Infants continually employ'd about them, for the time which is lost then, is never to be retriev'd.

Hor.: Yet we seldom remember any thing of what we saw or heard, before we were two Years old: then what would be lost, if Children should not hear all that Impertinence?

Cleo.: As Iron is to be hammer'd while it is hot and ductile, so Children are to be taught when they are young . . .[75]

Mention has already been made of Mandeville's feminism, and his refusal to accept the contemporary myths about women. But while we are on the modern flavour of some of his writing, it may be as well to quote a passage that would not be unworthy of the Women's Liberation Movement. It is from one of Lucinda's contributions to the *Female Tatler*:

The first Ages of the World found us the Servants of Imperious Mankind, keeping of Sheep and kneading of Dough were our ordinary Employments; after that we were condemn'd to the Distaff or the Seraglio, Elder and Chaster Monasteries than those founded on better Pretences; one while we were educated in a strong Desire of being Blind by Thirty, that our Names might live in a Point Cravat, and Posterity be Witness how much Time we took pains to throw away . . . Letters were denied us, lest we shou'd see and claim our great Prerogative and Equality with haughty Man, to whom we were created Friends, not Servants, and delighted to advise and assist them in the Government of the Earth.

She goes on to rejoice that some women are throwing aside this slavery: 'The Needle is justly quitted for the Pen, and the Spice Box removed to make room for the 'Scrutore. . . . How much better do Arts and Sciences become a Lady than Salves and Potions!'[76]

---

[75] Ibid., p. 169 (Fourth Dialogue).
[76] *Female Tatler*, no. 111, 29–31 Mar. 1710.

There is of course a touch of parody in this: Mandeville is not to be identified entirely with Lucinda. But the evidence suggests that he agreed with at least most of these remarks. He nowhere argues against them, and he makes Cleomenes insist that women are at least the intellectual equals of men, and that the differences are mainly due to education.

Modern psychologists have paid some attention to 'consumer research': what attracts and repels customers. Mandeville does not approach this subject with their solemnity; but the eighteenth century was not ignorant of the art of salesmanship, and Mandeville observes it with his usual amused detachment:

Those who have never minded the Conversation of a spruce Mercer, and a young Lady his Customer that comes to his Shop, have neglected a Scene of Life that is very Entertaining ... While she remains irresolute what to take he seems to be the same in advising her; and is very cautious how to direct her Choice; but when once she has made it and is fix'd, he immediately becomes positive, that it is the best of the sort, extols her Fancy, and the more he looks upon it, the more he wonders he should not before have discovered the preeminence of it over anything he has in his Shop. By Precept, Example and great Application he has learn'd unobserv'd to slide into the inmost Recesses of the Soul, sound the Capacity of his Customers, and find out their blind Side unknown to them: By all which he is instructed in fifty other Stratagems to make her overvalue her own Judgment as well as the Commodity she would purchase. The greatest Advantage he has over her, lies in the most material part of the Commerce between them, the debate about the Price, which he knows to a Farthing, and she is wholly Ignorant of: Therefore he no where more egregiously imposes on her Understanding, and tho' here he has the liberty of telling what Lies he pleases, as to the Prime Cost and the Money he has refus'd, yet he trusts not to them only; but attacking her Vanity, makes her believe the most incredible Things in the World, concerning his own Weakness and her superior Abilities; He had taken a Resolution, he says, never to part with that Piece under such a Price, but she has the Power of talking him out of his Goods beyond any body he ever sold to: He protests that he loses by his Silk, but seeing that she has a Fancy for it, and is resolv'd to give no more, rather than disoblige a Lady he has such an uncommon value for he'll let her have it, and only begs that another time she will not stand so hard with him. In the mean time the Buyer, who knows that she is no Fool and has a voluble Tongue, is easily persuaded that she has a very winning way of Talking, and thinking it sufficient for the sake of

Good-breeding to disown her Merit, and in some witty Repartee retort the Compliment, he makes her swallow very contentedly the Substance of every thing he tells her. The upshot is, that with the Satisfaction of having saved Ninepence *per* Yard, she has bought her Silk exactly at the same Price as any body else might have done, and often gives Sixpence more than, rather than not have sold it, he would have taken. It is possible that this Lady, for want of being sufficiently flatter'd, for a Fault she is pleased to find in his Behaviour, or perhaps the tying of his Neck-cloth, or some other dislike as Substantial, may be lost, and her Custom bestow'd on some other of the Fraternity. But where many of them live in a Cluster, it is not always easily determin'd which Shop to go to, and the Reasons some of the Fair Sex have for their choice are often very whimsical and kept as a great Secret. We never follow our Inclinations with more freedom, than when they cannot be traced, and it is unreasonable for others to suspect them. A Virtuous Woman has preferr'd one House to all the rest, because she had seen a handsome Fellow in it, and another of no bad Character for having receiv'd greater Civility before it, than had been paid her any where else, when she had no thoughts of buying and was going to *Paul's* Church: for among the fashionable Mercers the fair Dealer must keep before his own Door, and to draw in random Customers make use of no other Freedom or Importunities than an obsequious Air, with a submissive Posture, and perhaps a Bow to every well-dress'd Female that offers to look towards his Shop.[77]

Mandeville is perhaps at his best in passages like this, where he appears, not as a Newton of the moral sciences, but simply as an observer of the human comedy. He is certainly a shrewd and penetrating one.

[77] *Fable of the Bees*, ed. Kaye, vol. 1, pp. 351-3 (*Search into the Nature of Society*).

6

THE THEOLOGIAN

WHAT were Mandeville's real beliefs about religion? They should not be too difficult to discover, one would think: there is plenty of documentation. He wrote a whole book on the subject, running to some four hundred pages. And, quite apart from *Free Thoughts on Religion*, Horatio and Cleomenes discuss religion almost as much as duelling, or honour, or human pride and vanity.

Yet the evidence remains equivocal. In the dialogues Horatio appears as the sceptic and Cleomenes as the defender of the faith. There is no doubt, of course, that when these two discourse on self-liking, on the errors of Lord Shaftesbury, or even on the character of Cromwell, it is Cleomenes who is Mandeville's spokesman. Yet Kaye suggests that, when the conversation turns on miracles or on discrepancies between the Book of Genesis and scientific knowledge, the roles are reversed, and it is Horatio who represents Mandeville's real opinion.[1] He may well be right. Certainly these discussions do not end, like many of the others, with Horatio convinced and humbly recanting. On the other hand, Cleomenes' arguments are not so obviously weak as to put their disingenuousness beyond all question: after all, they are often borrowed from Christian apologists of undoubted sincerity.

As for *Free Thoughts on Religion*, Mandeville is careful to point out in the Preface that it is only 'bigots, and the enemies of truth' who 'would insinuate that Free Thoughts must be impious and atheistical, in the same manner as lewd debauchees by the words *good-natured lady* would have you understand a whore'.[2] If we look beyond the title to the contents, we find that there are two main themes: the need for tolerance as between one Christian sect and another (or at least between Anglicans and dissenters) and the misdeeds of the clergy. There is every reason to believe that

---

[1] *Fable of the Bees*, ed. Kaye, vol. 2, p. 21, n. 2 (Preface).
[2] *Free Thoughts on Religion, the Church, and National Happiness*, 2nd ed., 1729, p. iii Preface).

Mandeville was sincere both in his advocacy of tolerance and in his anti-clericalism. But either a Christian or an atheist might be saddened by the spectacle of Christians persecuting one another; and either might be indignant at the worldliness and hypocrisy of scheming prelates. Mandeville's overt stance, of course, is that of the stern rebuking Christian; but we have already seen in the first chapter that there is at least a case for not taking that at face value.

Mandeville's anti-clericalism, however, may very well give us a clue. Many sincere Christians have been anti-clerical, for the same reason that bitterness about the alleged temporizing of Labour governments is usually most pronounced among ardent and doctrinaire Socialists. If however someone advances the thesis that such temporizing is inevitable, because government cannot be carried on without it, and never will be, one may doubt whether he is really a Socialist. And Mandeville does seem to suggest that churches could not survive unless their priests departed from Christian practice. But of course the parallel is not exact. It is the business of political parties to govern, and a political theory that made government impossible would clearly be defective. On the other hand, it may be said, religion is not concerned with the things of this world at all: there is no reason why Christians should not simply lead obscure and humble lives, without seeking influence or authority. This position is, however, hardly tenable if it is part of the nature of religion that the churches should behave as they do.

What is religion? Mandeville defines it: 'Religion in general consists in an acknowledgment of an immortal power that, superior to all earthly dominion, invisibly governs the world, and a respectful endeavour to discharge such duties as everyone shall apprehend to be requir'd of him by that immortal power.'[3] The belief that there is such a power is, he tells us more than once, so deeply rooted as to be instinctive:

Cleo.: Every Mischief and every Disaster that happens to him, of which the Cause is not very plain and obvious; excessive Heat and Cold; Wet and Drought, that are offensive; Thunder and Lightning even when they do no visible Hurt; Noises in the dark, Obscurity itself, and every thing that is frightful and unknown, are all administring and contributing to the Establishment of this Fear. The wildest Man, that can

[3] Ibid., p. 1.

be conceiv'd, by the time that he came to Maturity, would be wise enough to know, that Fruits and other Eatables are not to be had either always or every where: This would naturally put him upon hoarding, when he had good Store: His Provision might be spoil'd by the Rain; he would see that Trees were blasted, and yielded not always the same Plenty: He might not always be in Health, or his young ones might grow sick, and die, without any Wounds or external Force to be seen. Some of these Accidents might at first escape his Attention, or only alarm his weak Understanding, without occasioning much Reflection for some Time; but as they came often, he would certainly begin to suspect some invisible Cause; and, as his Experience encreas'd, be confirm'd in his Suspicion. It is likewise highly probable, that a Variety of different Sufferings, would make him apprehend several such Causes; and at last induce him to believe, that there was a great Number of them, which he had to fear. What would very much contribute to this credulous Disposition, and naturally lead him into such a Belief, is a false Notion, we imbibe very early, and which we may observe in Infants, as soon as by their Looks, their Gestures, and the Signs they make, they begin to be intelligible to us.

Hor.: What is that, pray?

Cleo.: All young Children seem to imagine, that every thing thinks and feels in the same Manner as they do themselves: And, that they generally have this wrong Opinion of things inanimate, is evident, from a common Practice among them; whenever they labour under any Misfortune, which their own Wildness and want of Care have drawn upon them. In all such Cases, you see them angry at and strike, a Table, a Chair, the Floor, or any thing else, that can seem to be accessary to their hurting themselves, or the Production of any other Blunder, they have committed . . . It is not to be imagin'd, that this natural Folly should be so easily cured in a Child, that is destitute of all Instruction and Commerce with his own Species, as it is in those, that are brought up in Society, and hourly improv'd by conversing with others, that are wiser than themselves; and I am persuaded, that a wild Man would never get entirely rid of it, whilst he lived.[4]

It is not only wild men who cannot get rid of the belief in an invisible cause.

Every Individual, whether he is a Savage, or is born in a Civil Society, is persuaded within, that there is such an invisible Cause; and should any Mortal contradict this, no Multitude would believe a Word of what he said. Whereas, on the other Hand, if a Ruler humours this Fear and puts it out of all Doubt, that there is such an invisible Cause,

---

[4] *Fable of the Bees*, ed. Kaye, vol. 2, pp. 208–10 (Fifth Dialogue).

he may say of it what he pleases, and no Multitude, that was never taught any Thing to the contrary, will ever dispute it with him. He may say, that it is a Crocodile or a Monkey, an Ox, or a Dog, an Onion, or a Wafer.[5]

The belief is, he goes on to say, innate:

> The Fear of an invisible Cause is as real in our Nature, as the Fear of Death; either of them may be conquer'd perhaps; but so may Lust . . . When I hear a Man say, that he never felt any Fear of an invisible Cause, that was not owing to Education, I believe him as much as I do a young married Woman in Health and Vigour, who tells me, that she never felt any Love to a Man, that did not proceed from a Sense of her Duty.[6]

The innate disposition to fear an invisible cause 'that meddles and interferes in Human Affairs',[7] and the desire to placate it, are obviously very useful to the skilful politicians who want to control men's behaviour. It does not follow that all churches are bound to seek political power (since some of them might simply want to spread what they believe to be the truth about the invisible cause) but the converse does follow: all who do seek political power will find it necessary to take on some of the functions of a church, or to ally themselves with those who have them.

How unanimous soever, therefore, all Rulers and Magistrates have seem'd to be in promoting some Religion or other, the Principle of it was not of their Invention. They found it in Man; and the Fear of an invisible Cause being universal, if Governours had said Nothing of it, every Man in his own Breast would have found Fault with them; and had a Superstition of his own to himself. It has often been seen, that the most subtle unbelievers among Politicians have been forced, for their own quiet, to counterfeit their Attachment to Religion, when they would a Thousand Times rather have done without it.[8]

If politicians have consequently found themselves dependent on religion, the churches, Mandeville tells us, have shown no reluctance to engage in politics. 'But be the religion of a country what it will, it is always certain, that the greater the authority of the church is, the better the clergy are pleased; and it fails as seldom, that, wherever it is excessive, the laity are slaves, and the government precarious, unless it be in the hands of the clergy

---
[5] *Enquiry into the Origin of Honour*, 1732, pp. 21–2.
[6] Ibid., p. 25.   [7] Ibid., pp. 27 and 190.   [8] Ibid., p. 28.

themselves.'[9] All states, then, should be on guard against 'the sly and bold encroachments of the church'.

That the churches' ends are mainly political is shown by their policy of 'sticking close, and obstinately adhering to their friends, whether good men or bad'.[10] Mandeville gives a number of illustrations: Constantine, as the first Roman emperor to turn Christian, has been universally praised as a good man, and his many murders, including those of his own wife and child, glossed over. This, Mandeville thinks, is undeniable, even if one rejects the view of 'the heathen authors, who said, that *Constantine* finding no ways to expiate the execrable murders he had been guilty of, in the *Pagan* religion, but finding some in the christian, he forsook that of his ancestors, and made himself a christian'.[11] Even Gregory the Great, though 'a man of strict morals, and one of the best of popes' (though 'a cruel persecutor of human wit', who hated books and learning) condoned the cruelty and treachery of Phocas, when he usurped the throne of the emperor Maurice, because Maurice had declared for the patriarch of Constantinople and against the pontiff of Rome. Gregory also praised Queen, Brunebauld of France, 'the most wicked woman in the world' and attributed all kinds of virtue to her because, 'in the midst of her heinous crimes', she endowed many churches and convents, and 'shew'd an extraordinary magnificence towards churchmen'.[12] On the other hand, a virtuous, wise, and tolerant ruler like Julian (stigmatized as 'the Apostate'), who did not choose to embrace Christianity, has been traduced and vilified. Even within the church, Mandeville goes on, the reputation of reforming popes like Hadrian the Sixth, who wanted 'to curb the licentiousness of the clergy', has been systematically blackened.[13]

As they are taken from the early history of Christianity, these examples necessarily refer to the Roman Catholic Church; but one must not suppose that the Reformation has made much difference. Mandeville goes on to tell similar stories about Protestant churches. The French Huguenots were annoyed with Blondel, one of their ministers, when he showed that the story of Pope Joan was false.[14] And in general

The national clergy in all countries hate arguing, they are always angry with those who oppose them, or but call the truth of their system in

[9] *Free Thoughts on Religion*, p. 158. [10] Ibid., p. 170. [11] Ibid., p. 171.
[12] Ibid., pp. 173–7. [13] Ibid., pp. 183–4. [14] Ibid., p. 198.

question; and no church ever had the power to punish men for disbelieving her doctrine without making a severe use of it on the slightest occasions: from all which it is manifest, that if protestant church-men are so civil, as not to pretend to be infallible, they expect we should return the compliment, and treat them as if they were.[15]

Priests and clergymen of all religions, it appears, are everywhere the same: greedy for power, for themselves and their churches, and very ready to persecute anyone who opposes them.

It is evident then, that there is no characteristick to distinguish and know a true church from a false one. The arguments for toleration or persecution, as they are occasionally wanted, are the same in the one, as they are in the other; in the behaviour likewise between national churches and those who dissent from them, countries differ but little. The language and actions are very near the same throughout christendom. The schismaticks reject all human authority, quote scripture, talk of reason, and desire toleration: the orthodox stand upon their prerogative of eldership, punishing of hereticks, and desire the assistance of the secular arm: whenever the schismaticks can make their opinion national, they are orthodox, and serve all other innovators, just as they were serv'd before.[16]

Those who have made a profession of religion, then, have been distinguished chiefly by their whole-hearted and ruthless pursuit of power. And religion, as we have seen, is peculiarly suited to be an instrument of power, since it builds on that instinctive fear of an invisible cause which no man is without and which politicians ignore at their peril. Is there anything else to be said about religion? The disposition to believe in an invisible cause is innate, but it does not follow that the belief is true; indeed, since it is aided by an infantile animistic belief, which is apparently also due to an innate disposition, and which is plainly false, the presumption might seem to be that it is also false that there are invisible causes. In that case, we would have a false belief which all men are disposed to hold, and which, if properly exploited, makes men easy to govern. It would be easy to conclude that churches are nothing but devices for exploiting the belief, and that the ambitiousness of churchmen is an essential, and not an accidental attribute.

This is certainly a possible, and even a plausible interpretation

[15] Ibid., p. 212.   [16] Ibid., pp. 260–1.

of Mandeville. But it is not the only one. For, even if there is in fact no invisible cause, it is part of the argument that most men sincerely believe that there is; and some of these might well suppose that they had found out the truth about it, and might found churches with no other purpose but to spread this supposed truth. This is of course quite consistent with there being others who cynically exploit the credulity of their fellows. And there are intermediate possibilities: some sincere believers may yield to the temptation to modify their doctrine in ways that will make them popular and powerful.

There is another possibility too. Perhaps there really is an invisible cause: that has not been ruled out. Most accounts of the nature of this cause are no doubt false: indeed they must be, since there are many such accounts, all mutually inconsistent. Superstition and idolatry are no doubt perpetuated by scheming priests greedy for power. But perhaps there is also a true religion.

Horatio suggests that Christians are no better off than the believers in any other religion: 'we can say no more for ourselves, than what Men of all Parties and Persuasions have done in all Ages, every one for their Cause, *viz*. That they alone were in the Right and all that differ'd from them in the Wrong.'[17] Cleomenes replies that, just as nobody could have written Newton's *Principia* who was not a great mathematician, so nobody could have done what Moses did who was not inspired:

If in a Place, where I was very well assured, that no Body understood any thing of colouring or drawing, a Man should tell me, that he had acquired the Art of Painting by Inspiration, I should be more ready to laugh at him than to believe him; but if I saw him draw several fine Portraits before my Face, my Unbelief would cease, and I should think it ridiculous, any longer to suspect his Veracity. All the Accounts that other Lawgivers and Founders of Nations have given of the Deities, which they or their Predecessors convers'd with, contain'd Ideas that were unworthy of the Divine Being; and by the Light of Nature only, it is easily prov'd, that they must have been false: But the Image which *Moses* gave the Jews of the Supreme Being, that he was One, and had made Heaven and Earth, will stand all Tests, and is a Truth that will outlast the World.[18]

---

[17] *Fable of the Bees*, ed. Kaye, vol. 2, p. 218 (Fifth Dialogue).
[18] Ibid., p. 220 (Fifth Dialogue).

Is Mandeveille sincere in this or not? A little later Cleomenes admits that Moses does not always reach these heights:

Hor.: I never heard any Body entertain higher Notions or more noble Sentiments of the Deity, than at different times I have heard from you; pray, when you read *Moses*, don't you meet with several Things in the Oeconomy of Paradise, and the Conversation between God and *Adam*, that seem to be low, unworthy, and altogether inconsistent with the sublime Ideas, you are used to form of the Supreme Being?
Cleo.: I freely own, not only that I have thought so, but likewise that I have long stumbled at it.[19]

This comes after Horatio has subjected Cleomenes to a kind of catechism designed to show that the Old Testament is on the whole no more credible than classical mythology:

Hor.: Do you believe *Hesiod*?
Cleo.: No.
Hor.: *Ovid's* Metamorphosis?
Cleo.: No.
Hor.: But you believe the story of *Adam* and *Eve*, and Paradise.
Cleo.: Yes.
Hor.: That they were produced at once, I mean at their full Growth: he from a Lump of Earth, and she from one of his Ribs?
Cleo.: Yes.
Hor.: In short, you believe the Innocence, the Delight, and all the Wonders of Paradise that are related by one Man: at the same time that you will not believe what has been told us by many, of the Uprightness, the Concord, and the Happiness of a Golden Age.
Cleo.: That's very true.
Hor.: Now give me leave to shew you, how unaccountable, as well as partial, you are in this. In the first Place, the Things naturally impossible, which you believe, are contrary to your own Doctrine, the Opinion you have laid down, and which I believe to be true: For you have proved, that no Man would ever be able to speak unless he was taught it: that Reasoning and Thinking come upon us by slow Degrees; and that we can know nothing that has not from without been conveyed to the Brain, and communicated to us through the Organs of the Senses . . .[20]

Cleomenes can only answer that 'Adam was altogether the Workmanship of God; a preternatural Production'; everything about him was miraculous, and only his progeny were subject

[19] Ibid., p. 316 (Sixth Dialogue).   [20] Ibid., p. 308 (Sixth Dialogue).

to the ordinary laws of nature. This passage is cited by Kaye as one in which it is Horatio who is Mandeville's spokesman: he obviously thinks that Horatio wins the argument. Certainly it is difficult to maintain, in the light of all this, that the Old Testament is obviously superior to its rivals. In the *Origin of Honour* Cleomenes speaks slightingly of the Old Testament: the Christian clergy, he says, 'finding several Things, which they had a Mind to, denied them in the Gospel; and that many Conveniencies which all other Priests had ever, not only been fond of, but likewise enjoy'd, were in Express Words forbid, and absolutely prohibited in the *New Testament*, they had Recourse to the *Old*, and providentially took Care from thence to supply the Deficiencies of the *New*.'[21] This applies particularly to the encouragement of war:

whenever Pillage or shedding of Blood are to be justified or encouraged by a Sermon, or Men are to be exhorted to Battle, to the Sacking of a City or the Devastation of a Country, by a Pathetick Discourse, the Text is always taken from the *Old Testament*; which is an inexhaustible Fund for Declamation on almost every Subject and every Occasion: And there is no worldly End, which the most ambitious Man, or the most cruel Tyrant can have to serve, but from some Part or other of that Book a Divine of middling Capacity may find out a proper Text to harangue upon, that shall answer the Purpose.[22]

The claims of Moses to inspiration, then, must rest entirely on the doctrine of the unity of God. But even here Mandeville is equivocal. In *The Origin of Honour* Cleomenes says:

That there is but one God, the Creator of Heaven and Earth, that is an all-wise and perfectly good Being, without any Mixture of Evil, would have been a most rational Opinion, tho' it had not been reveal'd. But Reasoning and Metaphysicks must have been carried to a great Height of Perfection, before this Truth could be penetrated into by the Light of Nature. *Plutarch*, who was a Man of great Learning, and has in many Things display'd good Sense and Capacity, thought it impossible that one Being should have been the Cause of the Whole, and was therefore of Opinion, that there must have been Two Principles; the one to produce all the Good; and the other all the Evil that is in the World. And Some of the greatest Men have been of this Opinion, both before and since the Promulgation of the Gospel.[23]

---

[21] *Enquiry into the Origin of Honour*, p. 157 (Third Dialogue).
[22] Ibid., p. 158 (Third Dialogue).   [23] Ibid., pp. 26–7 (First Dialogue).

So far this might seem to support the claim that Moses was inspired. But in *Free Thoughts*, when Mandeville comes to discuss the problem of evil, he tells us that, if one sets revelation aside, the Manichean doctrine of two principles seems to provide the only solution:

> How opposite soever this opinion was to reveal'd religion, and the clearest ideas we have of the unity of GOD, when once this monstrous hypothesis was admitted, it explain'd the phaenomena of human life better than any other, and solv'd innumerable difficulties that were inexplicable to the orthodox, whilst both parties confin'd themselves to the light of nature.[24]

And again:

> The argument of *Epicurus*, without the help of reveal'd religion, is not to be answer'd by any other system but that of the two principles, which immediately clears that and all other difficulties concerning the origin of evil. How strange and deplorable is the fate of human reason, that the worst of hereticks, nay the heathens themselves, should, with an hypothesis altogether absurd and contradictory, be able to explain, what we experience, a hundred times better than orthodox christians do with a supposition so just, so necessary and so true, of one first principle, which is infinitely good and almighty![25]

Ultimately, then, the unity of God would seem to depend, after all, on revelation: if we trust to reason alone, or the light of nature, we shall have to reject it. (For obviously the phrases 'absurd and contradictory' and 'so just, necessary and so true' are not meant to be taken at their face value.) The doctrine of the unity of God, then, will not do as a touchstone by which to test the genuineness of revelation. Horatio was right, it seems, in suggesting that Christians have no more guarantee of the truth of their beliefs than anyone else.

Perhaps, however, we can find marks of genuine revelation in the New Testament? Cleomenes, it will be remembered, speaks with mock admiration of the feat of the church in making Christianity an instrument of worldly power, considering the intractably unworldly doctrine it had to work with. This does not, of course, prove the truth of Christianity, but it at least suggests the sincerity of those who formulated its original doctrine. Even this, however, Mandeville casts some doubt upon, at least

---

[24] *Free Thoughts on Religion*, p. 104. [25] Ibid., p. 112.

obliquely. 'Christ', he says 'was the first, who plainly taught that men shall rise again, and in another world be punished or rewarded for ever, according as their behaviour has been in this life.'[26] It would be hard to think of a doctrine more useful to those who want to control men's behaviour. Perhaps, then, Christianity is after all not ill suited to the purpose of politicians. Mandeville, of course, insists that true Christianity demands nothing less than sober, upright, and self-sacrificing lives. It is the clergy who, in their own interests, insinuate that something less exacting may procure salvation: the payment of money, as in the sale of indulgences, or diligent observance of the outward forms of worship. Even the doctrine that virtue demands the mortification of the flesh, which at first sight seems a fatal obstacle to the worldly ambitions of the clergy, may be made to serve them. To practise austerity is a sure way to gain the respect and adherence of ordinary men, who know that they themselves would not be capable of such self-denial. The churches have known how to make use of this by means of an adroit division of labour, in which some of the clergy lead rigorous and austere lives, while others enjoy the power and the wealth which are earned thereby. Mandeville proceeds, at some length and with considerable gusto, to chronicle all the misdeeds of the clergy, and to denounce them. No doubt the doctrine of rewards and punishments in a future life has been perverted. One is left, however, to wonder about it in its original, unperverted form. No doubt it is immensely serviceable to humanity: human nature being as it is, perhaps nothing else will persuade men to behave decently to one another. Since men, with their innate disposition to believe in an invisible cause, demand some religious doctrine, it is no doubt better that they should accept this one, which is wholesome and beneficient. The wise man, then, will pretend to believe it. But is there any reason to suppose that it is true?

From what Mandeville tells us about the body-mind relationship, the presumption might well be that it is not true. In the *Treatise of the Hypochondriack and Hysterick Diseases*, Mandeville says that it is hard to see how survival after death is possible, for how could we think without the brain?[27] 'The Soul', Cleomenes tells us in *The Fable*, 'cannot be said to think, otherwise than an

[26] *Free Thoughts on Religion*, p. 162.
[27] *Treatise of the Hypochondriack and Hysterick Diseases*, 3rd ed., 1730, p. 159.

Architect is said to build a House, where the Carpenters, Bricklayers, etc. do the Work, which he chalks out and superintends.'[28] That is to say, the actual work of thinking is done by the bodily organs. Furthermore, animals think, though less perfectly than men, and they have no souls. In them thought is superintended by something else, Life, which somehow animates the body in something the way that steam makes a lifeless mass of metal move.

Hor.: But after all, that Self, that Part of us that wills and wishes, that chuses one thing rather than another, must be incorporeal: For if it is Matter, it must either be one single Particle, which I can almost feel it is not, or a Combination of many, which is more than inconceivable. *Cleo.*: I don't deny what you say; and that the Principle of Thought and Action is inexplicable in all Creatures, I have hinted already. But its being incorporeal does not mend the Matter, as to the Difficulty of explaining or conceiving it. That there must be a mutual Contact between this Principle, whatever it is, and the Body itself, is what we are certain of *a posteriori*; and a reciprocal Action upon each other, between an immaterial Substance and Matter, is as incomprehensible to human Capacity, as that Thought should be the Result of Matter and Motion.[29]

But, if materialism is hinted at here, it is a long way from being asserted. Mandeville's main point is that 'the Soul is altogether incomprehensible, and we can determine but little about it, that is not reveal'd to us.'[30] This is itself, of course, a double-edged remark: it may well imply that there is no real reason to suppose that the soul exists. But the implication might also be (and this is certainly what Mandeville would say, if pressed) that, since physiology can tell us nothing here ("The most consummate Anatomist knows no more of it [the operation of thinking] than a Butcher's Prentice'),[31] we are free to accept revelations about it. There may, then, be a soul which is immortal and which can go on thinking without the aid of the body, for all that we can tell: it is hard to understand how this could be, but then thinking in general is hard to understand. Revelation has not been refuted. But it has not been supported either; and it is the truth of revelation that is at present in question.

[28] *Fable of the Bees*, ed. Kaye, vol. 2, p. 164 (Fourth Dialogue).
[29] Ibid., pp. 173-4 (Fourth Dialogue).
[30] Ibid., p. 168 (Fourth Dialogue).
[31] Ibid., p. 165 (Fourth Dialogue).

Immortality is only touched on by Mandeville; but he gives much more attention to free will and determinism and, by a natural transition of thought, to the problem of evil. In *Free Thoughts on Religion* the context is his plea for tolerance. One of his main points here is that what Anglicans and dissenters dispute about are the non-essentials of religion: an argument that gives him plenty of scope for sarcasms at the expense of both parties. 'A churchman receives the sacrament kneeling, a presbyterian sitting . . . What barbarous notions must a man have of the deity, who could imagine that, if both spoke sincerely, and otherwise took the sacrament conscientiously, tho' in different postures, GOD would be offended at either!'[32] It is high time, he adds, that Christians should 'distinguish between the spirit of GOD, and that of contradiction'.[33]

He does concede, however, that more substantial matters of doctrine are sometimes at stake. The dispute about free will and predestination is one of these, and Mandeville discusses it at length. His sympathies are pretty clearly on the side of determinism. He begins by defining the will, as Hobbes had done, as 'the last result of deliberation, either long or short, which immediately precedes the execution of, or at least the endeavour to execute the thing will'd'.[34] He concludes from this that the will cannot be free: 'for as soon as the will is made, the thing will'd is determin'd, and before it is made, it is no will yet; but only a deliberation, what to will.'[35]

This may seem sophistical. All that Mandeville seems to be saying is that to will X is simply to resolve to do X, and that a resolve to do X could not be a resolve to do other than X. But of course it does not follow that the deliberating process could not have resulted in willing something other than X. He does go on, however, to repeat the usual determinist arguments:

Give two men each a glass in his hand of some value, which, if he breaks it, he is to pay for: let the one be of a covetous nature, but no wrangler, and very pliable as to opinion; the other very positive, but lavish of his money. Dispute with either of these pretty warmly against free-will, and the power he has of dropping the glass, or keeping it in his hand. The first, depend upon it, will not let it fall; and, dare him to it never so much, he'll content himself with saying, that he is sure

---

[32] *Free Thoughts on Religion*, pp. 62 and 64.
[33] Ibid., p. 65.   [34] Ibid., p. 96.   [35] Ibid., p. 97.

he can do it if he will, but that he has no mind to throw away so much money to be laugh'd at. The other, 'tis ten to one, will dash it to pieces, and, if he dares speak his mind, tell you, that he had rather pay for the glass, than not have the pleasure to convince you of your folly, obstinacy, or what else his passion or manners shall give him leave to call it. I doubt not but both persons would be fully persuaded, and therefore might swear with a good conscience that they had acted from a principle of free-will, though it seems plain to me, that each of them was prompted to do what he did, and over-ruled by a predominant passion. I know very well, that it is possible that the covetous man might have broke the glass as well as the other, but then his love for money must have been less, or his desire of triumph greater than would be suitable to the character I required him to be of.[36]

The chief objection to determinism, in its theological guise of predestination, is that it makes God the author of evil. It also makes him unjust: 'It is certain, that whilst we only follow the light of nature, nothing can be more inconsistent with the ideas we have of the justice and goodness of GOD, than that a creature should be punished for sins, which from eternity it was decreed he should commit.'[37] But a belief in free will does not really help here: the difficulty is only postponed. 'From the simple question, what is the cause of sin? the result of a thousand disputes must at long run be this. GOD is eternal, and a being infinitely good, so there could be no evil before the world was made; God created the world, then whence comes evil?'[38]

From man's sinful nature? But 'if man was the workmanship of a principle infinitely good and holy, he should not only have been created without any actual evil, but also without any inclination, or the least propensity to evil, since that inclination is such a defect, as could not have such a principle for its cause.'[39] This is after all the lot of the blessed in paradise, who must none the less be supposed to have free will. And, even if moral evil is man's responsibility, God must certainly be blamed for natural evil. The answer of Lactantius, that pain and sorrow are necessary for man to gain wisdom, is inconsistent with the story of the Garden of Eden. The orthodox belief is not, as Lactantius maintains, that virtue and wisdom cannot belong to a man without physical evil, but, on the contrary, that man became subject to this evil only because he renounced virtue and wisdom.[40]

[36] Ibid., pp. 98–100.   [37] Ibid., p. 101.   [38] Ibid., p. 103.
[39] Ibid., pp. 105–6.   [40] Ibid., p. 111.

The only rational solution is the Manichean one, that there are two Gods, one responsible for good and one for evil. Since Christians are committed to rejecting that hypothesis, they had better admit that the whole matter is a mystery insoluble to merely human reason. After all, St. Paul (Mandeville demonstrates with some relish) was just as baffled by it as everyone else:

He establishes absolute predestination in the plainest and concisest manner. *He hath mercy on whom he will have mercy, and whom he will he hardeneth.* Upon this the apostle, who knew very well what would naturally be objected against such a doctrine, starts the difficulty himself, *thou wilt say then unto me, Why does he yet find fault? for who has resisted his Will?* ... God we know had first hardened the heart of *Pharoah* against all the threatenings and miracles of *Moses*, and afterwards punished him for disobedience. A conduct seemingly opposite to all our human notions of justice and goodness ... All the solution he gives to the objection proposed, is the sovereign power of God, and the right the Creator has to dispose of his creatures as it seems good to him, *Nay, but oh man! who art thou that repliest against* GOD? *Shall the thing form'd say to him that form'd it why hast thou made me thus?* ... St. Paul, inspired as he was, does not pretend that he is able to account for it any other way. He is at a loss himself, the great apostle of the *Gentiles*, in whom human learning was joined with divine inspiration ... This ought to put an end to all disputes, and impose a profound silence on our reason ... Must not both parties blush, when they pretend to teach with clearness what was a mystery to St. *Paul*?[41]

The moral is that we must be tolerant of all the conflicting opinions on this mysterious topic:

The impossiblity there is in our little knowledge of reconciling either the system of predestination, or that of free-will, to all the necessary attributes of GOD ought, if not to unite men, at least make them desist from quarrelling, and taxing one another with teaching of impious things and horrid blasphemies. Those who are against toleration of either side, might be bore with, if they could clearly prove their opinion, and answer all objections after a convincing manner, but that men should anathematise, banish and hang those that dissent from them, tho' to defend their own system each party is forc'd to fly to GOD's incomprehensibility, is a thing altogether inexcusable.[42]

Mandeville was no doubt sincere in wanting mutual toleration; but the reader may very well suspect that he did see a solution to

[41] *Free Thoughts on Religion*, pp. 122-4.   [42] Ibid., pp. 125-6.

the problem. God cannot have all the attributes assigned to him: not omnipotence as well as benevolence, or evil could not exist. Perhaps, then, he has no attributes at all: or at least not the basic one of existence. Then, of course, the problem disappears.

This suspicion is strengthened by the discussion of the problem of evil in Part 2 of the *Fable*. Society arose, Cleomenes suggests, out of the need of primitive men to band together against wild animals. Since he also sees the guiding hand of Providence in the slow evolution of civilization, Horatio protests that it is 'inconsistent with the Ideas we have of a perfectly good and merciful Being' to suppose that Providence required men to be eaten by lions and wolves as a means to civilizing their descendants. Cleomenes replies that it is only man's arrogance that makes him suppose that it is worse for 'a Wolf to eat a piece of a Man, than it is in a Man to eat part of a Lamb or a Chicken'.[43]

This answer, of course, makes natural evil even more of a problem for the theist, since no one supposes that the suffering of lambs and chickens are brought upon them by their own wicked wills. Cleomenes does indeed point out that death is necessary (at least to the plan the Creator has chosen for this globe) if there is to be room for succeeding generations, and that being eaten is not necessarily a worse death than any other. This is at best a half-hearted defence of the divine plan, especially since it is accompanied by asides such as 'Everything is easy to the Deity':[44] presumably, then, he might have devised some less grisly system of animal economy. The general tenor of the passage is that Nature is indifferent to man. One indication of this, he says, is that the sun is larger than necessary if its sole function is to warm the earth: it must be meant to serve other planets as well.

Hor.: I cannot believe, that Providence should have no greater regard to our Species, than it has to Flies, and the Spawn of Fish; or that Nature has ever sported with the Fate of human Creatures, as she does with the Lives of Insects, and been as wantonly lavish of the first, as she seems to be of the latter. I wonder how you can reconcile this to Religion, you, that are such a Stickler for Christianity.
Cleo.: Religion has nothing to do with it. But we are so full of our own Species, and the Excellency of it, that we have no Leisure seriously to consider the System of this Earth: I mean the Plan on which the

---

[43] *Fable of the Bees*, ed. Kaye, vol. 2, p. 243 (Fifth Dialogue).
[44] Ibid., p. 245 (Fifth Dialogue).

Œconomy of it is built, in relation to the living Creatures, that are in it and upon it.

Hor.: I don't speak as to our Species, but in respect to the Deity: Has Religion nothing to do with it, that you make God the Author of so much Cruelty and Malice?

Cleo.: It is impossible, you should speak otherwise, than in relation to our Species, when you make use of those Expressions which can only signify to us the Intentions things were done with, or the Sentiments human Creatures have of them; and nothing can be cruel, or malicious, in regard to him who did it, unless his Thoughts and Designs were such in doing it. All Actions in Nature, abstractly consider'd are equally indifferent; and whatever it may be to individual Creatures, to die is not a greater Evil to this Earth, or the whole Universe, than it is to be born.

Hor.: This is making the First Cause of Things not an Intelligent Being.

Cleo.: Why so? Can you not conceive an Intelligent, and even a most Wise Being, that is not only exempt from, but likewise incapable of entertaining, any Malice or Cruelty?

Hor.: Such a Being could not commit or order Things, that are malicious and cruel.

Cleo.: Neither does God. But this will carry us into a Dispute about the Origin of Evil: and from thence we must inevitably fall on Free-Will and Predestination, which, as I have told you before, is an inexplicable Mystery, I will never meddle with. But I never said or thought any thing irreverent to the Deity: On the contrary, the Idea I have of the Supreme Being, is as transcendently great, as my Capacity is able to form one, of what is incomprehensible; and I could as soon believe, that he could cease to exist, as that he should be the Author of any real Evil.[45]

This seems intentionally evasive; but the final remark is significant. That God is the author of evil is, in Mandeville's opinion, quite inescapable (unless we accept the Manichean solution, which has its own difficulties). Does he, then, accept the alternative, not indeed that an eternal and necessary being could cease to exist but that no such being ever did exist? Compare this exchange, in *The Origin of Honour*:

Hor.: It is better to have no Religion, than to worship the Devil.
Cleo.: In what Respect is it better?
Hor.: It is not so great an Affront to the Deity not to believe his

---

[45] *Fable of the Bees.* ed. Kaye, vol. 2, pp. 251-2 (Fifth Dialogue).

Existence, as it is to believe him to be the most Cruel and the most Malicious Being that can be imagin'd.
Cleo.: That is a subtle Argument, seldom made Use of but by Unbelievers.

This may be merely a gibe at Shaftesbury, who had caused some scandal by arguing that atheism produced less harm than false beliefs about God; but it is significant that Cleomenes does not bring any real argument against this view.[46] Mandeville is impressed, more than a century before Tennyson, with Nature's redness in tooth and claw, her care for the species, and her carelessness about the individual, impressed also, two centuries before Russell, with man's insignificance in the universe as a whole. If there is an intelligence controlling all this, it is incapable of malice and cruelty only in the sense that it is also incapable of kindness or justice. That kind of impersonal first cause could not be interested in dispensing rewards and punishments in a future life. And that is, for Mandeville, the central doctrine of Christianity.

There may indeed be even stronger reasons why the intelligence controlling the universe, if there is one, cannot be the Christian God. For, just as it is necessary (according to the plan on which the world is in fact organized) that animals should kill and eat one another, in order to prevent overcrowding, so, for the same reason, it is necessary that men should kill one another in war.[47] Wars, and the evil passions which cause them, are an essential part of the divine plan. Yet Mandeville is emphatic that war is entirely contrary to Christianity. Of course, this may just mean that God foreknew that most men would not practise Christianity; but this would, once again, raise a question about the justice of punishing them for not practising it.

Mandeville's official view, of course, is that these things are mysteries, beyond the comprehension of our finite human reason. Yet he also insists that reason is, after all, the final touchstone by which even revelation is to be tested.

It is very true, that our senses sometimes deceive us, that our reasons are false, and our judgment errs. This I confess is a mortifying reflection;

---

[46] *Enquiry into the Origin of Honour*, p. 154 (Third Dialogue).
[47] Ibid., pp. 253-4 (Fifth Dialogue).

but still the greatest certainty we can receive must come from them; for when once we begin to doubt of our reason, and our senses, we are no longer sure of any thing, an immediate revelation from GOD not excepted; for how shall we trust to a revelation, when we cannot depend, either on the senses by which we receive it, or our reason, the only touch-stone, by which we can assure ourselves of its being divine?[48]

He goes on, it is true, to make a distinction between what is above reason and what is against reason. As an example of a belief that is above reason, but not against it, Mandeville takes the assertion that a man once saw through an oaken plank two inches thick. He would not, he says, accept this on merely human testimony, but, if it came as a revelation from God, he would believe it, once he was satisfied that the revelation was genuine. The belief is at variance with the laws of optics, or at least hard to reconcile with what we know of them; but our knowledge of such laws is, after all, incomplete and fallible. (And, indeed, the discovery of X-rays, of which he could have had no inkling, may well vindicate Mandeville here.) One cannot, however, believe what is against reason: that is, 'the contrary of what he plainly apprehends to be true':[49] for example, that two and two make seven.

This would seem to restrict the province of reason quite severely: nothing vouched for by revelation need be disbelieved, however much it runs counter to scientific knowledge, unless it involves an actual contradiction. We understand so little about first causes and the like that we must just accept what we are told about them as mysteries, which we cannot hope to understand. Reason, however, still has the important task of deciding whether an alleged revelation is genuine. And this may be enough to nullify the concessions: presumably it would be within the competence of reason to decide (for example, on the ground that any first cause must be impersonal and indifferent to mankind) that no revelations are in fact genuine.

Some revelations may apparently be ruled out as being against reason: 'Nothing can be more shocking to human reason', Mandeville tells us, 'than the doctrine of the real presence in the eucharist.'[50] It was of course safe for him to say that, in a Prot-

---

[48] *Free Thoughts on Religion*, p. 70. [49] Ibid., p. 95.
[50] Ibid., pp. 86–7.

estant country; but in the context it is at least possible that he is glancing at another doctrine, much more dangerous to attack, the Trinity.

There is hardly a truth more easily apprehended, or which we are more fully convinc'd of, than that two and two make four: yet were men to be taught from their infancy that it was a mystery, that on a certain occasion two and two made seven, with an addition to be believ'd on pain of damnation, I am persuaded, that at least seven in ten would swallow the shameful paradox; and that if they had always seen others ill-treated for disbelieving of it, by that time they were come to years of maturity, they would not only assert it themselves, but likewise dislike, if not hate those, who should call it in question. We must suppose, that it has been inculcated to them with application and assiduity by parents, nurses, masters, and all that had the tuition of, or any direction over them. Few people are acquainted with the force of prejudice: we are little capable of examining any thing which is rooted in us by education and custom.[51]

Ostensibly, Mandeville may be talking about transubstantiation, to which he has just made a passing reference; but for several pages immediately before that he has been discussing the doctrine of the Trinity, emphasizing its mysteriousness and unintelligibility, and that it was established only by a more or less arbitrary decision of the Council of Nicaea, whose 'debates were as much influenced by private grudges and personal hatreds, as the love of truth, or any real piety'.[52] The Arians, he tells us, would have accepted a compromise; but 'the orthodox bishops fear'd, lest they should expound these terms in an ill sense, and therefore made an addition to it more binding; which when the *Arians* likewise would have subscribed to, the orthodox still found out more hampering terms, till at last from an incomprehensible mystery they made it in the opinion of the *Antitrinitarians*, a plain and intelligible contradiction.'[53] And indeed, there is not much difference between saying that two and two make seven, and saying that, 'on a certain occasion', one plus one plus one make one.

This is of course no minor matter, since it concerns the divinity of Christ. In one place Mandeville makes a remark that may be

[51] Ibid., pp. 87-8.   [52] Ibid., p. 79.   [53] Ibid., p. 81.

interpreted, without much straining, as a reference to the doctrine of the Atonement:

Hor.: A Man must be very stupid to believe, that his close Attachment to the World, and the loosness of his own Morals can be atton'd for by the recluse and strict Lives that are led in some Religious Houses. *Cleo.*: Not so stupid as you imagine: There is Nothing in it that clashes with the common Notions of Mankind. Ceremonies are perform'd by Proxy; Men are security for one another; and a Debt is not more effectually discharg'd when we receive the Money from him who borrow'd it, than when it is paid by his Bail, tho' the Principal himself runs away.[54]

It is obvious that Horatio has not been answered; and obvious too, that his remark does not apply only to Roman Catholic monasticism.

So far, then, there would seem to be quite a strong case for saying that Mandeville was a covert atheist. When he refers to atheism he is at least kinder than most of his contemporaries. We have seen that, in the Tyburn pamphlet, he appeals to the atheists among his readers as well as to the Christians. In *Free Thoughts* he tells us:

Atheists are either speculative or practical; speculative atheists are those unhappy people, who, being too fond of knowledge or reasoning, are first deluded into scepticism, till, unable to extricate themselves from the mazes of philosophy, they are at last betray'd into a disbelief of every thing they cannot comprehend, and become the most convincing evidences of the shallowness of human understanding. The number of these has always been very small; and, as they are commonly studious peaceable men, the hurt they do to the publick is inconsiderable.[55]

That a speculative atheist should be a quite moral man is no more surprising than that a Christian should lead a very wicked life. Even 'practical atheists', libertines who 'only deny a God because they wish there was none', are relatively rare, being found chiefly among 'sprightly youth' of good education.

In the *Origin of Honour*, Cleomenes, by way of reply to Horatio when he says that it is better to be an atheist than to believe in a cruel God, suggests that many of the Mexicans who worshipped

---

[54] *Enquiry into the Origin of Honour*, p. 111 (Second Dialogue).
[55] *Free Thoughts on Religion*, p. 4.

the cruel Vitzliputzli may have been deterred from perjury for fear of being punished by that God.

Hor.: Then not to have believed the Existence of that chimerical Monster was Atheism in *Mexico*.

Cleo.: It certainly was, among People that knew of no other invisible Cause.[56]

This hardly suggests that atheism is false, however inconvenient it may be to those who want to discourage perjury.

Does Mandeville give us any real reason to suppose that it is false? He tells us that atheism shows the shallowness of human understanding, that 'philosophy is the worst guide to eternity, and ought never to be mixed with theology',[57] that atheism and superstition have a common origin, ignorance of the divine essence.[58] But, since the divine essence is incomprehensible, theists are presumably ignorant of it too; and Shaftesbury himself could hardly have made the contrast between atheism and superstition more favourable to atheism:

Weak Minds, and those that are brought up in Ignorance, and a low Condition, such as are much exposed to Fortune, Men of slavish Principles, the Covetous and Mean-spirited, are all naturally inclin'd to, and easily susceptible of Superstition, and there is no Absurdity so gross nor Contradiction so plain, which the Dregs of the People, most Gamesters, and nineteen Women in twenty may not be taught to believe, concerning invisible Causes. Therefore Multitudes are never tainted with Irreligion; and, the less civiliz'd Nations are, the more boundless is their Credulity. On the contrary, Men of Parts and Spirit, of Thought and Reflection, the Assertors of Liberty, such as meddle with Mathematicks and natural Philosophy, most inquisitive Men, the disinterested, that live in Ease and Plenty; if their Youth has been neglected, and they are not well grounded in the principles of the true Religion, are prone to Infidelity; especially such amongst them, whose Pride and Sufficiency are greater than ordinary; and if Persons of this sort fall into the Hands of Unbelievers, they run great Hazard of becoming *Atheists* or *Scepticks*.[59]

It would seem that the good reasons are actually on the side of atheism: philosophy destroys theology. And, whatever may be said about the insufficiency of human reason and the shallowness

---

[56] *Origin of Honour*, p. 155 (Third Dialogue).
[57] *Free Thoughts on Religion*, p. 92.
[58] *Fable of the Bees*, ed. Kaye, vol. 2, p. 312 (Sixth Dialogue).
[59] Ibid., pp. 312–13 (Sixth Dialogue).

of human understanding, reason is, after all, quite inescapably, the touchstone of revelation.

Mandeville may not, however, have wanted to go so far as to say that there are no good reasons for believing in some kind of invisible cause.

Cleo.: ... Do you believe that there ever was a Man, who had made himself?
Hor.: No: That's a plain Contradiction.
Cleo.: Then it is manifest the first man must have been made by something; and what I say of Man, I may say of all Matter and Motion in general. The doctrine of *Epicurus*, that every thing is deriv'd from the Concourse and fortuitous Jumble of Atoms, is monstrous and extravagant beyond all other Follies.
Hor.: Yet there is no mathematical Demonstration against it.
Cleo.: Nor is there one to prove, that the Sun is not in love with the Moon, if one had a Mind to advance it: and yet I think it a greater Reproach to human Understanding, to believe either, than it is to believe the most childish Stories that are told of Fairies and Hobgoblins.
Hor.: But there is an Axiom very little inferior to a mathematical Demonstration, *ex nihilo nihil fit*, that is directly clashing with and contradicts the Creation out of Nothing. Do you understand, how Something can come from Nothing?
Cleo.: I do not, I confess, any more than I can comprehend Eternity, or the Deity itself: but when I cannot comprehend what my Reason assures me must necessarily exist, there is no Axiom or Demonstration clearer to me, than that the Fault lies in my want of Capacity, the Shallowness of my Understanding. From the little we know of the Sun and Stars, their Magnitudes, Distances and Motion; and what we are more nearly acquainted with, the gross, visible Parts in the Structure of Animals, and their Oeconomy, it is demonstrable that they are the Effects of an intelligent Cause, and the Contrivance of a Being infinite in Wisdom as well as Power.
Hor.: But let Wisdom be as superlative, and Power as extensive as it is possible for them to be, still it is impossible to conceive, how they should exert themselves, unless they had something to act upon.
Cleo.: This is not the only thing which, tho' it be true, we are not able to conceive: How came the first Man to exist? and yet here we are. Heat and Moisture are the plain Effects from manifest Causes, and tho' they bear a great Sway, even in the mineral as well as the animal and vegetable World; yet they cannot produce a Sprig of Grass, without a previous Seed.

Hor.: As we ourselves, and every thing we see, are the undoubted Parts of some one Whole, some are of the Opinion, that this all, . . . the Universe, was from all Eternity.
Cleo.: This is not more satisfactory or comprehensible, than the System of *Epicurus*, who derives every thing from wild Chance, and an undesign'd Struggle of senseless Atoms. When we behold things, which our Reason tells us could not have been produced without Wisdom and Power in a degree far beyond our Comprehension, can any thing be more contrary to or clashing with that same Reason, than that the things, in which that high Wisdom and great Power are visibly display'd, should be coeval with the Wisdom and Power themselves, that contriv'd and wrought them? Yet this Doctrine, which is *Spinosism* in Epitome, after having been neglected many Years, begins to prevail again, and the Atoms lose ground: for of Atheism, as well as Superstition, there are different Kinds, that have their Periods and Returns, after they have been long exploded.[60]

Does Cleomenes or Horatio get the better of the argument here? The difficulties seem fairly evenly balanced: on the one hand, the impossibility of creation out of nothing, on the other the difficulty of finding any other explanation for the existence of the universe, with the evidence it bears of design. Mandeville may have believed that the balance of probability was in favour of an intelligent first cause. That is to say, he may have been a deist. Deism is defined in *Free Thoughts* ('He who believes, in the common acceptation, that there is a God, and that the world is rul'd by providence, but has no faith in any thing reveal'd to us, is a deist')[61] but not discussed there. In the *Fable* we are told that deism, no less than atheism, prevents men from being frightened into good behaviour by threats of punishment in another world; and that 'nothing has contributed more to the growth of Deism in this Kingdom, than the Remissness of Education in Sacred Matters, which for some time has been in Fashion among the better sort.'[62] These are hardly arguments against its truth, especially if one considers religious education in the light of what Mandeville says in *Free Thoughts* about the ease with which people may be persuaded that two and two make seven, or Cleomenes' comments on what men can be brought to believe about the invisible cause. The only argument Mandeville gives

---

[60] Ibid., pp. 310–12 (Sixth Dialogue).
[61] *Free Thoughts on Religion*, p. 3.
[62] *Fable of the Bees*, ed. Kaye, vol. 2, p. 313 (Sixth Dialogue).

for going beyond deism to Christianity is that Moses must have been inspired, or he could not have thought of the unity of God. But he also tells us that a belief in the unity of God is itself unreasonable, if it is also believed that God is benevolent. The evidence which suggests that there may be an intelligent first cause also indicates that that intelligence is indifferent to man, and certainly did not make the universe for his sake;[63] in short, that the first cause is not at all like the God of Moses.

If Mandeville was an atheist, or at most a deist, it does not follow that he is entirely insincere in his endeavours to recall men to what he takes to be true Christianity. A main theme of *Free Thoughts* is that all that is really essential to Christianity is its moral teaching: the outward forms are unimportant (and certainly not worth quarrelling about) and the nature of God is so mysterious, and so difficult for finite intellects to comprehend, that in matters of doctrine all we can do is to accept what we find it possible to believe, and allow our neighbours to differ from us if they wish to. Mandeville's moral views will be discussed in a later chapter, but we may assume that he did think it desirable that men should try to love their neighbours as themselves. He also thought that men found it very hard to do this, and that they never did more than approximate to it, very imperfectly, and then only if they were induced to do so because their weaknesses, such as pride, had been pandered to.

One of these weaknesses was a tendency to believe in an invisible cause which meddled with and interfered in human affairs, and which required men to behave in certain ways. Anyone who wanted to influence men's conduct must take account of this belief: 'the most subtle Unbelievers among Politicians', it will be remembered, 'have been forced, for their own Quiet, to counterfeit their Attachment to Religion when they would a Thousand Times rather have done without it.'[64] Including, perhaps, Bernard Mandeville?

Only an educated few would accept Christian morality without its supernatural underpinning: even if Mandeville was himself an atheist or a deist, he may well have believed that it would be dangerous for most men to accept atheism or deism. Unfortunately, a belief in God was dangerous too. When men behaved

---

[63] Ibid., pp. 260–1 (Fifth Dialogue).
[64] *Enquiry into the Origin of Honour*, p. 28 (First Dialogue).

morally only because they thought that that was the way to please God, they might easily persuade themselves, or be persuaded by interested parties, that God could be pleased by something less exacting, such as attending church regularly, or buying indulgences. The clergy of course (not always insincerely) were also playing the game of pandering to men's superstitions, and persuading them that the way to please God was to please *them*. Mandeville, accordingly, finds it necessary to devote most of *Free Thoughts* to warning men against the machinations of the clergy. For Heaven's sake, he says in effect (or, more accurately, for goodness sake), don't be deluded into cutting one another's throats over this nonsense.

It is only a little less important that men should not be deluded into giving the clergy political power. Mandeville implores men to be tolerant of each other's religious beliefs; but his tolerance does not extend to clerical interference in politics.

I conjure all civil magistrates to believe, that nothing is more destructive to the peace of the society, or more dangerous to the publick welfare in general, than to let the clamours and audaciousness of malecontent clergymen go unpunished when they become criminal, and tamely to suffer that men, who, by their function, ought to stand by and strengthen the authority of the government in every thing that is not clashing with the laws of God, or their country, should openly traduce, and endeavour to render it odious to the people.[65]

The laity, he suggests, should be on guard against 'the least tendencies to sedition and civil discord'. He does not actually say (though perhaps he hints as much) that they should act as informers; but they should 'beware . . . how they give ear to such preaching'.

. . . let every person re-examine himself after sermon, and if he finds all calm within, and his mind not more disturb'd with anger, aversion, or other symptoms of animosity, against those of different opinions, or against his superiors, in going out than it was in coming into the church, the minister has acted the good shepherd, and done honestly by his flock, and we may be satisfy'd that his discourse was not design'd to destroy or endanger the publick repose: but if after the same precaution, you feel in your bosom some rancour or ill-will, either against the government, or any of the ministry, or against others whom

---

[65] *Free Thoughts on Religion*, p. 319.

you disagree with. If you feel a desire of revenge, and your charity to any sort of man is sensibly decayed, you may immediately, unless there is another visible cause of your change, lay the fault on your minister. 'Tis he who has seduc'd you from CHRIST, and you may assure yourself, that, to gratify some passion, or serve some other worldly end, he has endeavour'd to disturb the tranquillity of the people.[66]

The proper function of the clergy is 'to lead and encourage us in the difficult path of virtue, and show us the way to eternal happiness', to acquaint 'the rude multitude with the heinousness of sin' and when necessary 'scare them from evil doing with the terrors of hell'.[67] A belief in Christianity, Mandeville may have thought, is a necessary evil if men are to be cajoled or frightened into being virtuous: the difficulty is to prevent it from going beyond bounds.

In insisting that all that is essential to Christianity is the practice of virtue and self-denial, Mandeville naturally appeals to the scriptures. In exhorting Anglicans to be tolerant of Dissenters, for example, he points out that 'all ceremonies in use amongst christians, even the most decent and the least liable to censure, must be own'd to be of human invention, and that we had none we could with any certainty call apostolical.'[68] As a rule, he is careful to speak respectfully of the Bible, and especially the New Testament. He allows Horatio to enlarge upon the absurdities of the account of the Garden of Eden, or of Noah's ark, but Cleomenes always makes at least a show of defending them. When Horatio makes a facetious reference to the Beast of the Apocalypse and the Whore of Babylon, Cleomenes says primly: 'The Revelations of St. John are beyond my Comprehension, and I shall never laugh at Mysteries for not understanding them.'[69] In urging the contending sects to allow bygones to be bygones, he allows himself to say that the sins of heretics should not be 'like the sin of *Adam*, entail'd upon all their posterity to the world's end',[70] which hints at the unreasonableness of that belief; but it is no more than a hint.

There is one place, however, where he lets down his guard. It is in the *Modest Defence*, when he is trying to meet the objection that 'no Christian Government ought to authorize the Commis-

---

[66] *Free Thoughts on Religion*, pp. 321–2.   [67] Ibid., p. 289.
[68] Ibid., p. 57.   [69] *Enquiry into the Origin of Honour*, p. 89 (Second Dialogue).
[70] *Free Thoughts on Religion*, p. 251.

THE THEOLOGIAN 175

sion of the least known Sin, tho' for the greatest temporal Advantage'. His answer is, in part: *'Fornication* is, no doubt, a direct Breach of a *Gospel* Precept and therefore a Sin; but this Sin, barely as such, concerns the *Government* no more than the Eating of Black-puddings, equally prohibited in the same Text.'[71]

A footnote refers us to Acts 15 : 29: 'That ye abstain from Meats offer'd to Idols, and from Blood, and from Things strangled, and from Fornication; From which if ye keep yourselves, ye do well'.

It is hard not to see this as an open sneer. And even when Mandeville contents himself with hints, some of these suggest very serious criticisms of Biblical doctrine. As part of his plea for tolerance, he says that heretics were, very often, led astray by their good qualities:

When men of narrow views lye poring upon particular scripture places, and let go the main scope and drift of the gospel, they must commit errors, or when men, having in vain raised all their faculties to render the infinite sublimity of GOD and his attributes intelligible, and endeavouring to make him less incomprehensible, pull down, as it were, the Deity to the level of their weak intellects, they fall into miserable mistakes. This latter was the fault of *Origen*, who could not reconcile the eternity of damnation with the infinite goodness of GOD ...[72]

In some pious writers this could be sincere: in Mandeville it is surely meant ironically.

There is another passage not unlike it in the first chapter of *Free Thoughts*:

... the various punishments which human laws inflict on different crimes, are in most cases proportioned to the prejudice they are of to civil society, or the visible damage any of its members did or might sustain by them. It is not the same with offences done to Almighty GOD; the least of them, if we believe the gospel, wilfully committed, makes us liable to eternal damnation, if we do not repent of it before we dye.

How trifling, or at least how venial to human capacities would seem the sin of *Adam* should we only consider the act it self, by which it was committed? yet how great has been the punishment, and how terrible the consequences to himself and all his posterity! nothing

---
[71] *A Modest Defence of Public Stews*, p. 51.
[72] *Free Thoughts on Religion*, pp. 201-2.

could be more innocent than the eating of an apple: there was no Prejudice in it to human society, or any of the creation; and the whole enormity of *Adam's* crime was deriv'd from the bare prohibition.

What is a sin therefore is such, not as a mischief upon earth, but an affront to heaven.[73]

To be very touchy about affronts to himself, and to insist on punishing them very severely indeed, is, of course, one of the less estimable dispositions of the Man of Honour, and one of the more obvious ways in which self-liking manifests itself. Mandeville continually excuses what might appear to be divine shortcomings by appealing to the mysteriousness and incomprehensibility of God; but this behaviour is only too human and too easy to understand. Mandeville could hardly have respected such a God. Yet the point is quite crucial. The punishment of sin is for Mandeville the central doctrine of Christianity, and one he continually insists on. Ostensibly, indeed, this passage is meant to impress upon his readers the need to lead virtuous lives: he goes on immediately: 'The chief duty then of real religion among christians consists in the sacrifice of the heart and is a task of self-denial to be perform'd with the utmost severity against nature.'[74] Merely observing the outward forms of religion will not be enough to earn the clemency of a God like this.

It is perhaps barely possible that, in spite of all that has been said, Mandeville actually was the sincere Christian he professed to be. What must we suppose, for this to be true? First, that he was convinced by the argument from a first cause, and by the argument from design, that the universe is controlled by an intelligent being. It is not too unlikely that he did believe that. But, secondly, he must have persuaded himself, against (as it seemed to him) all the evidence, and for no other reason than that some (though by no means all) of the Old Testament seemed rather ahead of its time, that that intelligence cared about human behaviour, and more particularly human misbehaviour. Thirdly, he must have believed that the intelligence was both benevolent and omnipotent, though it seemed inescapable to him that it was the author of evil, and that the usual theological explanations of this were entirely inadequate. Fourthly, we must suppose that he accounted for this by reflecting that any first cause must in any case be mysterious and incomprehensible to us, since the origin of the universe

[73] *Free Thoughts on Religion*, pp. 15-16.   [74] Ibid., p. 16.

beggared human understanding: Hence we might believe anything we were told of it, provided that the authority was reputable, and the doctrine not actually against reason, as distinct from being beyond reason. The doctrine of the Trinity was, however, against reason, since it had been deliberately made so in order to dish the Arians; holding this, Mandeville must also have believed that some approximation to it must be true, in order to preserve the divinity of Christ, not to mention the Holy Ghost. Fifthly, since he was convinced that the history of Christianity as an organized religion was a long record of chicanery and power-seeking, he must have believed that the only reputable authority was the Bible, although he also believed that the Old Testament contained many crudities, and many texts which could be used by the clergy to justify war and other human iniquities, and that even the New Testament gave an account of the punishment of sin that was contrary to the most elementary notions of justice.

As I have said, it is barely possible that Mandeville did believe all that. In religious matters, it is never safe to assume, from the absurdities and inconsistencies involved in a belief, that it is not sincerely held, even by highly intelligent men of a generally sceptical temper. The alternative account I have given of Mandeville's views on religion does, however, seem very much more probable.

7
THE MORALIST

AT least five distinct, and indeed widely different, moral theories have been attributed to Mandeville: moral scepticism (variously referred to as Nihilism, Pyrrhonism, and anarchism); immoralism, a kind of inversion of accepted morality, according to which what is usually called virtue is really vice, and vice virtue; rigorism or asceticism, which insists that virtue is inseparable from self-denial; utilitarianism, the view that the rightness of actions consists in their contribution to the general welfare; and ethical egoism, the view that it consists in their contribution to one's own welfare.

The second of these is not usually distinguished from the first, though it is obvious that, if morality is an illusion and nothing is either good or bad, vice (so-called) is no more to be commended than virtue. Of course, if morality is thought of as a set of more or less arbitrary prohibitions preventing us from doing what our natures prompt us to, then the removal of its authority would presumably plunge us headlong into vice. This inference would seem to depend on the cynicism about human nature (and, one might add, about morality) that, when they encountered it in Mandeville, so distressed his critics. It was an inference some of them drew, none the less. In the wider (and, I think, preferable) sense of 'morality' in which it simply means the policy by which we think it advisable to lead our lives, this happy release from inhibition would not be a repudiation of morality, but the adoption of a morality of a particular kind: perhaps a hedonistic one.

1. MORAL SCEPTICISM

Those who accuse Mandeville of moral scepticism rely mainly on two passages: one in *A Search into the Nature of Society* which seems to put forward an extreme moral relativism, and the other in *The Origin of Moral Virtue* in which Mandeville explains how 'Moral Virtues are the Political Offspring which Flattery begot upon Pride.'[1]

[1] *Fable of the Bees*, ed. Kaye, vol. 1, p. 51 (*An Enquiry into the Origin of Moral Virtue*.)

In the first of these Mandeville begins by pointing out that, although most judges of painting will agree 'when a fine Picture is compared to the daubing of a Novice', they disagree very much about the relative merits of the recognized masters. Moreover, paintings are valued for the signatures on them rather than for their intrinsic merits: 'A noted Original will be ever worth more than any Copy that can be made of it by an unknown Hand, tho' it should be better.' Value will also be affected by the scarcity of an artist's work, and the eminence of the people who collect his paintings. Nevertheless, there is one constant standard which keeps fluctuations of taste within limits: 'Painting is an Imitation of Nature, a Copying of things which Men have everywhere before them',[2] and, to at least some extent, will be judged by its likeness to the original. With the works of nature themselves, however, there is no such standard.

How whimsical is the Florist in his Choice! Sometimes the Tulip, sometimes the Auricula, and at other times the Carnation shall engross his esteem, and every Year a new Flower in his Judgment beats all the old ones, tho' it is much inferior to them both in Colour and Shape. Three hundred Years ago Men were shaved as closely as they are now: Since that they have wore Beards, and cut them in vast Variety of Forms, that were all as becoming when fashionable as now they would be ridiculous. How mean and comically a Man looks, that is otherwise well dress'd, in a narrow-brim'd Hat when every body wears broad ones; and again how monstrous is a very great Hat, when the other extreme has been in fashion for a considerable time? . . . What Mortal can decide which is the handsomest, abstract from the Mode in being, to wear great Buttons or small ones?[3]

He goes on to give a striking example. When linen shrouds were made illegal (in order to protect the woollen industry) people were at first shocked, but now 'Burying in Linen being almost forgot, it is the general Opinion that Nothing could be more decent than Woollen, and the present Manner of Dressing a Corps: which shews that our Liking or Disliking of things chiefly depends on Mode and Custom, and the Precept and Example of our Betters and such whom one way or another we think to be Superior to us.'

[2] Ibid., p. 326 (*A Search into the Nature of Society*).
[3] Ibid., p. 328.

There follows immediately the paragraph that scandalized so many of his readers:

> In Morals there is no greater Certainty. Plurality of Wives is odious among Christians, and all the Wit and Learning of a Great Genius in defence of it has been rejected with contempt: But Polygamy is not shocking to a Mahometan. What Men have learned from Infancy enslaves them, and the Force of Custom warps Nature, and at the same time imitates her in such a manner that it is often difficult to know which of the two we are influenced by. In the *East* formerly Sisters married Brothers, and it was meritorious for a Man to marry his Mother. Such Alliances are abominable; but it is certain that, whatever Horror we conceive at the Thoughts of them, there is nothing in Nature repugnant against them, but what is built upon Mode and Custom. A Religious Mahometan that has never tasted any Spirituous Liquor, and has often seen People Drunk, may receive as great an aversion against Wine, as another with us of the least Morality and Education may have against lying with his Sister, and both imagine that their Antipathy proceeds from Nature. Which is the best Religion? is a Question that has caused more Mischief than all other Questions together. Ask it at *Peking*, at *Constantinople*, and at *Rome* and you'll receive three distinct Answers extremely different from one another, yet all of them equally positive and peremptory. Christians are well assured of the falsity of the Pagan and Mahometan Superstitions; as to this point there is a perfect Union and Concord among them; but enquire of the several Sects thay are divided into, Which is the true Church of Christ? and all of them will tell you it is theirs, and to convince you, go together by the Ears. It is manifest then that the hunting after this *Pulchrum et Honestum* is not much better than a Wild-Goose-Chace that is but little to be depended upon: But this is not the greatest Fault I find with it. The imaginary Notions that Men may be virtuous without Self-Denial are a vast inlet to Hypocrisy, which being once made habitual, we must not only deceive others, but likewise become altogether unknown to our selves . . .[4]

J. C. Maxwell says that this passage is merely a *reductio ad absurdum* of Shaftesbury's assimilation of moral to aesthetic judgements, and that 'Mandeville's ethical theory is not at any point sceptical, relativist or Pyrrhonist.'[5] This, he claims, is quite obvious from the context.

Let us, then, look at the context. It is true that Mandeville is

---

[4] *Fable af the Bees*, ed. Kaye, vol. 1, pp. 330–1.
[5] J. C. Maxwell, 'Ethics and Politics in Mandeville', *Philosophy*, 26 (1951), 245.

quite explicitly attacking Shaftesbury, of whom he says, in his opening paragraph:

He seems to require and expect Goodness in his Species, as we do a sweet Taste in Grapes and China Oranges, of which, if any of them are sour, we boldly pronounce that they are not come to that Perfection their Nature is capable of ... In respect to our Species he looks upon Virtue and Vice as permanent Realities that must ever be the same in all Countries and all Ages, and imagines that a man of sound Understanding, by following the Rules of good Sense, may not only find out that *Pulchrum et Honestum* both in Morality and the Works of Art and Nature, but likewise govern himself by his Reason with as much Ease and Readiness as a good Rider manages a well-taught Horse by the Bridle.[6]

Mandeville's main purpose, then, is to show, against Shaftesbury, that there are no such 'rules of good sense', either in aesthetics, or in morals: that a man cannot expect, simply by following his instincts, to reach infallible conclusions about either virtue or beauty; that what we take to be the deliverances of reason and common sense are, in these matters, actually the result of custom and education.

Mandeville is inclined to misrepresent Shaftesbury, making out his view of human nature to be more naïvely optimistic than it actually was; but it is true that he did think that both the sense of beauty and the moral sense were, in a way, instinctive. Men, he thought, feel a specific emotion when they contemplate a sunset or an old master: they put this emotion into words by talking about beauty, as if this were some kind of transcendental quality in the beautiful object. In fact, however, the only qualities to be found there are the quite ordinary ones of colour, symmetry, and proportion: beauty is not an additional quality, but a slightly oblique way of referring to the emotions these other qualities arouse in us. In the same way, when we contemplate, with our mind's eye, such mental qualities as courage or unselfishness we feel a different emotion: one we put into words by talking about virtue. These reactions are in some sense instinctive, or, as Shaftesbury would say, natural. One might suppose him to mean that the same objects evoke them in all men, just as the same light-rays, impinging on the retina, evoke the same colour impressions.

[6] *Fable of the Bees*, ed. Kaye, vol. 1, pp. 323-4 (*A Search into the Nature of Society*).

Perhaps he does mean this; but he also says that taste, both in art and in morals, may be corrupted, and may need cultivation:

> If *Civility* and *Humanity* be a TASTE; if *Brutality*, *Insolence*, *Riot*, be in the same manner a TASTE; who if he cou'd reflect, wou'd not chuse to form himself on the amiable and agreeable, rather than the odious and perverse Model? who wou'd not endeavour to *force* NATURE as well in this respect, as in what relates to a *Taste* or *Judgment* in other Arts and Sciences? For in each place the *Force on* NATURE is us'd only for its Redress. If a natural *good* TASTE be not already form'd in us; why shou'd not we endeavour to form it, and become *natural*?[7]

He is quite clear that standards, in both art and morals, are not arbitrary:

> Shou'd a Writer upon *Musick*, addressing himself to the Students and Lovers of the Art, declare to 'em, 'That the Measure or Rule of HARMONY was *Caprice* or *Will*, *Humour* or *Fashion*', 'tis not very likely he shou'd be heard with great Attention, or treated with real Gravity. For HARMONY is Harmony by *Nature*, let Men judg ever so ridiculously of Musick. So is *Symmetry* and Proportion founded still in *Nature*, let Mens Fancy prove ever so barbarous, or their Fashions ever so *Gothick* in their Architecture, Sculpture, or whatever other designing Art. 'Tis the same case, where *Life* and MANNERS are concern'd. *Virtue* has the same fix'd Standard. The same *Numbers*, *Harmony*, and *Proportion* will have place in MORALS; and are discoverable in the *Characters* and *Affections* of Mankind; in which are laid the just Foundations of an Art and Science, superiour to every other of human Practice and Comprehension.[8]

At bottom, it will be noticed, the sense of beauty and the moral sense are the same: there is a proportion, symmetry, and harmony to be found in men's actions as well as in paintings or landscapes. And it is, Shaftesbury believes, the same proportion and harmony: what evokes our admiration in each case (if our taste has not been corrupted) is the way in which a part (an individual) fits in with a whole (society, the human race, the universe). Consequently Shaftesbury and his followers talk about the beauty of actions.

One need not be a moral sceptic to disagree with all this. Certainly Mandeville's main point is that it is impossible to distinguish what we 'naturally' approve from what we have been taught to approve. We do not, he insists, have any natural

---

[7] Shaftesbury, *Characteristics*, 2nd ed., 1714, vol. 1, p. 339 (Advice to an Author).
[8] Ibid., p. 353.

tendency to seek the good of the whole, the public good. Man is fit for society only in the sense that grapes are fit for wine: that is to say, he may be made so, by skill and industry; but it is not enough simply to let nature take its course. Man is not naturally virtuous, but he is malleable. The many fluctuations of taste, both in art and in morality, show his malleability, as well as the lack of any constant, 'natural' standard. But to say that there is no constant standard of that kind is just to say that men need to learn what is right, and cannot discover it merely by following their natural instincts. Virtue, he goes on immediately to say, is not possible without self-denial. This would be an oddly inconsistent remark for a moral sceptic to make. Mandeville adds that those who think otherwise open the way to self-deception, and proceeds to give an example of such self-deception: Shaftesbury himself.

Shaftesbury, he suggests, was 'of a Quiet Indolent Nature', with studious tastes acquired under the tutorship of John Locke. His family position called him to an active public life, like that of his celebrated grandfather, the first Earl: in refusing to accept this role and living quietly in the country instead he was indulging himself, and possibly neglecting his duty.

It is probable he would answer that he lov'd Retirement, had no other Ambition than to be a Good Man, and never aspired to have any share in the Government, or that he hated all Flattery and slavish Attendance, the Insincerity of Courts and Bustle of the World. I am willing to believe him: but may not a Man of an Indolent Temper and Unactive Spirit say, and be sincere in all this, and at the same time indulge his Appetites without being able to subdue them, tho' his Duty summons him to it. Virtue consists in Action, and whoever is possest of this Social Love and kind Affection to his Species, and by his Birth or Quality can claim any Post in the Publick Management, ought not to sit still when he can be serviceable, but exert himself to the utmost for the good of his Subjects. Had this noble Person been of a Warlike Genius or a Boisterous Temper, he would have chose another Part in the Drama of Life, and preach'd a quite contrary Doctrine: For we are ever pushing our Reason which way soever we feel Passion to draw it, and Self-love pleads to all human Creatures for their different Views, still furnishing every individual with Arguments to justify their Inclinations.[9]

---

[9] *Fable of the Bees*, ed. Kaye, vol. 1, pp. 332–3 (*A Search into the Nature of Society*).

This passage was in a way turned against Mandeville by John Brown, who suggested that Mandeville's own opinions about human nature might be explained in this way no less than Shaftesbury's:

'Tis well known, that the Writer of the *Fable of the Bees* was neither a *Saint* in his Life, nor a *Hermit* in his Diet: He seems to have been Master of a very considerable *Sagacity*, much knowledge of the World, as it appears in populous *Cities*, extremely sensible to all the grosser bodily Enjoyments; but for Delicacy of Sentiment, Imagination or Passion, for an exquisite *Taste* either in *Arts* or *Morals*, he appears to have been *incapable* of it . . . The noble Writer is known to have been of a Frame the very Reverse of this: His *Constitution* was neither more nor less opposite to Dr. Mandeville's, than his Philosophy. His sensual appetites were weak, his Imagination all alive, noble and capacious; his Passions were accordingly refined, and his public Affections (in *Fancy* at least) predominant . . . Among the *Epicureans* we ever find Men of high Health, florid complexions, firm Nerves, and a Capacity for Pleasure: Of the *Stoic* Party are the delicate or sickly Frames, Men incapable of the grosser sensual Enjoyments, and who either *are* or *think* themselves *virtuous*.[10]

Brown is, on the whole, agreeing with Mandeville, but no one has accused him of moral scepticism; he is actually arguing for utilitarianism. The point is not that each man regards as virtuous whatever way of life his inclinations lead him towards, so that virtue is an illusion, a mere mask for self-indulgence. The point is that our inclinations may lead us to deceive ourselves about what is virtuous. Brown, like Mandeville, is arguing against Shaftesbury's contention that there is a natural tendency to virtue. Mandeville, unlike Brown, adds that we can be sure that we are really being virtuous only when we are practising self-denial.

Is Maxwell, then, right, and Mandeville quite free from moral scepticism or relativism? Certainly it is unfair to interpret him as saying, in this passage, that 'he who prefers Equity to Injustice, is but like him that chooses a *great Button* rather than a *small* one; and he who prefers Fidelity to Falseness, as whimsical as the *Florist*, who admires the *Auricula* more than the *Tulip*.'[11] Even if we take the remark about flowers out of its general context,

[10] John Brown, *Essays on the Characteristics*, 1752, Essay II, Section VII, pp. 117–18.
[11] William Law, *Remarks upon a late book, entitled* The Fable of the Bees, 1723. In *Works of the Reverend William Law*, 1762, vol. 2, p. 30.

the attack on Shaftesbury, Mandeville says of the florist that each year he prefers a new flower, 'though it is inferior' to the others 'both in Colour and Shape'. So that even here he is implying that there are standards for judging colour and shape: the stress is on the fickleness of taste, not on the absence of objective criteria. When he goes on to say 'In Morals there is no greater Certainty' he may be taken, then, to mean that men's judgement is uncertain, not that there are no true judgements to be made.

Yet Maxwell is hardly accurate when he says that 'the allegations are entirely based on one sentence': 'In Morals there is no greater Certainty.' There is also, after all, the account of the origin of the virtues, 'the Political offspring which Flattery begot upon Pride'. According to Mandeville the whole concept of virtue was dreamed up by 'skilful Politicians', in order that 'the Ambitious might reap the more Benefit from, and govern vast Numbers of them with the greater Ease and Security'.[12] This looks as if morality is a confidence trick, with no more basis in reality than the dicky-bird which, children used to be told, in the days before high-speed photography, would pop out of the camera if only they kept still and fixed their eyes on the right aperture. And the virtues Mandeville is talking about here are those which he acknowledged to be genuine virtues: the ones involving self-denial. Scorn is poured upon Shaftesbury because he is supposed to think that virtue is possible without self-denial, a view which, according to Mandeville, is 'a vast inlet to hypocrisy' and self-deceit. Yet even the virtue based on self-denial is, it would seem, a fabrication and a fraud.

But, of course, morality in any broad sense can hardly be that. For it is hard to see how we can live at all without passing judgement on our past actions (and those of others) and forming some policy to guide our future ones. Whatever policy we arrive at constitutes *a* morality, though it need not be the accepted policy which is reverentially called Morality. William Law accuses Mandeville of inconsistency in using the phrase: 'I lay it down as a first Principle that . . .' How, he asks, 'can you pretend to have a *first Principle* . . . after you have declared that the *moral Virtues* are all a Cheat, by making them *the Political Offspring which Flattery*

[12] *Fable of the Bees*, ed. Kaye, vol. 1, p. 47 (*An Enquiry into the Origin of Moral Virtue*).

begot upon Pride?'[13] Certainly Mandeville never gives up the appraisal of human actions. He is not backward, either, in advocating policies which, he tells his readers, they ought to follow: mutual toleration, for example, especially in matters of religion. He cannot do this without appealing to criteria and asserting values, and he can hardly believe that these criteria and those values are the fraudulent invention of ambitious politicians.

What was it, then, that the politicians invented? The short answer is that they invented virtue, but not goodness. When Horatio asks whether people cannot be good by choice, Cleomenes answers: 'There is an Ambiguity in the Word Good which I would avoid; let us stick to that of Virtuous, and then I affirm, that no Action is such, which does not suppose and point at some Conquest or other, some Victory great or small over untaught Nature; otherwise the Epithet is improper.'[14] Now what is the point of conquering the passions in this way? Why should anyone attempt so painful a task? The reason given by the skilful politicians, it will be remembered, was that men who were 'enslaved by voluptuousness' and 'yielded without resistance to every gross desire' were no better than brutes; whereas those who 'despised whatever they had in common with irrational creatures' and 'opposed by the help of reason their most violent inclinations' were 'the true representatives of their sublime species, exceeding in worth the first class by more degrees than that it self was superior to the beasts of the field'.[15]

Are these reasons genuine? Since they are described as an appeal to pride, and moreover as flattery, there is a presumption that they are not. In the Introduction to the 'Origin of Moral Virtue' Mandeville says: 'As for my Part, without any Compliment to the courteous Reader, or my self, I believe Man (besides Skin, Flesh, Bones, etc. that are obvious to the Eye) to be a compound of various Passions, that all of them, as they are provoked and come uppermost, govern him by turns, whether he will or no.'[16] And he adds that 'we all pretend to be ashamed' of this state of affairs. This rather looks as if we have no reason to pride ourselves on our superiority to the other animals. Especially since

---

[13] William Law, *Remarks upon* . . . The Fable of the Bees, 1723. In *Works*, 1762, vol. 2, p. 47.

[14] *Fable of the Bees*, ed. Kaye, vol. 2, p. 109 (Third Dialogue).

[15] Ibid., vol. 1, 43-4 (*Enquiry into the Origin of Moral Virtue*).

[16] Ibid., p. 39.

we are told that the reward we get for this painful self-denial is illusory:

> Oh! the mighty Prize we have in view for all our Self-denial! can any Man be so serious as to abstain from Laughter when he considers that for so much deceit and insincerity practis'd upon our selves as well as others, we have no other Recompence than the vain Satisfaction of making our Species appear more exalted and remote from that of other Animals than it really is; and we in our Consciences know it to be?[17]

The same point is made in the *Origin of Honour*, when Cleomenes says that 'Men are better paid for their Adherence to Honour than they are for their Adherence to Virtue: The First requires less Self-denial; and the Rewards they receive for that Little are not imaginary but real and palpable.'[18]

It seems clear, then, that the exaltation of virtue is a confidence trick. Yet it is not true to say that the tricksters were motivated only by personal ambition. In the *Origin of Moral Virtue* Mandeville says that their purpose was 'that the Ambitious might reap the more Benefit from, and govern vast Numbers of them with the greater Ease and Security'. But he also says that they wanted 'to render Men useful to each other as well as tractable'.[19] And in the *Origin of Honour* he tells us that all this was a slow evolutionary process, and that the politicians in question were 'All that, having studied Human Nature, have endeavour'd to civilize Men, and render them more and more tractable, either for the Ease of Governours and Magistrates, or else for the Temporal Happiness of Society in general'.[20] He also tells us there that

> All Human Creatures have a restless Desire of mending their Condition; and in all Civil Societies and Communions of Men there seems to be a Spirit at Work, that, in Spight of the continual Opposition it receives from Vice and Misfortunes, is always labouring for, and seeking after what can never be obtain'd whil'st the World stands.
> *Hor.*: What is that pray?
> *Cleo.*: To make Men compleatly Happy upon Earth.

In Part 2 of the *Fable* Mandeville gives an account of the origin of society, and of morality, that is quite close to Hobbes.

---

[17] Ibid., p. 145 (Remark N).
[18] *Enquiry into the Origin of Honour*, 1732, p. 43.
[19] *Fable of the Bees*, ed. Kaye, vol. 1, p. 47 (*Enquiry into the Origin of Moral Virtue*).
[20] *Enquiry into the Origin of Honour*, 1732, pp. 40-1.

Men are driven to combine first by the fear of wild animals and then by fear of one another. Slowly they come to realize that to live peaceably together they need governments, and laws which they all obey: above all, that they need to control their passions:

> The principal Laws of all Countries have the same Tendency; and there is not one, that does not point to some Frailty, Defect or Unfitness for Society, that Men are naturally subject to; but all of them are plainly design'd as so many Remedies, to cure and disappoint that natural Instinct of Sovereignty, which teaches Man to look upon every thing as centring in Himself, and prompts him to put in a Claim to every thing, he can lay his Hands on.[21]

Where Mandeville differs from Hobbes is that he does not think that the mere realization that self-control is necessary for peace and security will be enough to enable men to control themselves, even when reinforced, as Hobbes would reinforce it, by fear of temporal punishment. The fear of eternal punishment in another world will not be enough either:

> Men that to all outward Appearance are Believers, that go to Church, receive the Sacrament, and at the Approach of Death are observed to be really afraid of Hell ... yet ... are Drunkards, Whoremasters, Adulterers, and not a Few of them betray their Trust, rob their Country, defraud Widows and Orphans, and make wronging their Neighbours their daily Practice.[22]

The strongest influence on human nature is pride, the fear of shame, as duellists and soldiers amply testify. All rulers, Cleomenes tells Horatio, need to humour human nature. They must make men believe that 'we say Nothing to them, but what we know to be true.'[23] He does not, however, stipulate that what they say must actually be true. The story about man's superiority to the other animals is a fabrication intended to humour human nature: it supplies men with the only motive powerful enough to make them practise self-denial (though in some ways the invention of Honour, appealing to the same motive, does the job better). Yet the self-denial is really necessary: necessary to make men tractable. And they need to be tractable, not only so that ambitious

---

[21] *Fable of the Bees*, ed. Kaye, vol. 2, p. 271 (Sixth Dialogue).
[22] *Enquiry into the Origin of Honour*, 1732, p. 19.
[23] Ibid., p. 20.

men may govern them, but also that they may be useful to one another.

There is a sense, then, in which Mandeville does not deny the reality of virtue. There are genuine reasons for being virtuous, even though the reasons that persuade men to virtue (or to what they take to be virtue) are spurious. Conrad Suits calls attention to the full wording of the title-page of the second of the two 1714 editions: 'The Fable of the Bees: or, Private Vices Publick Benefits. CONTAINING, several Discourses, to demonstrate, That Human Frailties, *during the degeneracy of* MANKIND, may be turn'd to the Advantage of the CIVIL SOCIETY, and made to supply the Place of *Moral Virtues*'.[24] It would appear from this that there are genuine moral virtues, even if men are too degenerate to be capable of them.

What would genuine virtue be, according to Mandeville? Presumably, the practice of self-denial, not to gratify one's own self-esteem, but because one realized that it was necessary for human happiness. Mandeville indeed defines virtue as 'every Performance, by which Man, contrary to the impulse of Nature, should endeavour the Benefit of others, or the Conquest of his own Passions out of a Rational Ambition of being good'.[25] It is true that this is the definition arrived at by the skilful politicians. Perhaps, then, it applies only to the sham virtue that they invented? Mandeville's point, I think, is that virtue in this sense is genuine enough, since what the politicians saw was simply that it was necessary for human well-being. Virtue in this sense, however, is never practised, since men are (at least while degenerate) incapable of acting from 'a rational ambition of being good'. What takes the place of this motive is pride; what the politicians invented were spurious considerations that might appeal to pride. Consequently what was practised was not real virtue, since it sprang from a 'human frailty', but only a substitute for it: a fairly satisfactory substitute, since it had the same practical results. How does it come about, then, that the politicians and their pupils arrived at a definition of the genuine, and not the sham virtue? The answer is that, though they were not really

---

[24] Conrad Suits, 'The Meaning of *The Fable of the Bees*', [unpublished Ph.D. thesis], University of Chicago, 1961, p. 72. The title-page referred to is reproduced in Kaye, vol. 2, opp. p. 392.

[25] *Fable of the Bees*, ed. Kaye, vol. 1, pp. 48–9 (*Enquiry into the Origin of Moral Virtue*).

acting out of 'a rational ambition of doing good', they thought they were. Otherwise they could not have prided themselves on subduing their passions, and giving rein only to that nobler faculty, the reason, which alone distinguished them from the brutes.

One reason why Mandeville insists on the variability of men's moral judgements may be that he wants to deny that men are capable of acting from a rational ambition of being good, or even, as Hobbes would have it, from a rational concern for their own remote interest. Otherwise it might be objected that the politicians merely drew men's attention to truths about man's nature, and his superiority over the other animals, and that what motivated them was not vanity but a rational apprehension of those truths. Mandeville insists that men may pride themselves on (or be ashamed of) almost anything: 'valuing themselves upon Actions that were perform'd several Ages before they were born'[26] (by their ancestors) or 'bragging of their Vices and boasting of their Impudence',[27] if they happen to live among rakes. Everything depends upon what happens to win admiration in the circles in which they move: it is the love of admiration that influences men and not, as opponents like William Law would make out, a reasoned conviction that some kinds of action are, in some quite objective sense, admirable.

To say, however, that men are moved by their passions and not by the rational apprehension of eternal and immutable truths is a long way from moral scepticism. This position was actually defended by Hutcheson against Gilbert Burnet in the *London Journal* at the same time as he was bitterly attacking Mandeville in the *Dublin Weekly Journal*. Hutcheson, indeed, sneers at Mandeville for gravely putting forward tautologies as profound psychological truths: one of these is 'That Man never exerts himself but when he is roused by Desire'. 'A most important Maxim', Hutcheson says sarcastically.[28] When Hutcheson's illustrious follower reformulated the maxim as 'Reason is the slave of the passions' no one thought that it was a tautology. Mandeville anticipates Hume; but that does not of course make him a moral sceptic.

---

[26] *Enquiry into the Origin of Honour*, 1732, p. 95.
[27] *Fable of the Bees*, ed. Kaye, vol. 2, p. 90 (Second Dialogue).
[28] F. Hutcheson, *Reflections upon Laughter and Remarks upon* The Fable of the Bees, 1729, in *Collected Works*, Hildesheim, G. Olms, 1971, vol. 7, p. 166.

Neither the *Origin of Moral Virtue* nor the *Search into the Nature of Society*, then, need be interpreted as a repudiation of morality. But Adam Smith, in making Mandeville a representative (ultimately the sole representative) of 'licentious systems of moral philosophy' does not rely on the passages usually quoted from those works, but on Mandeville's thesis about self-denial. Mandeville, he points out, asserts that no actions are really virtuous, since none involve self-denial. Those which appear to be virtuous are really self-indulgent, since their purpose is to gratify vanity and pride. No actions, then, are ever virtuous. But to say this, Adam Smith protests, is 'to take away altogether the distinction between vice and virtue'. Consequently 'the tendency' of Mandeville's 'system' is 'wholly pernicious'.[29]

This makes Mandeville a sceptic, not about morality in the abstract, but about the actual occurrence of virtuous actions, a charge to which he might have pleaded guilty. To believe that all men are sinful is perhaps to be sceptical, but hardly about morality. But, it may be said, Mandeville goes further than that, and claims that all *actions* are sinful. And to say that is to say in effect that none are. It does not matter what we do, since anything we do is bound to be wicked in any case. The good Samaritan is just as wicked as the torturer: one is indulging his taste for benevolence, and the other his taste for inflicting pain. Since it is self-indulgence that is wrong, one is no better than the other.

As a *reductio ad absurdum* of Mandeville's asceticism, this has its force. But if it is intended as exposition rather than criticism, as an account of what Mandeville actually means his readers to conclude, it is at least open to question. Perhaps it is inconsistent of Mandeville to distinguish between the various forms of self-indulgence, to commend some and dispraise others, because in doing so he implies that there are other moral criteria besides the presence of self-denial. Nevertheless, that is what he does. Pity, though 'a Frailty', is, he says, 'of all our Weaknesses . . . the most amiable, and bears the greatest Resemblance to Virtue'.[30] 'There are not many Occasions on which we ought to conquer or curb it.'[31] To say, then, that something is a frailty (Mandeville does not

---

[29] Adam Smith, *The Theory of Moral Sentiments*, 1759. Facsimile reprint of 1853 ed., New York, Augustus M. Kelley, 1966, p. 451.
[30] *Fable of the Bees*, ed. Kaye, vol. 1, p. 56 (*Enquiry into the Origin of Moral Virtue*).
[31] Ibid., p. 260 (*Essay on Charity and Charity-Schools*).

call pity a vice) is not to imply that it, or the conduct prompted by it, ought always to be curbed. There are, it would seem, other criteria which help to determine what we ought to do. So that, even if Mandeville has in effect abolished the distinction between virtue and vice, he has not thereby abolished all moral considerations.

The definition of vice, indeed, makes it clear what these other criteria are. '. . . they agreed with the rest, to call every thing, which, without Regard to the Publick, Man should commit to gratify any of his Appetites, VICE; if in that Action there cou'd be observed the least prospect, that it might either be injurious to any of the Society, or ever render himself less serviceable to others.'[32] Mere indulgence of one's appetites, then, is not enough to make an action vicious: there must also be a lack of concern for the public good as a whole, and also (what is not quite the same thing) for possible harm to other individuals. In so far as this implies that the public good, simply as such, is the criterion of what we ought to do, Mandeville is plunging into another hornet's nest, as we shall see in the next section; since he also seems to say that private vices are public benefits. Perhaps immoralism, rather than scepticism, is the charge that Adam Smith really wants to bring. However that may be, the point at the moment is that the charge of moral scepticism hardly seems to have been made good.

2. IMMORALISM

Most of Mandeville's contemporary critics (Berkeley, Law, Bluet, for example) take it for granted that his object is to praise vice and denigrate virtue. The same view is taken by Norman Wilde, who suggests, in an article in *Mind* in 1898, that Mandeville was the mouthpiece of those 'men of wit and fashion' who resented the reform movement of the day, which was itself a reaction against the licentiousness of the Restoration.[33]

This seems to have been Berkeley's view of Mandeville. *Alciphron*, Berkeley's attack on the free thinkers of his day, pays special attention to Mandeville and Shaftesbury, as representing two opposite kinds of error. The book is in dialogue form. Lysicles, who expounds Mandeville's views, may be meant

[32] Ibid., p. 48 (*Enquiry into the Origin of Moral Virtue*).
[33] N. Wilde, 'Mandeville's Place in English Thought', *Mind*, N.S. 7 (1898), 224.

to represent a follower of Mandeville rather than Mandeville himself; but it is significant that he is described as a 'young gentleman . . . of lively parts and a general insight into knowledge, who, after having passed the forms of education and seen a little of the world, fell into intimacy with men of pleasure and free-thinkers, I am afraid much to the damage of his constitution and his fortune'. His mind has been corrupted 'by a set of pernicious principles, which, having been observed to survive the passions of youth, forestall even the remote hopes of amendment'.[34] In defending these principles, Lysicles identifies himself with Wilde's 'men of wit and fashion:'

Euphranor: I should wonder if men were not shocked at notions of such a surprising nature, so contrary to all laws, education and religion.
Lysicles: They would be shocked much more if it had not been for the skilful address of our philosophers, who, considering that most men are influenced by names rather than things, have introduced a certain polite way of speaking, which lessens much of the abhorrence and prejudice against vice.
Euphranor: Explain me this.
Lysicles: Thus, in our dialect, a vicious man is a man of pleasure, a sharper is one that plays the whole game, a lady is said to have an affair, a gentleman to be gallant, a rogue in business to be one that knows the world. By this means we have no such things as sots, debauchees, whores or rogues in the *beau monde*, who may enjoy their vices without incurring disagreeable appellations.
Euphranor: Vice then is it seems, a fine thing with an ugly name.
Lysicles: Assuredly it is.[35]

In accusing Mandeville of praising and promoting vice Berkeley was, of course, relying chiefly on the subtitle of the *Fable*: Private Vices Publick Benefits. He takes it for granted that Mandeville is advocating drunkenness, gambling, and highway robbery, because he points out that even these practices benefit some members of the community: brewers, locksmiths, the tradesmen who are enriched by the highwayman's lavish spending, the law officers who apprehend him, and so on. In his reply to Berkeley, *A Letter to Dion*, Mandeville accuses him of never having

---

[34] G. Berkeley, *Alciphron, or the Minute Philosopher*, 1732. *Works*, ed. A. A. Luce and T. E. Jessop, vol. 3 (1950), pp. 32–3.
[35] Ibid., p. 69.

read the *Fable*; and certainly anyone who had read *Alciphron* first would be surprised at what he actually found in Mandeville. He would have had no hint that Mandeville's tone is satirical, and that the satire is directed against fashionable rakes quite as often as against hypocritical clergymen; that Mandeville at least claims to be on the side of virtue and religion; or that his chief delight is the exposure of just the hypocrisy or self-deception that leads to euphemisms like those of Lysicles.

Probably Berkeley had at least glanced at the *Fable*, since some of Lysicles' remarks paraphrase passages in it, and in the *Discourse to Magistrates* there are three direct quotations, with page references. Two of these had been bandied about quite a lot by 1738 and were no doubt quoted by many people who had never read Mandeville, but the third is from Part 2 of the *Fable*, which had not been published when Dennis, Fiddes, Hutcheson, Law, and Bluet wrote their books against Mandeville. On the other hand, Berkeley misinterprets this quotation so grossly that it is hard to believe that he had ever read it in its context. Possibly he used the *Fable* as some politicians use their opponents' speeches, and went through it looking for damning quotations, without trying to take in the argument as a whole.

For in his attack on Shaftesbury and Mandeville Berkeley had a quite explicit political purpose. His *Discourse addressed to Magistrates and Men in Authority* was apparently occasioned by a public scandal in Dublin over a society of young men calling themselves the Blasters, who, it was reported to the Irish House of Lords (including the Bishop of Cloyne), offered up prayers to the Devil, publicly drank the Devil's health, and 'uttered the most daring and execrable blasphemies against the sacred Name and Majesty of God; and often made use of such obscene, blasphemous, and before unheard of expressions as the Lord's Committees think they cannot even mention to your Lordships, and therefore choose to pass over in silence'.[36] Berkeley seized the opportunity to urge action against writers who, by openly questioning the truth of Christian doctrines, might be supposed to encourage such excesses. After the usual genuflections to freedom of speech and the usual distinction between liberty and licence ('The profane

[36] Report to the Irish House of Lords, 10 March 1737, quoted in Berkeley, *Works*, ed. A. A. Luce and T. E. Jessop, vol. 6 (1953), p. 197 (Editor's introduction to the *Discourse on Magistrates*).

and lawless scorner is one thing, and the modest inquirer after truth another')[37] Berkeley cites some interesting Biblical precedents:

> Darius, a heathen prince, made a decree that in every dominion of his kingdom men should tremble and fear before God (Dan., vi, 26). Nebuchadnezzar, likewise, another heathen, made a decree that every people, nation and language which spoke anything amiss against God should be cut in pieces, and their houses made a dunghill (Dan., iii, 29). And if these things were done in Persia and Babylon, surely it may be expected that impious blasphemers against God and His worship should at least be discouraged and put out of countenance, in Christian countries.[38]

It is interesting, in the light of this, to notice the following passage in *Alciphron*:

> *Euphranor*: ... But methinks it would be dangerous to make such notions public.
> *Crito*: Dangerous! To whom?
> *Euphranor*: In the first place to the publisher.
> *Crito*: That is a mistake; for such notions have been published and met with due applause, in this most wise and happy age of free-thinking, free-speaking, free-writing and free-acting.
> *Euphranor*: How! May a man then publish and practise such things with impunity?
> *Crito*: To speak the truth, I am not so clear as to the practic part. An unlucky accident now and then befalls an ingenious man. The minute philosopher Magirus, being desirous to benefit the public by circulating an estate possessed by a near relation who had not the heart to spend it, soon convinced himself, upon these principles, that it would be a very worthy action to dispatch out of the way such a useless fellow, to whom he was next heir. But, for this laudable attempt, he had the misfortune to be hanged by an underbred judge and jury. Could anything be more unjust?
> *Euphranor*: Why unjust?
> *Crito*: Is it not unjust to punish actions when the principles from which they follow are directly tolerated by the public? Can anything be more inconsistent than to condemn in practice what is approved in speculation?[39]

---

[37] *Discourse to Magistrates*, 1738. Berkeley, *Works*, ed. Luce and Jessop, vol. 6, (1953), p. 218.
[38] Ibid., pp. 220-1.
[39] *Alciphron*, 1732. Berkeley, *Works*, ed. Luce and Jessop, vol. 3 (1950), pp. 73-4.

In the *Discourse to Magistrates* Berkeley did not scruple to accuse Shaftesbury and Mandeville of being directly responsible for encouraging crime:

We esteem it a horrid thing to laugh at the apprehensions of a future state, with the author of the *Characteristics*, or with him who wrote the *Fable of the Bees*, to maintain that 'moral virtues are the political offspring which flattery begot upon pride'; that 'in morals there is no greater certainty than in fashions of dress'; that, indeed, 'the doctrine of good manners teacheth men to speak well of all virtues; but requires no more of them in any age or country than the outward appearance of those in fashion'. Two authors of infidel systems these, who, setting out upon opposite principles, are calculated to draw all mankind, by flattering either their vanity or their passions, into one or other system. And yet the people among whom such books are published wonder how it comes to pass that the civil magistrate daily loseth his authority, that the laws are trampled upon, and the subject in constant fear of being robbed, or murdered, or having his house burnt over his head.[40]

It is hard to believe in Berkeley's honesty here, when one considers the third of his quotations from Mandeville. If he is not dishonest he is certainly blatantly inconsistent (always assuming that he had actually read the *Fable*); for Mandeville is explaining that good manners, like virtue, are founded on pride and flattery. Yet Berkeley takes this to be a recommendation of good manners and a disparagement of virtue. In the passage quoted Mandeville is indeed pointing out one difference between good manners and virtue: good manners (or politeness) are compatible with insincerity. Virtue is not. Like virtue, politeness makes it possible for men to live together fairly harmoniously, but it has its limitations, as Mandeville is pointing out. His whole tone when he treats of politeness is much less respectful than when he is talking about virtue. If Berkeley had read him at all carefully he could not possibly have continued to suppose that Mandeville was a spokesman for the world of fashion, rather than its satirist.

Berkeley's accusations against Mandeville, at least by implication, became even wilder. In the *Discourse to Magistrates*, he says: 'The magistrate, perhaps, may not be sufficiently aware that these pretended advocates for private light and free thought are in

---

[40] *Discourse to Magistrates*, 1738. Berkeley, *Works*, ed. Luce and Jessop, vol. 6 1953), p. 216.

reality seditious men, who set themselves up against national laws and constitutions.'[41] This may not be meant to apply to Mandeville (and even Berkeley could hardly have thought it true of Shaftesbury), though it comes only a few paragraphs after the reference to these two. He may merely mean that this is the unintended effect of their teaching. The sentence immediately before the one referring to Shaftesbury and Mandeville reads: 'We declare against those who would seduce ignorant and unexperienced persons from the reverence they owe to the laws and religion of their country; and, under the notion of extirpating prejudices, would erase from their minds all impressions of piety and virtue, in order to introduce prejudices of another kind, hostile to society.'[42] So that it may be that Lysicles is meant to be showing Mandeville's influence, but not expressing Mandeville's actual views when he says:

Weak men, indeed, are prejudiced towards rules and systems in life and government, and think if these are gone all is gone: but a man of great soul and free spirit delights in the noble experiment of blowing up systems and dissolving governments, to mould them anew upon other principles and in another shape. Take my word for it, there is a plastic nature in things that seeks its own end. Pull a State to pieces, jumble, confound and shake together the particles of human society, and then let them stand for a while, and you shall soon see them settle of themselves in some convenient order, where heavy heads are lowest, and men of genius uppermost.[43]

Yet Lysicles has been identified so closely with Mandeville that most readers are bound to take this as expressing Mandeville's opinion. If Berkeley himself thought that, it could only have been because Mandeville objected to the doctrine of passive obedience, which Berkeley defended. It is presumably that controversy that Horatio is referring to when, in the *Origin of Honour*, he mentions 'your Revolution-Principles' to Cleomenes, who replies: 'The illegal Sway of Magistrates is not to be justified from the Gospel, any more than the Resistance of the People.'[44] Since *Alciphron* was published in the same year as the *Origin of Honour*, it is just possible that, in using the phrase 'Revolution-Principles', Mandeville was thinking of Berkeley's attack on him.

[41] Ibid., p. 217. [42] Ibid., p. 216.
[43] *Alciphron*, 1732. Berkeley, *Works*, ed. Luce and Jessop, vol. 3 (1950), p. 100.
[44] *Enquiry into the Origin of Honour*, 1732, p. 170.

It is of course quite ludicrous to suppose that Mandeville would have agreed with what Lysicles says about the beneficial effects of revolution. His whole emphasis is on the fragile nature of civilization and the long ages of patient effort that have been needed to build it up. He does say that the state is like a knitting-frame or a turnspit, or like a clock which 'plays several Tunes with great exactness':[45] all these machines keep going by their own momentum, and need only a minimum of tending by people of no great capacity. But the whole point here is that, given a good constitution, a state can be governed very well by mediocre people. It took great skill and ingenuity to invent the knitting-frame, the clock, or the spit in the first place; and similarly 'great Pains and Consideration' are needed to evolve a smoothly working political system. It is only when that has been achieved that the state can be relied on to run itself. Obviously it would be the height of folly to smash this intricate structure and expect it to readjust itself with improvements.

Mandeville is quite justified when he says of Alciphron and Lysicles:

But there never were Two such Creatures in the World as those whom you have made the Champions for Free-thinking. I don't speak as to their Irreligion and Impiety, or their Incapacity of maintaining what they loudly assert; for such there are many among Rakes and Gamesters: But the Knowledge, good Sense and Penetration, which your Libertines display at some Times, are inconsistent with the Ignorance, Folly and Stupidity they shew at others. . . . No Mortal ever saw such Disputants before; they always begin with swaggering and boasting of what they'll prove; and in every Argument they pretend to maintain, they are laid upon their Backs, and constantly beaten to Pieces, till they have not a Word more to say; and when this has been repeated above half a Score times, they still retain the same Arrogance and *mal-a-pert* Briskness they were made to set out with at first; and immediately after every Defeat, they are making fresh Challenges, seemingly with as much Unconcern and Confidence of Success, as if Nothing had pass'd before, or they remember'd Nothing of what had happen'd. Such an Undauntedness in assaulting, and Alacrity in yielding, as you have made them display, never met in the same Individuals before.[46]

---

[45] *Fable of the Bees*, ed. Kaye, vol. 2, pp. 322, 323, and 325 (Sixth Dialogue).

[46] Mandeville, *A Letter to Dion*, 1732, pp. 51–3 (Facsimile reprint), Augustan Reprint Society publication no. 41, 1953.

To see what a straw man Lysicles actually is, consider this piece of dialogue:

Euphranor: ... some wise men have thought a family may be considered as a small kingdom, or a kingdom a great family. Do you admit this to be true?
Lysicles: If I say *yes*, you'll make an inference; and if I say *no*, you'll demand a reason. The best way is to say nothing at all. There is, I see, no end of answering.[47]

Berkeley, it is obvious, is not concerned to create a worthy exponent of Mandeville's views, or to examine them fairly and dispassionately. He is anxious to show a connection between religious doubt and crime and immorality, and Mandeville's reputation as an open advocate of vice plays into his hands. For Berkeley is only repeating the charges already made by Law, Bluet, and a good many others. As Mandeville said, in support of his contention that Berkeley had not read his book: 'After all, you have advanced Nothing in the second Dialogue concerning me, which it may not be proved to have been said or insinuated over and over in Pamphlets, Sermons and Newspapers of all sorts and Parties.'[48]

For example, William Law's book about Mandeville begins:

Sir, I have read your several Compositions in favour of the Vices and Corruptions of Mankind; and hope I need make no Apology, for presuming to offer a Word or two on the Side of Virtue and Religion. I shall spend no Time in Preface, or general Reflections, but proceed directly to the Examination of such Passages as expose *moral* Virtue, as a Fraud and imposition, and render all Pretences to it, as odious and contemptible.[49]

And George Bluet says in the preface to his book on Mandeville:

There needs no great Wit, and much less Logick, to recommend the Practice of Vice. Treatises of Impiety will subsist, and find Applause from their own intrinsick Value, without the Gloss of good Sense to set them off. What Occasion is there for any exact Talent of reasoning to convince young Fellows, that in the midst of their Debauchery they are promoting the publick Good? That the Magistrate neglects his

---

[47] *Alciphron*, 1732. Berkeley, *Works*, ed. Luce and Jessop, vol. 3 (1950), pp. 74–5.
[48] *Letter to Dion*, 1732, p. 6.
[49] W. Law, *Remarks upon a Book entitled* The Fable of the Bees, 1724. *Works of the Reverend William Law, M.A.*, vol. 2, 1762 (reprinted 1892), p. 3.

Duty to them in not providing better for their Pleasures, by tolerating a sufficient Number of Temples of Venus, where without the Trouble and Pains of employing People to bawd for them, they may constantly offer up their Devotions? That if ever through a general Practice of Virtue, or the want of good Government, they should fall under so great a Misfortune as to find a Scarcity of English Whores, it is the proper Business of the Magistrate to look out and procure a sufficient Number from foreign Parts? The pupils such Lectures are designed for, carry Intentions about with them, that will easily excuse the want of a good reasoning Head in their Tutor.[50]

Bluet relies chiefly on Mandeville's argument about private vices and public benefits, and on his account of the origin of virtue. The two are, he suggests, connected: 'The Task our Author has Undertaken, is to represent Virtue as base and contemptible in Theory, and mischievous in practice.'[51] He adds that the two contentions are actually inconsistent:

He says, the Distinctions between Good and Evil, Virtue and Vice, were the Contrivance of *Politicians*; and again, *Moral Virtues are the political Offspring which Flattery begot upon Pride*, or the Offspring which the Flattery of Politicians begot upon Pride; and again, *the first Rudiments of Morality* were *broached by skilful Politicians to render men useful to each other*. Whoever these Politicians were, or in what Age or Country soever they lived, they were certainly (according to his Scheme) but sorry Bunglers at their Work; the introducing such a Distinction, or concurring in the Production of *Moral Virtues*, being only creating, according to him, so many Sources of Distress and Poverty to a People. If all modern Politicians are as *cunning* as these first, he may be very right in his Opinion, that the *Governors of Societies, and those in high Stations, are greater Bubbles than any of the rest*.[52]

The last quotation from Mandeville may help to explain why he was thought to be subversive. In the original it reads '... greater Bubbles *to Pride* than any of the rest', and occurs in a discussion of Honour, not virtue. In it Mandeville is doing something to correct the impression that his 'politicians' were simply playing a confidence trick.

Law and Berkeley also base their charges against Mandeville on his account of the usefulness of vice and the genesis of virtue.

---

[50] [G. Bluet], *An Enquiry whether a general practice of Virtue tends to the Wealth or Poverty, Benefit or Disadvantage of a People*, 1725, Preface.

[51] Ibid., p. 23. [52] Ibid., p. 22.

They also find evidence of immoralism in Mandeville's insistence on man's resemblance to his fellow animals. Berkeley makes Lysicles assert that 'a wise man pursues only his private interest, and that this consists in sensual pleasure' and that 'as other animals are guided by natural instinct, man too ought to follow the dictates of sense and appetite.'[53] Law says:

Your Goodness would not suffer you to see this part of Christendom deluded with such false Notions, of I know not what *Excellence* in Virtue, or *Evil* in Vice, but obliged you immediately to compose a *System* (as you call it) wherein you do these three things.
1st. You consider Man, *merely* as an *Animal*, having, like other Animals, nothing to do but follow his Appetites.
2dly. You consider Man as cheated and flattered out of his natural State, by the Craft of Moralists, and pretend to be very sure, that the '*moral Virtues are the political offspring which Flattery begot upon Pride*'.
So that Man and Morality are here both destroyed together. Man is declared to be only an *Animal*, and Morality an Imposture. According to this Doctrine, to say that a Man is dishonest, is making him just such a Criminal as a Horse that does not dance.
But this is not all, for you dare further affirm in praise of immorality, '*That Evil, as well moral as natural, is the solid Basis, the Life and Support of all Trades and Employment without exception; that there we must look for the true Origin of all Arts and Sciences; and that the Moment Evil ceases, the Society must be spoiled, if not dissolved*'.
These are the principal Doctrines, which with more than Fanatic Zeal you recommend to your Readers; and if lewd Stories, profane Observations, loose Jests, and haughty Assertions, might pass for Arguments, few People would be able to dispute with you.[54]

Whether or not these are Mandeville's principal doctrines, they are certainly the principal reasons for accusing him of immoralism. In order to see whether the accusation is justified, then, we shall need to consider these three charges against him.

His account of the origin of virtue has already been discussed in the last section. On the whole, Mandeville's object does not seem to be the discrediting of virtue and morality. He says that morality has a human origin; but it is hardly an imposture, since it represents the knowledge, slowly and painfully acquired over

---

[53] *Alciphron*, 1732. Berkeley, *Works*, ed. Luce and Jessop, vol. 3 (1950), p. 85.
[54] W. Law, *Remarks upon a Book entitled* The Fable of the Bees, 1724. *Works of the Reverend William Law, M.A.*, vol. 2, 1762 (reprinted 1892), pp. 3–4.

the centuries, of how men can subdue their appetites sufficiently to live together in something like harmony. In a sense, it is true, men cannot subdue their appetites at all: the best they can do is to set one appetite to catch another. Hence pride has to be called in. But if one's motive is pride, then one is not really acting virtuously. So that virtue, strictly speaking, does not exist. But the substitute for it does the job reasonably well, and may require a good deal of self-discipline, even if the ultimate motive is self-gratification. It is, moreover, self-gratification of a peculiarly refined kind: 'The Enjoyments that arise from being virtuous are of that Nicety, that every ordinary Capacity cannot relish them.'[55] If to say all this is to praise pride, which is a vice, it is to praise it only when it leads men to behave in a way that is indistinguishable from truly virtuous conduct. This is hardly the scoffing at virtue and the glorifying of vice that Law would lead us to expect.

But, it may be objected, does not Mandeville deride virtue when he laughs at men for being so simple as to practise self-denial 'for the vain Satisfaction of making our Species appear more exalted and remote from that of other Animals, than it really is'?[56] It is, however, the spurious inducement to virtue that Mandeville is deriding, and not virtue itself. No doubt a truly rational being would be virtuous because of the actual benefits to society; poor silly Man has to be offered additional (and illusory) inducements, like a child who will only eat wholesome food if given a sticky sweet as a bribe. So far as Mandeville's remark applies to virtue in general, there is no need to suppose that he is saying more than that. In the passage in question, however, he is talking more specifically about sexual desire. It is at least arguable that many of the restraints that have been placed on this appetite in the name of virtue do no good to anybody. Since Freud we are far more ready to agree that here at least the refusal to admit the existence of a natural appetite that man shares with the other animals may do much more harm than good.

Another, more cogent objection is that Mandeville assigns much the same origin to Honour as he does to virtue. Honour, moreover, like virtue, has the effect of making men useful to one another and fit for society. Indeed, he says that Honour is

---

[55] *Origin of Honour*, 1732, p. 44.
[56] *Fable of the Bees*, ed. Kaye, vol. I, p. 145 (Remark N).

more useful than virtue. Yet Mandeville is undoubtedly ridiculing Honour. Must he not, then, be ridiculing virtue as well?

Honour is, however, only more useful than virtue in the sense that it is easier to persuade men to embrace it: there are 'twenty men of real Honour to one of real virtue'. The reason for this is that Honour makes fewer demands on men; and, precisely because of that, its usefulness to society is limited.

... without Doubt, there is a noble Pleasure in forgiving of Injuries, to Speculative Men that have refin'd Notions of Virtue; but it is more Natural to resent them; and in revenging one's self, there is a Pleasure which the meanest Understanding is capable of tasting. It is manifest then, that there are Allurements in the Principle of Honour, to draw in Men of the lowest Capacity, and even the vicious, which Virtue has not.[57]

And Again

... A Man may be just and chaste, and yet not be able to convince the World that he is so; but he may pick a Quarrel, and shew, that he dares to Fight when he pleases, especially if he converses with Men of the Sword. Where the Principle of Honour was in high Esteem, Vanity and Impatience must have always prompted the most proud and forward to seek after Opportunities of signalizing themselves, in order to be stiled Men of Honour. This would naturally occasion Quarrelling and Fighting.[58]

If Honour is ridiculed, then, it is less for what it has in common with virtue than for its departures from virtue.

Is it true that Mandeville's account of the origin of virtue is inconsistent with his thesis about private vices and public benefits, as Bluet (and later Hume) maintained? We have yet to consider what that thesis really amounts to; but in the meantime it may be pointed out that the alleged inconsistency rebounds upon Bluet. For, if Mandeville is praising vice when he points out that it is sometimes useful to society, then he must also be praising virtue when he makes the same claim for it. Perhaps the degradation of virtue consists in making it out to be a human invention; but vice, too, is surely a human contrivance to satisfy our appetites? Perhaps Bluet's point is that virtue is degraded by being shown to be vice (vanity and pride) in disguise; but if Mandeville really

[57] *Origin of Honour*, 1732, p. 44.   [58] Ibid., p. 63.

glorifies vice, this could not be a degradation. If 'private vices, public benefits' is taken seriously as an exaltation of vice, it is hard to see how the *Origin of Moral Virtue* can be a denigration of virtue.

This does not, of course, answer Hume's question: 'Is it not very inconsistent for an author to assert in one page, that moral distinctions are inventions of politicians for public interest, and in the next page maintain, that vice is advantageous to the public?'[59] But that must wait until we consider what Mandeville means by 'private vices public benefits'.

Before doing that, let us have a look at the argument based on Mandeville's acceptance of man's animal nature. This takes slightly different forms in Law and in Berkeley. Law draws attention to Mandeville's assertion that man is 'a Compound of various Passions that all of them as they are provoked and come uppermost, govern him by turns whether he will or no'. This is of course inconsistent with the Rationalist view of morality which Law himself accepts, according to which the grasping by reason of eternal and immutable moral truths is enough to move men to action. But in insisting that men are influenced by reason only through the mediation of some desire, Mandeville was no more advocating immorality than Hutcheson or Hume. In saying that men are putting some constraint on their natures in practising virtue, Mandeville does perhaps lay himself open to the gibe that in that case 'to say that a man is dishonest is making him just such a criminal as a horse that does not dance'; he himself uses the analogy with horses. But we do regard a horse as vicious who kicks, bites, or throws his rider instead of tamely submitting to be a beast of burden, which is hardly more natural to a horse than dancing. To regard a vicious man in the same light is perhaps to rob vice of the Mephistophelean horror (and glamour) that surrounds it; but it is not to preach immoralism. Mandeville does not identify the natural with the good: he is constantly protesting against precisely that identification.

Berkeley's assertion that Mandeville values only sensual pleasure possibly derives from Remark O in the *Fable*, in which Mandeville discusses 'real pleasures', and dismisses the Stoic view that these can be enjoyed only by the virtuous. If so, this is

---

[59] D. Hume, *Of Luxury. Essays and Treatises on Several Subjects*, Part 2, 1752. 1758 ed., p. 163.

another example of the apparent inability of Mandeville's opponents to appreciate his satirical purpose.

> I expect to be ask'd why in the Fable I have call'd those Pleasures real that are directly opposite to those which I own the wise Men of all Ages have extoll'd as the most valuable. My Answer is, because I don't call things Pleasures which Men say are best, but such as they seem to be best pleased with; how can I believe that a Man's chief Delight is in the Embellishments of the Mind when I see him ever employ'd about and daily pursue the Pleasures that are contrary to them? *John* never cuts any Pudding, but just enough that you can't say he took none; this little Bit, after much chomping and chewing, you see goes down with him like chopp'd Hay; after that he falls upon the Beef with a voracious Appetite, and crams himself up to his Throat. Is it not provoking to hear *John* cry every Day that Pudding is all his Delight, and that he don't value the Beef of a Farthing?
> I could swagger about Fortitude and the Contempt of Riches as much as Seneca himself, and would undertake to write twice as much in behalf of Poverty as ever he did, for the tenth Part of his Estate.[60]

It seems clear that all Mandeville is saying here is that men really value material pleasures, and their protestations to the contrary are either hypocritical or self-deceiving. This is not to say that men ought to value these pleasures, and indeed the satire might lose some of its force if an addiction to these pleasures were not a real weakness.

It may be urged against this, however, that Mandeville's satire is directed against the pretentiousness of those who claim to despise sensuality, not against sensuality itself. Man's chief enjoyment, he may be saying, does lie in worldly pleasure, and it is far better that he should frankly acknowledge this fact, and not vainly pretend to be something he is not. This interpretation of Mandeville is plausible. Indeed, it is more than that: as far as it goes, it is perfectly correct. But it does not follow that there are never good reasons for denying oneself: for example, to prevent someone else from suffering even greater privation. To admit that men do have physical appetites and worldly desires and that, other things being equal, there is no harm in gratifying them, is not to preach immorality, unless one's morality is of a peculiarly ascetic kind.

It is a little confusing that Mandeville himself professes to hold

[60] *Fable of the Bees*, ed. Kaye, vol. 1, pp. 151–2 (Remark O).

just such an ascetic morality. If we take him seriously in this, then we must suppose that he is not saying that there is no harm in indulging our appetites, but only that we cannot in fact refrain from indulging them, and that it is better to admit this than pretend to be more virtuous than we are. Certainly Mandeville, here as elsewhere, speaks respectfully of genuine self-denial: he merely denies that it occurs, except perhaps very rarely. He pours scorn on the plea that bishops and other dignitaries accept wealth and luxury only to inspire respect for the church or other institution they represent. In fact, he says, there is no surer way of gaining respect from the ordinary man, who knows himself to be incapable of such self-denial, than by showing oneself to be genuinely contemptuous of riches. In the *Origin of Honour* he says that the Roman Catholic Church cunningly takes advantage of this by assigning the role of poverty to some of their clergy, who thus gain prestige for the whole church: the principle of division of labour enables the other clergy to enjoy the riches which accrue from such prestige. This does not perhaps show that Mandeville thinks self-denial genuinely admirable; but at least he is sure that it is genuinely admired.

Does Mandeville's emphasis on man's animal nature mean that he thinks only physical pleasures real? It is hard to see how anyone could suppose this when one considers that, for Mandeville, the supreme pleasure, for the sake of which human beings are prepared to sacrifice ease, comfort, and even life itself, lies in the knowledge that one is esteemed and admired by other people. This is clearly a mental and not a physical pleasure, even if Mandeville (like Hume) does seem to think that animals are capable of feeling it.[61] The 'worldly-minded, voluptuous and ambitious Man' described in Remark O aims at far more than merely physical satisfaction: he 'covets Precedence everywhere, and desires to be dignified above his Betters'; he 'employs none but the ablest and most ingenious Workmen, that his Judgment and Fancy may appear in the least Things that belong to him'; he likes to have 'witty, facetious and polite people to converse with'.[62] Berkeley and Law would no doubt regard these as ignoble aims, but they are distinctively human, and can hardly be said

---

[61] Ibid., vol. 2, pp. 130–2 (Third Dialogue). Cf. Hume, *Treatise of Human Nature* Book II, Part I, Section xii.
[62] Ibid., vol. 1, p. 148 (Remark O).

'to make man a mere animal'. Mandeville indeed anticipates Veblen in drawing attention to the highly immaterial nature of the satisfactions men pursue.

Berkeley's Euphranor argues against Lysicles that, since reason is what distinguishes man from the other animals, 'rational pleasures' must be 'more agreeable to human-kind than those of sense'.[63] In spite of its antiquity, this argument is of doubtful validity: there is no reason to suppose that the lyre-bird gets more pleasure out of displaying its lyre-shaped tail than from any of its other activities, merely because it is this tail that distinguishes it most obviously from other birds. But in any case the conclusion depends on twisting the meaning of 'rational' so that it means something like 'good'. The most that could fairly be inferred is that man's chief pleasures must require the exercise of his powers of reflection; and there seems no reason, as far as the argument goes, why what he reflects on should not be his own superiority to his fellows. Lysicles is, of course, too much a man of straw to point this out.

Mandeville's account of what most moves men is not, of course, acceptable to Berkeley and Law. No doubt they believe his views on human nature to be mistaken, and unduly cynical, and they are of course entitled to say so. But they do not have much justification for supposing him to be advocating what he is obviously satirizing. What man actually aims at need not be, in Mandeville's view, what he ought to aim at. And it is in any case a distortion of Mandeville to say that, according to him, man is a mere animal who can (and so ought) to seek only physical gratification.

So far, then, it would seem that the charge of immoralism cannot be made out by appealing either to Mandeville's account of the origin of virtue or to his views on man's nature. But, of course, the ground that is most relied on is neither of these, but Mandeville's thesis that private vices make for public benefits.

'It seems', says Hume, 'upon any system of morality, little less than a contradiction in terms, to talk of a vice, which is in general beneficial to society.'[64] A practice which is beneficial to society, that is to say, cannot be a vice in the proper meaning of

---

[63] *Alciphron*, 1732. Berkeley, *Works*, ed. Luce and Jessop, vol. 3, p. 86.
[64] D. Hume, *Of Luxury, Essays and Treatises on Several Subjects* Part 2, 1752. 1758 ed., p. 163.

the term. Mandeville, his contemporaries concluded, must mean that the practices commonly thought of as vices are not really vices at all, but virtues. Even his attempt to patch things up in the title-page of the second 1714 edition hardly helps; for if vices can be made to take the place of virtues, how can they be vicious?

George Bluet's favourite quotation from the *Fable*, which he triumphantly reproduces more than once in his book, is the couplet:

> Thus every Part was full of Vice
> Yet the whole Mass a Paradise.[65]

Many agreed with his apparent belief that nothing more was necessary to establish Mandeville as an immoralist.

Yet there is clearly another way of resolving the paradox Hume calls attention to. Instead of insinuating that what are commonly thought of as vices are not really vicious at all, Mandeville may mean us to draw the opposite conclusion: that what we think of as benefits are not really beneficial. In *A Letter to Dion* Mandeville tells Berkeley that he means precisely that:

If it be urged, that these Benefits are worldly, I own it; and Every body may see, in whose Sense I call them so; in the Language of the World, the Age and the Time I live: This one of my Adversaries perceived plainly and endeavoured to take Advantage of it against me, by saying, that Nothing could be a real Benefit, that did not conduce to a Man's eternal Happiness; and that it was evident, that the Things, to which I gave that Name, did not. I agree with him, that a Man's Salvation is the greatest Benefit he can receive or wish for; and I am persuaded that, speaking of things Spiritual, the Word is very proper in that sense; the same may be said of the Words Profit, Gain, and, if you please, Lucre; but I deny that without any Addition, this is the common Acceptation of them; in which, I hope, I may have the Liberty to make use of Words with the Rest of my Fellow-Subjects. All temporal Privileges and worldly Advantages whatever, are call'd Benefits, and a Thousand Things are beneficial to the Body, that have nothing to do with the Soul. So a Felon may have the Benefit of the Clergy; such are Benefit-Tickets; and so a Man may go to the Country for the Benefit of the Air. I would ask this wise Gentlemen, when he reads, that a Play is to be acted for the Benefit of such a one; which he thinks it is,

---

[65] *Fable of the Bees*, ed. Kaye, vol. 1, p. 24. See Bluet, op. cit., pp. 50–104, 137.

the Money the Person receives, or the Performance it self, that contributes most to his eternal Happiness.[66]

Mandeville goes on to argue that eternal happiness cannot, in any case, be a *public* benefit:

> But this eternal Happiness cannot at the soonest commence till after this Life; and when a Man is dead, he ceases to be a Member of the Society and is no longer a Part of the Publick; which latter is a collective Body of living Creatures, living upon this Earth, and consequently, as such not capable of enjoying eternal Happiness.[67]

Mandeville's defence, then, is that he is only saying that the way of life most people esteem, in particular the kind of prosperity that can be attributed to nations as a whole, depends upon vice. To say this is not to advocate vice: it is merely to point out to people that they need to choose, and that they are deluding themselves when they suppose that they can be virtuous and also enjoy the flesh-pots. If anyone asks Mandeville: 'which, then, shall I choose?' his answer is clear: 'Tho' I have shewn the Way to Worldly Greatness, I have, without Hesitation, preferr'd the Road that leads to Virtue.'[68] What the reader should say to himself is:

> Since this worldly Greatness is not to be attain'd to without the Vices of Man, I will have Nothing to do with it; since it is impossible to serve God and Mammon, my choice shall be soon made: No temporal Pleasure can be worth running the Risque of being eternally miserable; and, let who will labour to aggrandize the Nation, I will aim at higher Ends, and take care of my own Soul.

The Moment such a Thought enters into a Man's Head, all the Poison is taken away from the Book, and every Bee has lost its Sting.[69]

How convincing is this defence? There is, I think, little doubt that Mandeville's main purpose is to expose the hypocrisy and self-deception of those who profess to have no concern for worldly pleasures while taking care to enjoy as many of them as possible. One example of this is the clergyman who says that he wants high pay, not for his own sake, but for the sake of the prestige of the church. Mandeville's parable of small beer is

---

[66] *A Letter to Dion*, 1732, pp. 38–9.   [67] Ibid., p. 39.
[68] Ibid., p. 31. Mandeville is quoting from Remark T of the *Fable of the Bees*. See Kaye, vol. 1, p. 231.
[69] Ibid., p. 22.

directed against this sort of thing: he tells it in Remark T of the *Fable*, and quotes the whole passage in *A Letter to Dion*. In it he supposes a community in which

> the chief moral Evil ... was Thirst, and to quench it, a Damnable Sin; yet they unanimously agreed, that Every one was born Thirsty more or less. Small Beer in Moderation was allow'd to All; and he was counted an Hypocrite, a Cynick, or a Madman, who pretended that One could live altogether without it; yet those who owned they loved it, and drank it to Excess, were counted Wicked. All this while the Beer itself was reckon'd a Blessing from Heaven, and there was no Harm in the use of it; all the Enormity lay in the Abuse, the Motive of the Heart, that made them drink it. He that took the least Drop of it to quench his Thirst, committed a heinous Crime, while others drank large Quantities without any Guilt, so they did it indifferently, and for no other Reason than to mend their Complexion.[70]

Mandeville's main target here is certainly the desire to renounce one's cake and eat it too; the ambivalent attitude of Christians to worldly prosperity, that blessing of God that it is none the less sinful to value; and, in general, the smugness and complacency of making out England (or Europe) to be a Christian community when clearly it was nothing of the sort. Yet this does not quite end the matter. For, after all, the sensible thing for the 'heathens' in his parable to do was surely to admit that they were thirsty, and that there was no harm in quenching thirst.

Perhaps Mandeville protests a little too much in *A Letter to Dion*. One of the passages he quotes in his defence is the paragraph in the *Essay on Charity and Charity-Schools* in which he says that the poor should be virtually compelled to go to church on Sunday, and all other amusements prohibited:[71] it is very hard to believe that he meant this seriously. Again, he says that, in saying of the Spartans: 'There never was a Nation whose Greatness was more empty than theirs',[72] he only meant 'that such a Way of Living and a Glory to be obtain'd by so austere a self-denial, were not the Things which Englishmen wanted and desired'.[73] Sparta was, of course, a counter-example to Mandeville's contention that national greatness resulted from luxuriousness, and not fru-

---

[70] *A Letter to Dion*, pp. 25–6. And see Kaye, vol. 1, p. 235.
[71] Ibid., p. 41.
[72] *Fable of the Bees*, ed. Kaye, vol. 1, p. 245.
[73] *A Letter to Dion*, 1732, p. 32.

gality. But does not Mandeville, too, think Sparta's greatness empty and not to be desired? Almost everything he says about Honour, and military honour in particular, would lead one to suppose that here he agrees with the Englishmen.

Is Mandeville, then, after all an advocate of vice? The answer is, I think, that sometimes he is and sometimes he is not. 'Vice', as he uses it, is a blanket term, covering a multitude, not always of sins. Sometimes he is thinking of crimes like murder, rape, and highway robbery, whose viciousness no one would question; sometimes about practices condoned by society but condemned by Christian morality, like duelling, war, and luxurious living; sometimes he means any action at all for which the motive is self-gratification, in the widest possible sense of the term. Since human beings are incapable of acting from any other motive, according to Mandeville, the last category makes all human behaviour vicious, including the behaviour Mandeville approves of. But he does not of course approve (or, for that matter, disapprove) of every human action. Probably he is equally selective about the vices which fall into the first two categories: I doubt if Mandeville really sees much harm in what he calls luxury, which includes everything not immediately necessary for subsistence; but it does not follow that he is advocating highway robbery or duelling.

If vice is a blanket term, 'private vices public benefits' is a blanket phrase, under which Mandeville includes a number of distinct theses. These are:

1. The commercial prosperity of modern states like England depends upon luxury, and would be destroyed if people really practised frugality, instead of merely paying lip-service to it.

The modern reader is not likely to find this a very shocking contention. It had a considerable impact on Mandeville's readers because, in the eighteenth century, luxury was generally denounced, from the pulpit and elsewhere. Hutcheson complains that Mandeville's definition of luxury is absurdly wide, since it includes 'everything not immediately necessary to make man subsist as he is a living Creature'. Mandeville admits that this is rigorous, but says that

if we are to abate one Inch of this Severity, I am afraid we shan't know where to stop. When People tell us they only desire to keep themselves sweet and clean, there is no understanding what they would be at; if they made use of these Words in their genuine proper literal Sense, they might soon be satisfy'd without much cost or trouble, if they did not want Water: But these two little Adjectives are so comprehensive, especially in the Dialect of some Ladies, that no body can guess how far they may be stretcht.[74]

What is luxury to one person, that is to say, will be bare decency to another. Hutcheson protests that 'Intemperance and Luxury are plainly Terms relative to the Bodily Constitution, and Wealth of the Person.'[75] It is only exceeding one's income that is luxury. But the denunciations of luxury seem to suppose that something more than imprudence is involved: what is condemned is a weakness of character, luxuriousness, an attachment to the things of this world. One does not lose this attachment by being rich.

Very probably Mandeville did not think an attachment to worldly comforts reprehensible. To that extent he is genuinely praising, or at least condoning, one of the things he chooses to call vice. But if that makes him an immoralist, Hutcheson is equally one.

2. Apart from luxury, there are some pernicious practices which help to contribute to the community's prosperity, or at least to the prosperity of some members of it.

Thieves provide work for locksmiths; drunkards benefit brewers, and also contribute to the duty on malt; robbers and highwaymen spend more freely than the cautious citizens they rob, and so circulate money more effectively; and so on.

Bluet argues against this that it is absurd to suppose that non-productive labour can add to the national wealth. 'I have known an Overseer of the Poor in the Country, when a lusty Fellow has complain'd to him of his want of Work, employ him for a whole Day together in turning a Grindstone tho' nothing was all that while ground upon it. I believe it won't be said that the Parish was the richer for the Fellow's Labour.'[76] Suppose, he

---

[74] *Fable of the Bees*, ed. Kaye, vol. 1, p. 107 (Remark L).
[75] F. Hutcheson, *Reflections upon Laughter and* The Fable of the Bees. *Collected Works*, vol. 7, Opera Minora, G. Olms, 1971, p. 146.
[76] [G. Bluet], *An Enquiry whether a general Practice of Virtue tends to . . . Wealth or Poverty . . .* , 1725, p. 5.

adds, that a man employs a large number of shepherds to guard his flock against wolves.

Afterwards by the care and Skill of the Government, or the Assistance of his Neighbours, the Wolves are all destroyed. Would the Countryman complain that by this Means his Servants were left without Employment? ... The worst that could happen from the Want of Employment being only that some of his Shepherds would be turned into Footmen, and wait at their Master's Table, instead of watching his Flocks.[77]

What this overlooks is that the countryman might indeed see no cause for complaint, but, having no great desire for extra attendance at table, might (especially if he lived in the less feudal society towards which eighteenth-century England was hastening) simply dismiss his shepherds and save himself the expense of their wages. This would not of course alter the amount of wealth in the community; but it would affect its distribution, with effects of some kind (possibly harmful, possibly not) on the production of further wealth. Bluet assumes that the community will always provide some useful work for those willing to do it, or, failing that, will pay them anyway. If disease were suddenly to disappear, he asks, 'Would any one scruple to pay Physicians as much to sit still, as he pays them at present for Advice and Physick, in consideration of such a Blessing?'[78] The answer is that, unless they believed that disease would miraculously reappear if doctors were not paid, many people might refuse to support them in idleness. Mandeville is concerned, not with an ideal society, but with the motives which actually operate to keep the existing society going. He may well be right in thinking that sympathy for the redundant doctor (or shepherd) would not be as powerful a motive as the fear of disease (or of the loss of the flock). This would obviously apply also to the redundant locksmith or policeman.

At the same time, Mandeville does not show that the community as a whole would be less prosperous if robbery, drunkenness, etc. did not occur. The contention that some incidental benefits may nevertheless accrue to some people is not particularly exciting; it is, I believe, of importance to Mandeville mainly because it contributes to the more general thesis labelled 5 below.

[77] Ibid., p. 7.   [78] Ibid., p. 8.

And also, of course, because it was calculated to shock. A large part of Mandeville's reputation for cynical immorality derives from this contention. Yet it does not of course follow that Mandeville is commending and advocating highway robbery or drunkenness. He himself points this out by means of two quite ingenious analogies. The filthiness of the streets of London is a necessary consequence of 'the great Traffick and Opulency of that mighty City',[79] but this does not make dirt any the less objectionable: the question is simply whether it is worth putting up with for the sake of having a prosperous city. He finds another example in the castrati who were at that time delighting English audiences with the purity of their singing:

Nothing is more effectual to preserve, mend and strengthen a fine Voice in Youth than castration: The Question is not, whether this is true, but whether it is eligible; whether a fine Voice is an equivalent for the Loss, and whether a Man would prefer the Satisfaction of singing, and the Advantages that may accrue from it, to the Comforts of Marriage, and the Pleasure of Posterity, of which Enjoyments it destroys the Possibility.[80]

Bluet argues that the analogy with the dirt of London is irrelevant because here Mandeville is talking about an effect, not a cause. 'To say, as the Dirt of the Streets is the *Effect* of the Wealth of the City, so Vice or Wickedness is the *Cause* of the Wealth of a Society, is a sort of Logick peculiar to himself.'[81] It is hard to see how this affects Mandeville's argument. He is claiming that wealth cannot occur without a given cause and that equally wealth, in the city of London, is bound to have a given effect. Inseparability is a symmetrical relation. Of course one might find some means of preventing an effect which would leave the cause still in existence (as an entity, if not as a cause); but if this does not apply to causes Mandeville's case is actually strengthened, since then one might have wealth without dirt, but not without vice. In any case, the other analogy, with castrati, avoids the objection.

Mandeville's point is, first, that, when two things inevitably occur together, you must choose between having neither or

[79] *Fable of the Bees*, ed. Kaye, vol. 1, p. 11 (Preface).
[80] Ibid., vol. 2, p. 106 (Third Dialogue).
[81] [G. Bluet], *Enquiry whether . . . Virtue tends to . . . Wealth or Poverty . . .*, 1725, p. 17.

having both; and, secondly, that, even if you choose to have both, you are not thereby denying that one of them is an evil, though presumably you must think it a lesser evil than the absence of its concomitant. What his own choice would be cannot be deduced from the mere fact that he points out a concomitance. I have said above that he probably has no great objection to luxury; but that is an impression gained from his general attitude to it, not from the mere fact that he thinks that commercial prosperity depends upon it. It seems very unlikely that he would think that the obvious evils of highway robbery could be outweighed by any slight stimulation it might give to the circulation of money and to the manufacture of the kind of finery coveted by the mistresses of highwaymen. The Tyburn pamphlet is positive evidence that he does not think so.

3. Unworthy motives (self-love and self-liking in their various forms: in Mandeville's words, 'Avarice, Profuseness, Pride, Envy, Ambition, and other Vices')[82] do far more to keep society going than public spirit, or disinterested benevolence.

Cleomenes, in the course of his ironical defence of Shaftesbury, exclaims at the benevolence of the elderly and wealthy barrister who shortens his life by overwork 'in endeavouring to secure the possessions of others';[83] of the doctor who visits the sick from morning till night; of the clergyman who indefatigably insists on holding several livings and ministering to a number of parishes, though one is enough to keep him busy; of the merchant who supplies the rich 'with an infinite variety of superfluous Knicknacks and elaborate Trifles',[84] being so filled with affection for his fellows that he cannot bear to see them lacking, not only the necessaries of life, but any trifle they may happen to fancy.

Actually, of course, these men do these things to make money: a motive which far more often than philanthropy spurs men to endure the most arduous hardships. 'What a Bustle', Mandeville exclaims 'is there to be made in several Parts of the World, before a fine Scarlet or crimson cloth can be produced, what Multiplicity of Trades and Artificers must be employ'd!' Apart from the wool-combers, spinners, weavers, dyers, chemists, and the workmen who supply these tradesmen with their tools, there are

---
[82] *Fable of the Bees*, ed. Kaye, vol. 2, p. 106 (Third Dialogue).
[83] Ibid., p. 47 (First Dialogue).   [84] Ibid., p. 52 (First Dialogue).
ABM—H

the sailors who make dangerous voyages to get the dyes and other things needed:

> How widely are the Drugs and other Ingredients dispers'd through the Universe that are to meet in one Kettle! . . . While so many Sailors are broiling in the Sun and sweltered with Heat in the *East* and *West* of us, another set of them are freezing in the *North* to fetch Potashes from Russia.
>
> When we are thoroughly acquainted with all the Variety of Toil and Labour, the Hardships and Calamities that must be undergone to compass the End I speak of, and we consider the vast Risques and Perils that are run in these Voyages, and that few of them are ever made but at the Expence, not only of the Health and Welfare, but even the Lives of many: When we are acquainted with, I say, and duly consider the things I named, it is scarce possible to conceive a Tyrant so inhuman and void of Shame, that beholding things in the same View, he should exact such terrible services from his Innocent Slaves; and at the same time dare to own, that he did it for no other Reason, than the Satisfaction a Man receives from having a Garment made of Scarlet or Crimson Cloth. But to what Height of Luxury must a Nation be arrived, where not only the King's Officers, but likewise his Guards, even the Private Soldiers should have such impudent Desires![85]

These, then, are the motives that actually set the wheels of industry turning: the sheer urge to survive, in the sailors and the labouring poor, but, in the wealthy barrister, the grasping parson, and the obsequious merchant, avarice; and, in those who employ them or cause them to be employed, all sorts of petty desires, often for the most trifling and unnecessary things. This combination can bring it about that men perform feats of self-denial which neither their own benevolence nor the tyranny of others would drive them to.

This picture of the affluent society is not unfamiliar to us now: it seems a long way removed from the innocent economic enthusiasm of Adam Smith. Yet Mandeville almost certainly influenced Smith, and has been hailed as one of the originators of *laisser-faire*. Not only does self-interest provide the motive power which keeps society going, but the misfortunes of individuals are an essential part of the self-regulating mechanism:

> Philosophers, that dare extend their Thoughts beyond the narrow compass of what is immediately before them, look on the alternate

---

[85] *Fable of the Bees*, ed. Kaye, vol. 1, pp. 357–8 (*A Search into the Nature of Society*).

Changes in the Civil Society no otherwise than they do on the risings and fallings of the Lungs; the latter of which are as much a Part of Respiration in the more perfect Animals as the first; so that the fickle Breath of never-stable Fortune is to the Body Politick, the same as floating Air is to a living Creature.[86]

Actually Mandeville goes beyond Smith to Veblen, since he insists that men are moved not only by the desire for economic advantage in the narrower sense, but also by the less material satisfactions that come from conspicuous consumption and conspicuous waste. 'The poorest Labourer's Wife in the Parish, who scorns to wear a strong wholesom Frize, as she might, will half starve her self and her Husband to purchase a second-hand Gown and Petticoat, that cannot do her half the Service; because forsooth, it is more genteel.'[87] The worldly-minded voluptuous and ambitious man wants 'the chief Officers of his Household ... to be Men of Birth, Honour and Distinction, as well as Order, Contrivance and Oeconomy; for tho' he loves to be honour'd by every Body, and receives the Respects of the common People with Joy, yet the Homage that is paid him by Persons of Quality is ravishing to him in a more transcendent manner.'[88]

Does all this make Mandeville an immoralist? *Laisser-faire* has been called immoral often enough. Yet any slight spots there may be on Adam Smith's reputation in consequence leave it snow white in comparison with the pitch-hued denigration of Mandeville. Even the lesser opprobrium would seem to be undeserved, at least on this score. In his attack on charity schools, it is true, Mandeville does oppose any tampering with the economic structure of society. Even here, however, he may be merely pointing out that palliatives are of no use: the hardships of the labouring poor are the base on which society is built, and we had better recognize that fact. Certainly that is his usual stance: he is describing how society works, not praising it. His tone, indeed, is usually condemnatory. Certainly the affluent society, as he describes it, is not particularly attractive. The passage about the scarlet cloth is quoted by Mandeville in *A Letter to Dion* in order to persuade Berkeley that he is not really in favour of vice.

The most that could be said against Mandeville here, I think, is that his pessimistic realism, his insistence that men are such

[86] Ibid., p. 250 (Remark Y).
[87] Ibid., p. 129 (Remark M).
[88] Ibid., p. 149 (Remark O).

that they cannot be moved except by motives like avarice and pride, while doing nothing to white-wash a wicked society, at least discourages attempts to improve it. But even this is doubtful. The moral Mandeville draws is that, since men are like that, we had better channel their avarice and their vanity into activities that will not be harmful to others. His description of existing society hardly suggests that this enterprise could be accomplished without making any changes.

4. Apart from the part played in society by self-love and self-liking in general, some particular practices, pernicious in themselves, may be of advantage to the community.

One obvious example is prostitution. 'If Courtezans and Strumpets were to be prosecuted with as much Rigour as some silly People would have it, what Locks or Bars would be sufficient to preserve the Honour of our Wives and Daughters?'[89] Mandeville gives another example in *A Letter to Dion*:

It is the Business of all Law-givers to watch over the Publick Welfare, and, in order to procure that, to submit to any Inconveniency, any Evil, to prevent a much greater, if it is impossible to avoid that greater Evil at a cheaper Rate. Thus the Law, taking into Consideration the daily Encrease of Rogues and Villains, has enacted that, if a Felon, before he is convicted himself, will impeach two or more of his Accomplices, or any other Malefactors, so that they are convicted of a Capital Crime, he shall be pardon'd and dismiss'd with a Reward in Money. There is no Doubt but this is a good and wise Law; for without such an Expedient, the Country would swarm with Robbers and Highwaymen Ten-times more than it does; for by this Means we are not only deliver'd from a greater number of Villains, than we could expect to be from any other; but it likewise stops the Growth of them, breaks their Gangs, and hinders them from trusting one another ... All this while it is evident, that in this case the Law has only regard to the Publick Good, and to procure that, sets aside all other Laws, and proceeds rather contrary to the Common Notions we have of Justice; which, according to the *Civilians*, consists *in a constant and perpetual Desire of giving every one his Due*: For instead of Hanging, which is a Felon's due, it pardons him; and for Fear he should have some Goodness left, and that natural Compassion might make him unwilling to destroy his dearest Friends, and perhaps his Brother, with his Breath, the Law invites him to it by a large Sum of Money, and actually bribes

---

[89] *Fable of the Bees*, ed. Kaye, pp. 95–6 (Remark H).

him to add to the Rest of his Crimes that Piece of Treachery to his Companions, whom he has sworn Fidelity to, and perhaps drawn into the Villainy.[90]

All that Mandeville is saying here is that a lesser evil may sometimes have to be tolerated, and even encouraged, for the sake of avoiding a greater one. He tells Berkeley that this is the kind of thing he means when he says that, by skilful management, private vices may be turned into public benefits. Just as many critics of *laisser-faire* have thought it immoral, so many critics of utilitarianism have thought the maxim about lesser and greater evils to be immoral. But this is clearly not the kind of immoralism that Mandeville is accused of by Berkeley, Bluet, Law, and the rest.

5. Some evils go deep into the basis of society, and it is idle to suppose that they can be got rid of easily.

This has already been implied by 3 above, but Mandeville goes further than saying that avarice and pride, or more generally, self-love and self-liking, are the basic human motives. In part his point is the one made by Bernard Shaw in *Mrs. Warren's Profession* and *Major Barbara*: the comfort and prosperity of respectable people are bound up with such things as prostitution, sweated labour, armament manufacture, and slum tenements; we are all in it together, and it is not enough to be self-righteous about Merchants of Death or Scarlet Women. In part too he is saying that the respectable occupations are not so very different from the criminal ones:

To pass by the innumerable Artifices, by which Buyers and Sellers outwit one another, that are daily allowed of and practised among the fairest of *Dealers*, shew me the *Tradesman* that has always discover'd the Defects of his Goods to those that cheapen'd them; nay, where will you find one that has not at one time or other industriously conceal'd them, to the detriment of the *Buyer*? Where is the Merchant that has never against his Conscience extoll'd his Wares beyond their Worth, to make them go off the better?[91]

None of this, perhaps, goes beyond 3, though there is an obvious difference between Shaw's analysis of society and Adam

---

[90] *A Letter to Dion*, 1732, pp. 42-4.
[91] *Fable of the Bees*, ed. Kaye, vol. 1, p. 61 (Remark B).

Smith's. The moral emphasis is certainly very different. Mandeville, however, wants to advance a much more general thesis: one that is only incidentally about the economic and moral complexity of society. His statement of it provides Bluet and Law with the ammunition they are looking for: 'The short-sighted Vulgar in the Chain of Causes seldom can see further than one Link; but those who can enlarge their View, and will give themselves the Leisure of gazing on the Prospect of concatenated Events, may, in a hundred Places, see *Good* spring up and pullulate from *Evil*, as naturally as Chickens do from Eggs.'[92] This applies to natural evil (pain and suffering) as well as to moral evil:

After this I flatter my self to have demonstrated that, neither the Friendly Qualities and kind Affections that are natural to Man, nor the real Virtues he is capable of acquiring by Reason and Self-Denial, are the Foundation of Society; but that what we call Evil in this World, Moral as well as Natural, is the grand Principle that makes us sociable Creatures, the solid Basis, the Life and Support of all Trades and Employments without Exception: That there we must look for the true Origin of all Arts and Sciences, and that the Moment Evil ceases, the Society must be spoiled, if not totally dissolved.[93]

It might be thought that only that part of the thesis that concerns moral evil is relevant to the contention that private vices make for public benefits. For Mandeville, however, the two are bound up together. His main purpose is to oppose the view that man is a godlike being whose amiability and rationality (his instinctive tendency as a rational being to seek the rational life, which is the good life) lead him to construct a harmonious society in which each will seek the good of all. On this view there is a clear contrast between man's animal nature and his reason, which enables him to transcend that nature. It is reason that has produced civilization.

As against this, Mandeville argues that man stumbled into civilization, slowly and painfully, with very little foresight of the consequences of each step, as the result of his very frailties and weaknesses. His defencelessness against wild animals, and his fear of them, led him to take the first step, and join with his fellows for mutual protection. Horatio, it will be remembered,

---

[92] *Fable of the Bees*, ed. Kaye, vol. 1, p. 91 (Remark G).
[93] Ibid., p. 369 (*Search into the Nature of Society*).

has his doubts about a Providence which makes men sociable by the grisly expedient of allowing a large number of individuals to be eaten by lions. Cleomenes can give him only cold comfort: being eaten is perhaps no more painful than other kinds of death, and death is necessary if the world is not to be intolerably overcrowded. This is a good example of the way in which good and evil are inextricably intertwined.

Defencelessness and fear are frailties, but not moral faults. The next step to society, however, is the fear men have of one another, and this is the direct result of man's aggressiveness and self-seeking. By a slow and painful process of trial and error, they gradually arrive at the Hobbist solution, and accept restraints upon their own desire to dominate. But they do this as the result, not of some shining vision of the good society presented to them by Reason, but of a series of expedients aimed at gratifying their passions.

This view of society goes together with a view of the universe: the one which makes Mandeville sympathetic to Manichaeism. We simply do not live in the kind of world that would have been designed by a benevolent being in sole control: good and evil are so mixed in it that it is often hard to see where one ends and the other begins. We can only make the best of an imperfect world, including the imperfections of our own natures. Man is moved by his appetites and passions, not, as William Law protested, by the excellence of his nature, the result of his having been made in God's image.[94] By good luck and good management, these passions and appetites, many of them cruel and destructive, may be made to produce some good. Let us be thankful for that, and not pine for an imaginary creature who acts 'according to Order Truth and Reason', because he is at least to some degree like God, 'who is Truth and Reason itself'.[95] Above all, let us not flatter ourselves so grossly as to believe that we are that creature.

To Law and those who think like him, no doubt such a view is ultimately destructive of morality; but it does not make Mandeville the cynical immoralist they describe.

6. Since all human actions aim at self-gratification, they are all vicious: virtue itself is built upon the vice of pride.

[94] W. Law, *Remarks upon* The Fable of the Bees, 1723, in *Works*, 1762, vol. 2, pp. 5–6.
[95] Ibid., p. 17.

This is the thesis of the *Origin of Moral Virtue*. I have stated it in its most extreme form: actually Mandeville modifies it, at least in his more careful moments. The extreme thesis, however, is sometimes found in Mandeville: the gratifications men seek are either material pleasures, which, so far as they go beyond what is needed for bare subsistence, constitute luxury, which is a vice; or they are the immaterial pleasures of pride, which is a vice. Later, in the *Origin of Honour*, Mandeville admits that pride is only one manifestation of self-liking: it is only when it is 'excessive, and so openly shewn as to give Offence to others' that 'it is counted a Vice and call'd Pride'.[96] Even in the *Origin of Moral Virtue*, his actual definition of vice is 'everything which, *without Regard to the Publick*, Man should commit to gratify any of his Appetites'.[97] Mandeville's more considered opinion, then, is that self-gratification need not make an action vicious: it only prevents it from being virtuous. It follows that virtue does not really exist: what we count as virtue is really (according to the extreme thesis) vice; or at least a frailty. As we have seen, the contention that private vices make for public benefits is bound up with (and perhaps not always clearly distinguished from) the wider view that civilization itself (and so all public benefit) derives from human weaknesses and inadequacies.

If virtue itself is one of the public benefits Mandeville is talking about, the assertion that private vices make for public benefits can hardly be regarded as immoralism. Moreover, the account of the origin of virtue, so far from being inconsistent with that assertion, is part of what he means by it. It might still, of course, be inconsistent with some of the other things he means. Our consideration of those other things, however, suggests that it is not. Virtue is the practice of self-denial, which makes men useful to their fellows. Men are not capable of complete self-denial, but they may be induced to gratify one desire, for praise and esteem, by suppressing other, more harmful desires. In its more rarefied form, the esteem they seek is simply self-esteem. This is the nearest men can come to virtue, and in fact they seldom come so near. But there are other ways in which men do, often enough, deny themselves a good deal in order to gratify a ruling passion:

---

[96] *Enquiry into the Origin of Honour*, 1732, p. 3.
[97] *Fable of the Bees*, ed. Kaye, vol. 1, p. 48 (*Enquiry into the Origin of Moral Virtue*). My italics.

avarice, for example. This too may make them useful to their fellow men. The difference between the two cases is that the virtuous man could not get the self-esteem he seeks unless he genuinely did deny himself for the sake of others; it is just that that he prides himself on. The avaricious man does in fact make himself useful to others, but that is incidental: what he cares about is not that, but the money he gains. It is also incidental that the benefit to others outweighs any harm done to them. Sometimes it does, as with the merchant or the informer; sometimes it does not, as with the highwayman. The informer is no more meritorious than the highwayman. If the merchant is, it is not because his activities actually tend to the public good (since that is not what motivates him) but because, while he pursues self-gratification 'without regard to the publick', his disregard is less wanton and reckless: less complete. It may be objected that the virtuous man, too, is not really moved by concern for the public good, but by the desire for esteem. It is just to the extent that this is so that Mandeville says that he is not genuinely virtuous. But while a man who prides himself on acting for the public good is no doubt acting out of pride, and a desire for self-esteem, he may also be said to be acting out of a concern for the public good. His case is different from that of the man who gives a large donation to charity for the sake of his public reputation, and who would not really care if the reputation could be gained in some other way. If the virtuous man could gain self-esteem in some other way, he would not be the man he is: would not in fact be virtuous.

When the distinction between virtue and vice is made in this way, it is not inconsistent to say that both may make for public benefit.

3. RIGORISM

How sincere is Mandeville's repeated assertion that virtue consists in self-denial? Most of his contemporary critics brush it aside as patently insincere, and so do a good many of their successors. On the other hand Selby-Bigge points out that Mandeville is primarily a satirist concerned to show that 'material progress by no means implies spiritual advance' and thereby to attack 'the complacent cant which sees in the accumulation of private wealth the height of social virtue'.[98] His satire would lose its sting, he

[98] L. A. Selby-Bigge, ed., *The British Moralists*, 1897, p. xv.

argues, if Mandeville did not really believe that 'spiritual advance is impossible without self-sacrifice.

Kaye also thinks Mandeville's rigorism sincere, though in conflict with 'his real persuasion'.

It is a suit of clothes made for some one else which he has put on the living body of his thought . . . Mandeville's *feeling* is throughout anti-ascetic. He *rejoices* in destroying the ideals of those who imagine that there is in the world any real exemplification of the transcendent morality which he formally preaches. He is delighted to find that the rigoristic creed which he has adopted is an absolutely impracticable one.[99]

Mandeville, in short, thinks he is a rigorist, but is at heart a utilitarian.

It is of course common enough for a man to be mistaken about his own moral beliefs, especially when the ones he thinks he holds constitute the official morality of his community. This is, indeed, the kind of self-deception that Mandeville himself delights in exposing. But for that very reason it seems unlikely that he should be so grossly guilty of it himself. Granted that it is easier to see faults in others than in ourselves, Mandeville was especially sensitive to self-deception, and given to probing for hidden motives and unacknowledged beliefs. He was far too interested in, and far too adept at, self-analysis to be the kind of man that Kaye describes.

There is, however, a good case for the contention that Mandeville's cast of mind is fundamentally utilitarian. Kaye seems to mean by this that he is an empiricist, with a distaste for any suggestion of transcendentalism. But there is another trait, equally characteristic of the utilitarian mentality, that is strong in Mandeville: humanitarianism. As Bonamy Dobrée notices, 'he wrote a most moving account of a slaughtered ox'[100] (in Remark P of the *Fable*). The same Remark contains the amusing fable about the lion and the traveller, in which the lion exclaims: ''Tis only Man, mischievous Man, that can make Death a Sport'.[101] Again, consider Mandeville's recipe for making men fight:

First, take care they are persuaded of the Justice of their Cause; for no Man fights heartily that thinks himself in the wrong; then shew them

---

[99] *Fable of the Bees*, ed. Kaye, vol. 1, p. liii (Introduction).
[100] B. Dobrée, *Variety of Ways*, Oxford, Clarendon Press, 1932 (Reprinted by Books for Libraries Press Inc., Freeport, New York, 1967), p. 103.
[101] *Fable of the Bees*, ed. Kaye, vol. 1, p. 178 (Remark P).

that their Altars, their Possessions, Wives, Children and every thing that is near and dear to them, is concerned in the present Quarrel, or at least may be influenced by it hereafter; then put Feathers in their Caps, and distinguish them from others, talk of Publick-Spiritedness, the Love of their Country, facing an Enemy with Intrepidity, despising Death, the Bed of Honour, and such like high-sounding Words, and every Proud Man will take up Arms and fight himself to Death before he'll turn Tail, if it be in Daylight. One Man in an Army is a check upon another, and a hundred of them that single and without witness would be all Cowards, are for fear of incurring one another's Contempt made Valiant by being together. To continue and heighten this artificial Courage, all that run away ought to be punish'd with Ignominy; those that fought well, whether they did beat or were beaten, must be flatter'd and solemnly commended; those that lost their Limbs rewarded, and those that were kill'd ought, above all, to be taken notice of, artfully lamented, and to have extraordinary Encomiums bestowed upon them; for to pay Honours to the Dead, will ever be a sure Method to make Bubbles of the Living.[102]

What strikes one here is Mandeville's half-amused, half-horrified wonder at the way men throw their lives away. He is also making the paradoxical point that martial courage is a form of cowardice, when it is not vanity; but it is hard to believe that what he really sees wrong in this is that the spirit of self-sacrifice is not more whole-hearted. The concluding aphorism tells heavily against that interpretation. It was suggested in an earlier chapter that in *Free Thoughts on Religion* Mandeville is saying in effect: Believe this nonsense if you must, but for goodness sake don't cut each other's throats over it! What is really important, on the Utilitarian view, is to prevent suffering: all the cant about Virtue and Honour is mischievous unless it serves that end. It is very much in that spirit that Mandeville surveys the follies and pretences of mankind. It is a spirit not at all consistent with a zeal for the mortification of the flesh.

Why, then, does Mandeville insist that virtue consists in self-denial? Two main explanations have been advanced.

The first, and most obvious, is that this suits his satirical stance. Mandeville's chief concern always is to point out the contrast between what men say they are (what, indeed, they often believe themselves to be) and the way they actually behave. He looks round him at a society full of self-seeking and self-

[102] Ibid., pp. 210–11 (Remark R).

indulgence, in which men go to great pains to satisfy the most trivial desires and do not hesitate to trample on other men in the process. He sees that almost the only way to touch them is by appeals to their inordinate vanity: men will do anything for the sake of praise. Then he listens to the exhortations from the pulpit and to the account men give of their own behaviour. He finds that they claim to admire only self-abnegation, and that they represent themselves as being influenced, in most of their actions, by a selfless concern for the public good. It is exactly as in his parable of small beer: men quench their thirst as often and as copiously as they can, while pretending always that they drink for some other reason, and do not really enjoy it.

Clearly one way, and probably the most effective way, of bringing out this contrast between actions and professions is to adopt the standpoint of an uncompromising believer in self-abnegation, and to condemn the backsliders out of their own mouths. Mandeville's own beliefs, it might be said, are irrelevant; just as it is irrelevant that the author of *Gulliver's Travels* was in fact an Anglican Dean and not a sea-captain, that Montesquieu's *Lettres persanes* were not actually written by a Persian bringing a fresh eye to the spectacle of French society, or that Oliver Goldsmith was not really an itinerant Chinaman.

This is undoubtedly at least part of the truth. But it does not quite dispose of Selby-Bigge's point. For it is not a question of what external evidence may reveal to us about Mandeville's real opinions, but of the impression of those opinions we gain from reading him. There is, actually, very little reliable external evidence; the stories of his loose living and the like seem to be mainly inferences from his writings. Mandeville, it appears, does not strike the reader as a whole-hearted supporter of rigorism; and one might expect that to weaken the impact of his satire. Yet actually it could hardly be more forceful.

It might be said that this is because the satire is aimed at pretentiousness and hypocrisy, not at self-indulgence. We laugh at the heathens in the parable of small beer, not because they are thirsty but because they will not acknowledge their thirst, or because, when they do (for on Sundays they chant in church that they are the thirstiest of men) they obviously do not believe it and are affronted if anyone takes the admission seriously. Obviously the sensible thing for them to do would be to recognize their thirsty desires, and satisfy them openly, without guilt or concealment.

But if that were all that Mandeville is saying, he could hardly, having once made his point, go on deriding thirst in book after book (or pretending to do so) as he does deride vanity, Honour, avarice, and the rest. The joke would wear thin. If it does not, it is because these things are not only derisory from the point of view of an austere and ascetic Christian: they are also derisory from the reader's point of view, and from the author's point of view. It is certainly pretentiousness that Mandeville is attacking; but the pretentiousness consists in making oneself out to be better than one is. And 'better' here must really mean better and not just refer to some fanciful standard that no one could take seriously.

The same objection applies to the second explanation: that Mandeville is satirizing asceticism itself, and not merely the hypocrisy of those who profess to believe in it. Mandeville, Kaye tells us, 'achieved a practical *reductio ad absurdum* of the rigoristic attitude'.[103] (Kaye, indeed, thinks that he did this without realizing what he had done; but we may ignore that complication.) For it follows from the rigorist account of virtue that no one ever is virtuous. A careful examination of what passes for virtue shows that it is based on pride. As Adam Smith pointed out, this obliterates the distinction between virtue and vice, for all practical purposes. In practice, one is forced to adopt other criteria by which to judge actions. Thus the hypocrisy or self-deception of the rigorist is not accidental, but forced on him by the facts of life. For in fact it is impossible to live up to the rigorist morality, or to avoid adopting a different morality in practice.

It is hard to believe that Mandeville was as blind to these implications as Kaye believes. Nor do I think that he was wholly blind to them. At the same time, as was pointed out above, it is hard to believe that he does not genuinely think the professions of the rigorists to be better than their practice. And indeed, Mandeville does not as a rule criticize asceticism: he merely doubts whether it is ever practised. One does not find him sneering, in the manner of Voltaire or Anatole France, at the folly and barbarity of cultivating piety by wearing hair shirts or eating dry

[103] *Fable of the Bees*, ed. Kaye, vol. 1. p. li (Introduction).

bread. One possible exception is a passage in *Free Thoughts on Religion* in which he is discussing the celibacy of the clergy: he takes the opportunity to recount some of the weirder legends about the fortitude of saints in a tone that is hardly admiring:

> St. *Aldhelme*, an *English* friar, who lived in the eighth century, and was for his learning and piety made a bishop, got so perfect a mastery over the flesh, that the finest woman made no impression upon him: and not to flinch from the most dangerous temptations, he went to bed to a young girl, and lying by her side repeated the whole psalter, whilst the motions of his heart tended only to heaven.
>
> This invincible fortitude of St. *Aldhelme*, has been look'd upon as an example rather to be admired than imitated; and I believe not, that many, who have hazarded themselves to such trials of virtue, are come off conquerors, tho' several experiments have been made of it since the time of this saint. About the year 1437, the countess of *Guastala* by the advice of *Baptist de Crema*, a Jacobin monk, founded a society call'd, *That of the victory over ones self against the flesh*. To gain this victory, a certain lady named *Julia*, put a young fellow into bed with a young girl, and laid a crucifix as a barrier betwixt them; which, if it kept them virtuous, ought not to be omitted in the catalogue of the miracles that have been wrought by crucifixes. This society of *Guastalians* multiply'd prodigiously for some time, till being look'd upon as libertines, they were every where expell'd.[104]

Even here, however, the ostensible point is that the stories are fabrications, and that such attempts at self-mortification are bound to fail; it is only the tone that suggests that they are not worth the effort in any case. Mandeville's main objection to the celibacy of the clergy is that it is a pretence ('Had chastity been the church's aim, she would not have connived at the lewd transgressions of the clergy as she has done') and that the real object is political: 'if a society of a hundred men, who have all vow'd celibacy, will keep up their number, and, as any die, chuse other single men, under the same obligation in the room of the deceas'd it must be immortal, and, if they have a certain income exceeding their yearly expences . . . this society, at long run, will get into their clutches the greatest if not all the wealth of the country they live in.'[105]

Mandeville seems to think that the practice of self-mortification, when institutionalized by the churches, always does have a

[104] *Free Thoughts on Religion*, 1729, pp. 217–18. [105] Ibid., p. 214.

political purpose. Usually it is to gain respect and admiration, which are then turned to the advantage of those sections of the clergy who never dream of mortifying the flesh. But this device would not succeed unless men did genuinely admire and respect austerity of living. That they do so might, of course, be the result of superstition, or of the sentiment inspired by W. S. Gilbert's Bunthorne: 'If he's content with a vegetable love that would certainly not suit *me*, why, what a remarkably pure young man this pure young man must be!' Mandeville sometimes hints at this explanation:

All Multitudes will sooner believe a Man to come from God, who leads an Austere Life himself, and preaches Abstinence and Self-denial to others, tho' they themselves, I mean the Hearers, don't practise it, or take any Pains to comply with his Precepts, than they will another, who takes greater Liberties himself, and whose Doctrine is less severe. This the wise Architects of the Church of *Rome*, who were thoroughly skill'd in Human Nature, were well aware of.[106]

But he also seems to be implying that austerity of life really is worthy of respect. Consider, for example, Cleomenes' recipe for stopping the drift to Rome by reviving 'the Maxims of the Reformation':

Hor.: This is a fine Secret, and what, I dare say, the Clergy would be glad to know. Pray, which are those Maxims?
Cleo.: The Sanctity of Manners and exemplary Lives of the Reformers, their Application and unwearied Diligence in their Calling, their Zeal for Religion, and Disregard of Wealth and Worldly Enjoyments, either real or counterfeited, for that God only knows.
Hor.: I did not expect this. The Bench of Bishops won't thank you for your Prescription: They would call it an Attempt to cure the Patients by blistering the Physicians.[107]

A counterfeit renunciation, it will be noticed, will do the trick; but is there any doubt that Mandeville thinks real renunciation more worthy of respect?

He that harangues on the Contempt of Riches, and the Vanity of Earthly Enjoyments, in a rusty thread-bare Gown, because he has no other, and would wear his old greasy Hat no longer if any body would give him a better; that drinks Small-beer at Home with a heavy

---

[106] *Enquiry into the Origin of Honour*, 1732, p. 110.   [107] Ibid., p. 125.

Countenance, but leaps at a Glass of Wine, if he can catch it Abroad; that with little Appetite feeds upon his own coarse Mess, but falls to greedily when he can please his Palate, and expresses an uncommon Joy at an Invitation to a splendid Dinner: 'Tis he that is despised, not because he is Poor, but because he knows not how to be so with that Content and Resignation which he preaches to others, and so discovers his Inclinations to be contrary to his Doctrine. But when a Man from the greatness of his Soul (or an obstinate Vanity, which will do as well) resolving to subdue his Appetites in good earnest, refuses all the Offers of Ease and Luxury that can be made to him, and embracing a voluntary Poverty with Chearfulness, rejects whatever may gratify the Senses, and actually sacrifices all his Passions to his Pride in acting this Part, the Vulgar, far from contemning, will be ready to deify and adore him.[108]

Here again we are made to feel that the second clergyman, even though he acts from 'an obstinate Vanity', is more admirable than the first. No doubt it is his integrity we admire; but I am not sure that it is wholly that. It is not merely that he is consistent, but that he does have the strength of mind to subdue his appetites.

What, then, is the truth about Mandeville's rigorism? So far I have agreed with Kaye that Mandeville's temper is utilitarian, while rejecting his proviso that Mandeville was unaware of this, and was consciously a rigorist. On the other hand, I have agreed with Selby-Bigge that without the rigorism Mandeville's satire would lose some of its sting, and have rejected both the view that the rigorism is affected for the sake of the satirical stance, and the view that Mandeville's object is to satirize rigorism by reducing it to absurdity. How can these apparently conflicting positions be reconciled?

To answer this we need to look more closely at the rigorism Mandeville is said to have adopted. So far I have been using the term simply as a convenient way of referring to the belief that there can be no virtue without self-denial. But Kaye means more than that by it. Rigorism, he tells us, is a 'blend of asceticism and rationalism'.[109] Asceticism is the view that virtue is 'a transcending of the demands of corrupt human nature, a conquest of self, to be achieved by divine grace', and rationalism is the view that

---

[108] *Fable of the Bees*, ed. Kaye, vol. 1, p. 157 (Remark O).
[109] Ibid., p. xlviii (Introduction).

'virtue was conduct in accord with sheer reason.'[110] This is a vague phrase, but Kaye makes it clear that he has in mind the doctrines of the contemporary ethical rationalists, who held that moral truths are 'eternal and immutable', like mathematical truths, and are grasped by reason; that they are not, that is to say, merely expressions of preferences, or generalizations about what human beings happen to find satisfying, or about what they need to do to gratify their desires, as Hobbes held; that consequences, indeed, do not determine the value of actions, but only motives. Reason is often contrasted with desire: to act from desire is to be influenced by man's animal nature, and to act from reason to be influenced by that part of him which resembles God.

How far is it true that 'Mandeville adopted both of these conceptions', i.e. both asceticism and rationalism?

One part of the rationalist position he quite explicitly repudiates:

All Propositions, not confin'd to Time or Place, that are once true, must be always so; even in the silliest and most abject Things in the World; as for Example, It is wrong to under-roast Mutton for People who love to have their Meat well done. The Truth of this, which is the most trifling Thing I can readily think on, is as much Eternal, as that of the Sublimest Virtue. If you ask me where this Truth was, before there was Mutton, or People to dress or eat it, I answer, in the same Place where Chastity was, before there were any Creatures that had an Appetite to procreate their Species.[111]

This is the line that Hobbes took: moral propositions are generalizations about how men must behave if they are to live together peacefully, and so have some chance of gratifying their desires. They are eternal and immutable in the way that sociological or psychological laws are, but that does not prevent them from being relative to human tastes and preferences. If human nature were different, they would be different. The truths of psychology and sociology are of course discovered and not invented: they are about human desires, but they are what they are whether men like it or not. There is, however, some room for invention: we can, if we know the laws of psychology, devise means of getting men to do what we want them to, just as a

[110] Ibid., pp. xlvii (Introduction) and p. cxii, n. 1.
[111] *Enquiry into the Origin of Honour*, 1732, p. viii.

poultry farmer, say, might invent an incubator which would make the eggs behave as he wants them to. The invention will only be successful if it takes account of the physiological laws which apply to avian embryos. Similarly, the devices by which we try to get men to do what we want will only work if they are based on a sound knowledge of human nature.

For Hobbes the social contract is such a device. To that extent it is a human invention. The contract consists in an agreement between men to follow certain rules of behaviour: such rules as, keep your promises, treat others as your equals, be just, be compassionate, etc. Hobbes calls these rules Laws of Nature. In a sense these rules have been invented too; but, since it is only by following these rules that men will succeed in living together in society, they may also be regarded as discoveries. What has been discovered is that this is the only way to attain a given end. That you ought to follow these rules if you want to attain that end is, then, an eternal and immutable truth. Since you do in fact want to attain that end (so far as you are a rational being, at any rate, since the end is keeping society from falling apart, and if it falls apart you will have no chance of gratifying *any* of your desires) it is eternally and immutably true that you ought to keep promises, treat others as equals, etc., etc.

This is not of course what the rationalists mean by eternal and immutable truths. Moral propositions, they insist, are not instructions about how to gratify our desires: they state facts about actions, just as mathematical propositions state facts about lines and angles, and have nothing to do with our desires. Some actions are right or fitting and others are wrong or unfitting, whether or not performing them will lead to human gratification. They state laws that apply to God as well as to man: to all rational beings, just so far as they are rational beings. To be rational is not just to understand how to gratify your desires, to reason about *that*; purely rational beings, like God, have no desires. Desires are part of animal, not rational nature. God has a will, but it is not different from his understanding: to say that God wills men to be virtuous is just to say that he realizes that it is fitting that they should be virtuous. 'Fitting' does not mean 'fitting for some purpose'; it is the name of a quality (or perhaps a relation) of goodness or rightness that actions and dispositions have, just as lines and angles have mathematical qualities and relations. These are apprehended by reason in the way that reason tells us that two straight lines cannot enclose a space.

> As the Mathematician [William Law tells us], seeing the acknowledged Differences and Proportions of Lines and Figures, proceeded upon them to enlarge Men's Knowledge in such matters; so the moral Philosophers, seeing the acknowledged Difference between Right and Wrong, Good and Evil which the common Reason of Man consented to, they proceeded to enlarge and improve upon them . . . As *things* are different by their own proper Natures, independent of our Wills, so *Actions* have their own peculiar Qualities from themselves, and not from our Thoughts about them. In these immutable Qualities of Actions, is founded the fitness and reasonableness of them, which we can no more alter, than we can change the Proportions or Relations of Lines and Figures.[112]

Law is quite right when he says that Mandeville's account of the origin of virtue is inconsistent with this view of morality. Mandeville is quite close to Hobbes. He doubts, however, whether the mere realization that observing certain rules will lead to a peaceful society will be an adequate incentive to obey them. It is also necessary to appeal to vanity. What his skilful politicians invent (and this is pure invention and not partly discovery, in the way that Hobbes's Laws of Nature are discoveries) is the reason for priding oneself on self-denial: the story about the difference between man and the animals. Men are exhorted to pride themselves on 'despising whatever they had in common with irrational Creatures' and opposing 'by the Help of Reason their most violent Inclinations'.[113]

Since this difference between man's animal nature (the source of his desires) and his rational nature (the source of his apprehension of moral law) is part of the rationalist account of morality, it would seem that here too (as Law also pointed out) Mandeville departs from ethical rationalism. But this needs qualification. It is after all part of his definition of virtue that it is 'contrary to the impulse of nature', and that its motive is 'a Rational Ambition of being good'.[114] The only trouble is that virtue, so defined, does not exist. Since man is actually 'a compound of various Passions,

---

[112] W. Law, *Remarks upon* The Fable of the Bees, 1723. *Works*, 1762, vol. 2, pp. 12–14.
[113] *Fable of the Bees*, ed. Kaye, vol. 1, p. 44 (*Origin of Moral Virtue*).
[114] Ibid., pp. 48–9 (*Origin of Moral Virtue*).

that all of them, as they are provoked and come uppermost, govern him by turns, whether he will or no'[115] he cannot in fact act out of 'a Rational Ambition of being good', thus 'opposing Reason to his most violent inclinations' and subduing them: his most violent inclinations are bound to govern him. The most that can be attained is the ersatz virtue that results from provoking vanity so that it comes uppermost and becomes his most violent inclination. It is of course an essential part of this manœuvre that he should not realize that his motive is vanity, but should believe that he is acting from the rational part of his nature. That is why this remains as part of the definition of virtue.

If the reasons given for self-abnegation are largely spurious, there are nevertheless real reasons. They are Hobbes's reasons. Civilization does demand the subjugation of 'the instinct of Sovereignty' that makes us want to dominate others. It is indeed part of the skilful politicians' exhortation that men should 'make a continual War with themselves to promote the Peace of others', and aim at 'no less than the Publick Welfare' as well as 'the Conquest of their own Passion'.[116] The ersatz virtue, then, does serve a useful purpose. And while the man who is virtuous in this sense does indeed act (as all men must) from the dominant passion of the moment, he is nevertheless, in allowing his vanity to come uppermost, making a genuine, and quite arduous effort to control his other inclinations and to bring about the public good. There are reasons, then, for admiring the second of the two clergymen, even if he does act, not from 'greatness of soul' but 'from an obstinate vanity, which will do as well'. There are no such reasons for admiring the first clergyman, who does not control his inclinations at all.

Can Mandeville consistently say that the second clergyman would be even more admirable if he did act from greatness of soul? What does he mean by greatness of soul? Presumably not the apprehension of the kind of eternal and immutable moral truths that Law talks about. Mandeville does not believe that there are any such truths. And presumably not, either, the ability to sacrifice oneself for the sake of others, for, as we have seen, the second clergyman does that even if he acts out of an obstinate vanity. What greatness of soul seems to mean is the

---

[115] *Fable of the Bees*, ed. Kaye, vol. 1, p. 39 (*Origin of Moral Virtue*, Introduction).
[116] Ibid., p. 44 (*Origin of Moral Virtue*).

ability to exercise such self-control without the aid of vanity, simply for the sake of the public good. It is true that that is impossible, in Mandeville's opinion; but one may, after all, admire an ideal man who does not exist, and even one who cannot exist, human nature being what it is. Mandeville opposes Shaftesbury's view that it is possible to act out of a quite disinterested concern for the public good, because he thinks that this is a dangerous delusion, 'a vast inlet to hypocrisy and self-deception'; but that is quite consistent with thinking that, if only such a concern did exist, it would be admirable. Mandeville's portrait of man is, after all, a satirical one: he does not deny that it would be better if men were what they claim to be; he is only opposing the preposterous suggestion that they are like that.

There is no reason, either, why Mandeville should not genuinely accept the view that the virtue of an action depends on its motive, and not on its consequences. Not, indeed, if that is interpreted as the rationalists interpret it, to mean that what makes an action right is, ultimately, independent of its consequences. What makes self-denial right is that it is necessary if men are to be useful to others. If that were not so, there would be no point in it. It is not, as the rationalist maintains, that there is an eternal and immutable truth to the effect that self-denial is right or 'fitting', which leaves no more to be said. I do not believe that Mandeville approves of self-denial for its own sake. That is why I doubt if he has any genuine objection to luxury as such. But it is quite consistent to hold that, while self-denial is right only because of its consequences for the good of others, a man who denies himself not for that reason but for the sake of enriching himself is not virtuous, even if he does, incidentally, promote the public good. On the other hand, a man who denies himself for the sake of others is virtuous, even if, through bad luck, his sacrifice does not have the intended effect.

The belief that the virtue of an action depends on its motive is, of course, one reason why genuine virtue does not exist. The ersatz virtue is not true virtue just because its motive is vanity. It was suggested above that it may still come fairly close to true virtue, even by the criterion of motive, since what the man in question prides himself on is his concern for others. Leaving that aside, and granting that true virtue is not possible, what is possible is the avoidance of vice. Mandeville, it will be remembered, defines vice as 'everything which without Regard to the Publick, Man should commit to gratify any of his Appetites . . . if in that Action there cou'd be observed the least Prospect, that it might either be injurious to any of the Society, or even render himself less serviceable to others'.[117]

Hutcheson, who quotes only the first part of this definition, says that 'without regard to the Publick' must mean '*pernicious* to the Publick, unless he can shew that all Men have agreed to call eating when one is hungry, or going to sleep when one is weary, vitious, whenever he does not think of a Community'.[118] This, he says, is inconsistent with the thesis that vices make for public benefits. But it is clear that Mandeville's proviso would rule out the innocent actions of eating and sleeping, and that he does mean without thinking about the public good in situations when, if we did think about it, we would see that our actions might be harmful, not necessarily to the public good as a whole, but to individual members of the public. This makes the action of a man who murders his rich relative and puts his hoarded gold into circulation still vicious, even though it does in fact promote the public good.

We have, then, this position. No action is truly virtuous, since all actions are done from selfish motives. A selfish motive may however be innocent, if the man who acts from it does so only after assuring himself that no harm will be done to others. In the Preface to his medical treatise, Mandeville defends himself against a possible charge of self-advertisement with this reflection: 'Wherefore as Times go, and the World is degenerate, I don't think, that he is either a bad Subject or a useless Member of Humane Society, who, without detriment to the Publick, serves his own Ends, by being beneficial to those that employ him: More I don't pretend to.'[119] This probably represents his real attitude to self-seeking and self-indulgence. As we have seen, he at least hints that the selfish motive may include, as an essential part of it, a concern for others, or at any rate a belief that considering others instead of oneself is a good thing.

But such Men, as without complying with any Weakness of their own, can part from what they value themselves, and, from no other Motive

---

[117] *Fable of the Bees* ed. Kaye, vol. 1, p. 48 (*Origin of Moral Virtue*).
[118] F. Hutcheson, *Reflections upon Laughter and Remarks upon* The Fable of the Bees. *Works*, Olms, 1971, vol. 7, Opera Minora, p. 400.
[119] *Treatise of the Hypochondriack and Hysterick Passions*, 1711, pp. xiii–xiv.

but their Love to Goodness, perform a worthy Action in Silence: Such Men, I confess, have acquir'd more refined Notions of Virtue than those I have hitherto spoke of; yet even in these (with which the World has yet never swarm'd) we may discover no small Symptoms of Pride, and the humblest Man alive must confess that the reward of a Virtuous Action, which is the Satisfaction that ensures upon it, consists in a certain Pleasure he procures to himself by Contemplating on his own Worth . . .[120]

It then becomes positively meritorious, if (so far as the motive is, after all, pride) not strictly virtuous.

To what extent does all this amount to accepting rigorism? I think it is clear that Mandeville did not accept the central rationalist contention, that moral principles are eternal and immutable truths, as contrasted with devices for making men useful to one another. To that extent Kaye is right about his utilitarian temper, though wrong in supposing that Mandeville himself did not realize or acknowledge this attitude to morality. But Mandeville probably does accept asceticism, the view that virtue consists in 'a conquest of self' and 'a transcending of the demands of corrupt human nature', in the utilitarian form that a fully virtuous man (if only he existed) would act from a disinterested concern for the public good. Since such men do not in fact exist, the best we can hope for is that men will control their desires so as to prevent them from conflicting with the good of others, and will play one corrupt passion, pride, against the others so that, by priding themselves on that degree of self-control, they make it possible. That this is the best we can hope for really is to man's discredit. There really is something degrading about the way men are led by the nose by desires, often quite trivial and transient ones. But, since men *are* like that, it is dangerous to ignore the fact and useless to repine at it.

4. UTILITARIANISM AND EGOISM

What has just been said suggests that Mandeville is a utilitarian. J. M. Robertson calls him 'one of the real founders of utilitarianism';[121] Bonamy Dobrée goes a step further and says that 'he is the father of Utilitarianism'.[122] It is not clear that either of them

---

[120] *Fable of the Bees*, ed. Kaye, vol. 1, p. 57 (*Origin of Moral Virtue*).
[121] J. M. Robertson, *Essays towards a Critical Method*, 1889, p. 224.
[122] B. Dobrée, *Variety of Ways*, 1932 (1967 reprint), p. 115.

means that he knew what he was founding or begetting: their point seems to be that, by insisting that all actions are prompted by passion and desire, Mandeville opened the way for the theory that the distinction between virtue and vice depended on the consequences of actions, and not on the presence or absence of self-denial. The same point is made by Kaye, who thinks that Mandeville's influence on the development of utilitarianism was very great indeed, while at the same time explicitly denying that he was a conscious utilitarian.

In the last section I have gone further than this in suggesting that Mandeville not only opposes the rationalist contention that moral principles express eternal and immutable truths, but regards them as devices for making men useful to one another. That by itself might merely make him a cynic; but it seems clear that he also regards it as a good thing that men should be useful to one another.

Does he, then, accept one eternal and immutable truth after all: namely, that men ought to be useful to one another? What, in short, is the status of the basic utilitarian principle itself? Most utilitarians have been, like Mandeville, opposed to rationalism, and have consequently found this question awkward. The most obvious way of answering it is to say that human welfare is something that men just happen to want, not something a passionless faculty called Reason instructs them that they ought to want. This is Hobbes's starting-point: we begin by asking what men actually want, and how they may get it. It turns out that men have little chance of getting any of the things they want unless they live together more or less peaceably in a society, and that the only way to do that is to agree to follow certain rules. We call these rules 'morality'.

This gives us a firmly naturalistic account of morality, fits it in with the rest of human behaviour, and saves us from having to regard it as somehow mystical. For the utilitarian, however, it has one grave defect. What men want, no doubt, is welfare, happiness, the gratification of desire: but it is their own welfare, their own happiness, not that of other people. For Hobbes it is the gratification of one's own, egoistic desires that is the ultimate justification of morality. The rules tell us to consider the welfare of others, but only as a means to an end: the maintenance of society; and that in its turn is a means to one's own, individual welfare. The utilitarian wants to make the general welfare an end, not a means, and to say that, when one's own happiness conflicts with the general happiness, one ought to prefer the latter. Usually, he also wants to give a naturalistic account of morality. It is not easy to see how he can do both.

This is notoriously a stumbling-block for Bentham and Mill, who try to base utilitarianism on egoism. It is usually said that they fail and that Mill in particular was betrayed into gross logical errors by his desperate and futile attempt to reconcile the irreconcilable. It is arguable, however, that Mill's reconciliation makes more sense than has been supposed. For what after all would be the next step in a Hobbist society? Once men have discovered that their welfare depends on forming a society and observing certain rules in order to keep it from disintegrating, they will take care to inculcate these rules in the next generation, and to reinforce them by the usual mechanism of punishment and reward. In a generation or two, men will cease to think of morality as a means to an end: in the modern jargon, the rules will be 'internalized'; in Mill's words: 'Not only does all strengthening of social ties, and all healthy growth of society give to each individual a stronger personal interest in practically consulting the welfare of others; it also leads him to identify his *feelings* more and more with their good, or at least with an even greater degree of practical consideration for it. He comes, as though instinctively, to be conscious of himself as a being who *of course* pays regard to others.'[123] As Mill also puts it, the welfare of others, from being a means, becomes an end: it is desired for its own sake. That this has come about through a process of conditioning (or, as Mill would say, association) does not make it any the less an end. Men do not naturally and instinctively desire the general happiness, but as members of society they are inevitably conditioned to do so: the general happiness becomes a part of their individual happiness, in the sense that they feel unhappy if they attain their individual goals in a way that runs counter to the general happiness. This is the phenomenon known as conscience.

Mandeville's account of the development of civilization and of morality is not unlike Hobbes's. Is he then an egoist rather than a utilitarian? His insistence that men can act only from self-love or self-liking suggests that he is. And certainly what

[123] J. S. Mill, *Utilitarianism*. Everyman edition, 1910, ed. A. D. Lindsay, p. 30.

provoked him to attack Shaftesbury was his opposition to the view that men naturally and instinctively aim at the public good. Against the rationalists he makes the point, later developed by Hume, that Reason manifests itself, not in apprehending mystical truths, but in reasoning, and that what we reason about is the consequences of our actions. Mandeville sees those consequences in terms of individual pleasure and pain.

Hor.: Would you prefer that Goodness, built upon Selfishness and Mercenary Principles, to that which proceeds from a Rectitude of Thinking, and a real Love of Virtue and the Reasonableness of Mens Actions?
Cleo.: We can give no better Proof of our Reasonableness, than by judging rightly. When a Man wavers in his Choice, between present Enjoyments of Ease and Pleasure, and the Discharge of Duties that are troublesome, he weighs what Damage or Benefit will accrue to him upon the Whole, as well from the Neglect as the Observance of the Duties that are prescrib'd to him; and the greater the Punishment he fears from the Neglect, and the more transcendent the Reward is which he hopes for from the Observance, the more reasonably he acts, when he sides with his Duty. To bear with Inconveniences, Pain and Sorrow, in Hopes of being eternally Happy, and refuse the Enjoyments of Pleasure, for Fear of being Miserable for ever, are more justifiable to Reason, and more consonant to good Sense, than it is to do it for Nothing.[124]

Here the attack on rationalism is combined with one on Shaftesbury's assertion that virtue is its own reward. In this Mandeville is voicing a common opinion, shared by many of the clergy: Shaftesbury's views alarmed them because they did not believe that the motive to act virtuously would be strong enough if there were no material rewards or punishments. But this view about human motives did not necessarily imply that the virtuous act is virtuous only because it promotes self-interest. Men were incapable of being virtuous unless they thought it was in their interest, but what made an action virtuous was not that, but its conformity to God's will. Mandeville, however, seems to agree with Hobbes that the real reason for being virtuous (i.e. considering others and restraining 'the instinct of sovereignty') as distinct from the motive (vanity or fear of Hell) or the spurious reasons (demonstrating man's superiority to the other animals or

---

[124] *Origin of Honour*, 1732, p. 32.

avoiding punishment after death) is the maintenance of society. And perhaps, if pressed, he would also agree that the reason for not allowing society to collapse is that everyone, and consequently oneself, would be unhappy if it did.

Mandeville does, however, depart from (or at least supplement) Hobbes in a way which suggests that he is, at least to some extent, anticipating Mill. It is only after a long, slow conditioning process that man becomes fit for society. He does not consciously promote the interests of his fellow man in order to maintain society, in order to serve his own interests: not even the skilful politician is as clear-sighted as that about what he is doing. Instead men simply come to identify their own well-being with considering the interests of others. Mandeville's view is significantly different from Mill's, in that it is not so much that men develop benevolent feelings, and still less a dispassionate concern for the public good, but that they come to pride themselves on their self-denial and their disinterestedness. Mandeville, then, is still more an ethical egoist than a utilitarian.

Yet, although he stresses man's essential selfishness, he never makes much of the point that the ultimate reason for bothering to keep society going is the contribution it makes to one's own individual happiness, as distinct from the happiness of men in general. He is prepared to take the extreme utilitarian view that one may, without injustice, sacrifice an innocent individual to the good of the community as a whole. For example, he says that it is not unjust to kill the shipwrecked crew of an infected ship if that is the only way to preserve the health of the nation. Perhaps this is not inconsistent with egoism, since even Hobbes admits that in entering society the individual runs a risk of being sacrificed for the general good: the justification for running it is that in the only alternative (the state of nature, i.e. an anarchic absence of society) the risks he runs are much greater. In Hobbes, however, this is a grudging admission. Mandeville's readiness to accept the most austere consequences that may be drawn from utilitarianism does suggest that he is less of an individualist than Hobbes, and attaches more importance to the public good as such. After all, even Richard Fiddes, who wrote a rationalist *Treatise of Morality* (complete with a 144-page preface against Mandeville) concedes that 'no Man can be obliged to any Duties of Society, which will more than over-balance the Benefits, which he can propose to reap from Society. For this would be to propose an End (which no wise, or reasonable Man will do) of less Value, than that which is expended or given up, in order to attain it.'[125]

J. C. Maxwell argues that Mandeville's utilitarianism is meant to apply only to governments and legislators and that it is not inconsistent with Mandeville's rigorism, which he takes at face value. On Mandeville's view, he says, a statesman is in a special position: he has an *ex officio* concern for human welfare. Politicians are not more disinterested than anyone else, but the content of their duty is different. 'They ought to aim at the temporal good of society as a whole, whereas private citizens ought simply to follow the precepts of moral law.'[126] The statesman ought to be ascetic himself, but it is not his duty to promote asceticism in the community as a whole.[127]

There is certainly some evidence in Mandeville's writings to support this view. In *A Letter to Dion*, Mandeville agrees that nothing can be a benefit to an individual that 'might destroy, or any Ways interfere with his eternal Happiness';[128] but, he says, eternal happiness cannot be a *public* benefit. This suggests that public good is not just the sum of private goods, and may indeed conflict with private good. But Mandeville also makes the point that by 'public benefits' he just means what people usually think of as benefits: he agrees that they may really be harmful. Perhaps, then, it is not these alleged benefits that it is the duty of a statesman to promote, but real ones. There is, however, a somewhat more substantial piece of evidence in the *Modest Defence* when he says, in answer to the objection that a Christian Government ought not to connive at the sin of fornication:

To this Objection, I answer, that it is universally allow'd as one of the greatest Perfections of the Christian Religion that its Precepts are calculated to promote the Happiness of Mankind in this World as well as the next; if so, then it is a direct Arraignment of the Lawgiver's infinite Wisdom, i.e. a Contradiction to assert that, in matters of Law and Government, the Public Breach of any Gospel Precept can pos-

---

[125] R. Fiddes, *A General Treatise of Morality, form'd upon the Principles of Natural Reason only, with a Preface in Answer to two Essays lately published in the* Fable of the Bees, 1724, p. xcviii.
[126] J. C. Maxwell, 'Ethics and Politics in Mandeville', *Philosophy*, 26 (1951), 251.
[127] Ibid., p. 247.
[128] *A Letter to Dion*, 1732, p. 39.

sibly be for the temporal Good of any *Society* whatever: And therefore we may with Confidence affirm, that no sinful Laws can be beneficial, and *vice versa*, that no beneficial Laws can be sinful. Now we have already given sufficient Proof of the Benefit the *Publick* would receive by licensing the *Stews*, and therefore ought to conclude such licence lawful. . . .[129]

This looks like a straight utilitarian account of sinfulness, but perhaps Mandeville means it to apply only in 'matters of Law and Government'? That is Maxwell's interpretation. It is the particular function of a statesman he says, 'to promote . . . not what would be the public welfare if man were virtuous, but what is in fact the welfare of fallen man with his inordinate desires'.[130] The suggestion seems to be that it is not sinful for governments to aim at the gratification of those desires, though sin is committed by the citizen who has them and indulges them. 'Since man, in the state of nature, is entirely corrupt, a legislature can never, properly speaking, be said to promote or encourage sin: men will sin in any case, and the legislator's sole business is to prevent their sin from being harmful to society.'[131] But what, we may ask, is meant by 'harmful to society' here? If the criterion is 'the public welfare of fallen man with his inordinate desires', it would seem that the absence of sin would be harmful to society. And this is rather difficult to reconcile with the remark about its being one of the greatest perfections of Christianity that its precepts promote happiness in this world as well as the next. Mandeville can hardly mean that the happiness of corrupt man is in fact sinful, but that it is the duty of legislators to promote it just the same, since they will not increase the actual commission of sin. He does make the point that the substitution of public whoring for private will lessen rather than increase the total amount of fornication, and that it is futile to try to stamp out fornication altogether. Better, then, to control it. But, if Mandeville's asceticism is sincere, as Maxwell maintains, and luxury is really sinful, it becomes the duty of the legislators, in promoting public prosperity, to do more than merely control sin. They will be actively promoting it; for they will be making luxury, or a greater degree of luxury, possible where it was not so before. (Incidentally, it may be doubted whether Mandeville believed

[129] *A Modest Defence of Publick Stews*, 1725, p. 51.
[130] Maxwell, op. cit., p. 247.
[131] Ibid., p. 249.

fornication as such to be sinful, any more than luxury. Almost immediately after the passage quoted above, he points out that the text forbidding fornication also forbids black puddings. Maxwell omits this sentence, though he quotes the passages immediately before and after it.)

It is hard to believe, then, that Mandeville thought self-denial good in itself, and not merely as a means of making men useful to one another, and that his utilitarianism applies only to statesmen. What does seem possible, however, is that he distinguishes between the duties of governments and those of private citizens when it comes to sacrificing innocent individuals for the public good. At first sight, it seems to follow from utilitarianism that it is right to sacrifice them, but many utilitarians have denied that this does follow. One argument is that the loss of security, if everyone knows that he may, through no fault of his own, suffer severe privations or even death at the hands of his fellow citizens, will outweigh any possible gain to the public good. Another possibility is to amend utilitarianism, as Sidgwick did, so as to make the equal distribution of happiness good in itself, as well as the maximization of happiness; so that it is not necessarily right to increase the general happiness at the cost of the total destruction of the happiness, and perhaps the life, of some unfortunate individual. The problem is a real one, as anyone may see by asking himself what he would do if he had it in his power to avert a world war, say, by allowing an innocent hostage to be killed. The fact that few, if any, of us are actually forced to make such hard choices does not affect the point: which is that there is real doubt about which course would be the right one. It might conceivably be argued that the answer would depend on whether one was acting as a public official or a private citizen; and it may be that this is what Mandeville is saying.

Consider the whole of the passage in which he introduces the example of the shipwrecked, infected sailors:

First, then, I expect to be attack'd with that old moral Precept, of *Not doing Evil that Good may come of it*. This may be answer'd with another old Saying, equally authentick, and more applicable to the present Purpose, that *of two Evils we ought to chuse the least*. The Case is this: A private Member of a *Society*, may, doubtless, commit a Crime with a Design to promote the Good of that *Society*, which was partly the Case of *Felton* against the Duke of *Buckingham*; and this evil Action may possibly answer the Goodness of the Intention, but is universally condemn'd as an unwarrantable Presumption, and falls justly under the Censure of doing a certain Evil, for the Prospect of an uncertain Good. But as to the *Legislature*, there is a vast Difference; for they, and they only, are entrusted with the Welfare of the *Society*: This Publick Welfare is, or ought to be, the whole End and Scope of their Actions; and they are fully impowered to do whatever they judge fully conducive to that end. If their intentions come up to this, they are certainly in their Consciences acquitted. But as to the World, their Actions, that is, their Laws, are judg'd good or bad, just or unjust, according as they actually prove beneficial or detrimental to the *Society* in general: And therefore it is the grossest Absurdity, and a manifest Contradiction in Terms, to assert, That a *Government* may not commit Evil that Good may come of it; for, if a Publick Act, taken in all its Consequences, really produces a greater Quantity of Good, it must, and ought to be term'd a good Act; altho' the bare Act consider'd in itself, without the consequent Good, should be in the highest Degree wicked and unjust. As for Instance: A Ship performing Quarantine, and known to be infected, is sunk by a Storm; some of the Crew, half drown'd, recover the Shore; but the moment they land, the *Government* orders them to be shot to Death. This Action, in itself, is no less than a downright unchristian and inhuman Murther; but since the Health and Safety of the Nation is secured by this severe Precaution, it is no Wonder, if we allow the Action to be not only justifiable, but, in the strictest Sense of Morality, just.[132]

It is not clear just what the difference is, according to Mandeville, between the Government and a private citizen like John Felton (who, in the reign of Charles I, assassinated the Duke of Buckingham, partly because he had a personal grudge against him, but partly for political reasons). If Felton did a certain evil for the sake of an uncertain good, so did the hypothetical authorities who shot the sailors. Mandeville says that governments are judged by whether they do actually succeed in promoting the public good; but he is not prepared to apply the same criterion to Felton. I think that Mandeville is uncertain, not indeed whether the rightness of actions depends on their consequences for happiness (which is all that is essential to utilitarianism), but how far harm to one individual may be permissible in order to prevent harm to others.

This leads to an ambiguity in his definition of vice. It is vicious

[132] *A Modest Defence of Publick Stews*, 1725, pp. 49-50.

to gratify one's appetites 'without regard to the Publick' if there is any prospect of injuring, not just the public good as a whole, but any individual, or even rendering oneself less serviceable to others. Where does this leave Felton? He certainly injured an individual, and no doubt he rendered himself less useful to others, since he was put to death, as he no doubt foresaw. But did he do so without regard to the public good? Mandeville concedes that Felton did consider the effect of his action on the public good, and acted partly for that reason. But he does not therefore excuse him. Why, then, does 'regard to the publick' figure in Mandeville's definition at all? Presumably because one is sometimes justified in injuring an individual for the sake of the public good, even if one gratifies one's own desires at the same time: for example when, full of indignation and possibly wanting revenge, we hand over to the police the criminal who has robbed us. Sometimes; but not, it seems clear, always, in Mandeville's view.

Perhaps, however, he is merely making Hobbes's point that, considering all that is at stake, and the grave consequences of making a mistake, it had better be left to the Government to judge when the public good justifies penalizing some individual? I think that more than that is involved. Mandeville wants to justify the channelling of vicious motives into publicly useful directions without thereby denying that they are vicious. The businessman whose avarice leads him to be entirely ruthless to his competitors and his workmen alike may be contributing to the commercial prosperity of the nation, and may even realize that fact, but he is still acting viciously. In the last section mention was made of the heir who murders his miserly relative and puts his gold into circulation, thereby doing a public service. The point then was that, since it is not the public good that he is thinking of, his action is still vicious. But the example was suggested by *Alciphron*, where the heir is supposed to be a disciple of Mandeville's, who has realized the contribution he can make to the public good. His action would still not be justified on utilitarian principles, of course, since the injury done to the relative is too great to be compensated for by the rather dubious benefit to the community. But, even apart from that, it seems clear that Mandeville does not justify such actions. It seems unlikely that he would regard them as justified even if performed by a Government faced by a fiscal problem. He is concerned with the happiness of individuals, and not merely with the public good, even though he realizes that there are sometimes difficult situations in which the happiness of one, or of a few, individuals conflicts with the happiness of many.

One difficulty in regarding Mandeville as a utilitarian is his treatment of pity. If he believes that the real reason for being virtuous is to make oneself useful to other men, why does he decry pity, and say that it is a weakness? His ostensible reason is that pity is a passion, like any other, and that to give way to it is to be self-indulgent. How can he say that, if he does means to think self-denial good in itself, but good only as a not really promoting the happiness of others? Pity obviously does that.

One reason, of course, is that Mandeville is anxious to maintain that civilization arises out of man's weaknesses and vices, not out of any Godlike qualities. He does not want to make any concessions to Shaftesbury's thesis that man's natural disposition is on the whole good. While it is going much too far to say, as Wilde does, that 'Mandeville cannot be treated as a systematic writer' and that 'it is idle to point out inconsistencies in his theories . . . Any theory is good enough for him if it will afford him a weapon against some phase of current morality and religion',[133] it is true that, in maintaining a thesis (or a paradox) he does sometimes seize on any argument that comes to hand.

Yet his arguments against pity are actually utilitarian ones. Pity is obviously objectionable when it impels us to keep away from the object of pity, to avert our eyes from the beggar's sores instead of doing something to relieve him. Even when pity moves us to more positive action, it may do more harm than good, aiding and abetting the corruption of judges, the seduction of virgins, the spoiling of children. What is needed to correct these excesses, Mandeville argues, is a dispassionate concern for the public good as a whole. This is clearly a utilitarian ideal. It is true that Mandeville's main purpose is to show that such a dispassionate concern never actually occurs, in spite of all the sophistries of my lord Shaftesbury. But to say that, because of human frailty, the utilitarian ideal can never be fully realized is not to deny the truth of the utilitarian account of what morality is.

While Mandeville is much more of a systematic writer than Wilde supposes, it is true that he is not primarily concerned to

[133] N. Wilde, 'Mandeville's Place in English Thought', *Mind*, 7 (1898), 223.

develop a system of moral philosophy. He is a satirist, whose main targets are human folly, human pretentiousness, and the human capacity for self-deception. His explicit statements about morality are at least sometimes part of his satiric stance, even if it is not safe to assume that they are always or only that. To arrive at his moral philosophy we need to consider not only what he actually says but his purpose in saying it, and the underlying moral attitudes which he reveals, both consciously and unconsciously. One can hardly expect the result to be a neat and tidy system, with all the inconsistencies resolved, and all the difficulties met. But, when that has been said, Mandeville's underlying moral theory seems to come closest to utilitarianism: a utilitarianism based, to at least some extent, on Hobbist ethical egoism.

8
THE REAL MANDEVILLE?

WHAT conclusions, if any, can we now reach about the question asked in the first chapter: which of the representations of Mandeville is the true one?

So far we have considered only the evidence of his own writings. There is not much to be added from external evidence, which is scanty, unreliable, and sometimes conflicting. Records show that he was baptized at Rotterdam on 20 November 1670, and that he matriculated at the University of Leyden in October 1685.[1] He presented a dissertation in 1689 on the consciousness of animals, taking the Cartesian view (which he afterwards abandoned) that they were automata, and another one in 1691 on the chylification of the blood, after which he took the degree of Doctor of Medicine. He seems to have gone to England shortly afterwards. He married there in 1699. We know from his medical treatise that, in specializing in nervous disorders, he was following in the footsteps of his father, who had practised medicine in Amsterdam and Rotterdam for more than thirty-eight years.[2] He died in London on 21 January 1733. The *Gentleman's Magazine* has the briefest of entries in its list of deaths for January:[3]

21st. Dr. Mandeville, author of *The Fable of the Bees* and other pieces.

The traces of feminism shown by Mandeville in *The Virgin Unmask'd* and elsewhere did not extend to his will: of five hundred pounds he had in South Sea Annuities, he left one hundred to his wife and the remainder, together with the rest of his estate, to his son Michael; to his daughter Penelope he left 'twenty shillings for a Ring'.[4]

In his article on Mandeville in the *Dictionary of National*

---

[1] *Fable of the Bees*, ed. Kaye, vol. 1, pp. xvii–xx. Most of the facts mentioned in this paragraph come from Kaye.
[2] *Treatise of the Hypochondriack and Hysterick Passions*, 1711, pp. xii and 40.
[3] *Gentleman's Magazine*, 3 (1733), 46.
[4] *Fable of the Bees*, ed. Kaye, vol. 1, facing p. xx (reproduction of Mandeville's will).

Biography Leslie Stephen says that the only personal details of Mandeville's life that have been preserved are to be found in brief references in Benjamin Franklin's *Autobiography*, Sir John Hawkins's *Life of Samuel Johnson*, and Jeremiah Whitaker Newman's *Lounger's Commonplace Book*. Of these Hawkins's account is the most circumstantial, even though most of it is contained in a footnote (to a remark about the effect on 'the moral conduct of the young and unthinking' of such writers as 'Collins, Mandeville, Morgan and Tindal; the first pair deists, and the latter infidels'). Mandeville, he tells us, 'lived in obscure lodgings in London and was never able to acquire much practice'; he made a living by writing 'sundry papers in the *London Journal* and other such publications, to favour the custom of drinking spirituous liquors, to which employment of the pen it is supposed he was hired by the distillers'; he was 'coarse and overbearing in his manners where he durst be so; yet a great flatterer of some vulgar Dutch merchants who allowed him a pension'. He adds that 'this last information comes from a clerk of a city attorney, through whose hands the money passed.'[5]

Such of this as can be checked would seem to be false: Kaye went through the files of the *London Journal* and other contemporary journals without finding the articles commissioned by the distillers.[6] Mandeville's known writings, he points out, contain vivid warnings of the evil effects of excessive drinking, notably Remark G of the *Fable*. Since Kaye's researches, Paul Bunyan Anderson, who discovered Mandeville's contributions to the *Female Tatler*, has unearthed a pamphlet called *A Dissertation upon Drunkenness*, which he also attributes to Mandeville, mainly because of its close verbal resemblance to Remark G.[7] The title-page includes the words: 'Also an Account of the Pride, Insolence and Exorbitance of Brewers, Vintners, Victuallers, Coffee-House-Keepers, and Distillers, with the various Arts and Methods by which they allure and excite People to drink and debauch themselves.'[8] It now seems established that Anderson's attribution was mistaken, and that the author of the pamphlet was not Mandeville, but someone who plagiarized freely from

---

[5] Sir John Hawkins, *The Life of Samuel Johnson*, LL.D., 1787, p. 263.
[6] *Fable of the Bees*, ed. Kaye, vol. 1, p. xxiii, n. 3.
[7] P. B. Anderson, 'Bernard Mandeville on Gin', *PMLA* 54 (1939), 775–84.
[8] Ibid., p. 777.

the *Fable*. But the mere fact that the attribution could be made, with some plausibility, tells heavily against Hawkins's story.

In his medical treatise, Mandeville extols the medicinal qualities of wine, while deploring the fact that people render themselves immune to its curative effects by drinking it when they have no need of them. He also introduces a rhetorical eulogy of it:

... it is not only in the power of this Vegetable to make the Slave fancy himself to be free, the Poor to be Rich, the Old Young, and the Miserable Happy; but it likewise actually mends visible Imperfections; renders the Infirm Strong, the Decrepit Nimble, and the Stammerer Eloquent; and what neither *Circe's* nor *Medea's* Art could ever perform; turns Vices into Virtues, and by the Charm of it, the Coward, the Covetous, the Proud, and the Morose become Valliant, Generous, Affable, and good Humour'd.[9]

But, apart from the obvious irony of this, it is made quite clear that it is not meant seriously: 'I am no Critick', Philopirio adds immediately afterwards, 'but well assured that, Poetical Flights apart, the innumerable mischiefs which Wine, as it is managed, creates to Mankind, far exceed whatever *Horace*, or any body else can say in commendation of it.'[10]

This part of Hawkins's story, then, seems unlikely to be true. As for the Dutch merchants, Kaye makes the plausible conjecture that they were John and Cornelius Backer, mentioned in Mandeville's will as holding the South Sea Annuities for him, and that they were not his patrons but merely his business agents.

Kaye also thinks it unlikely that Mandeville lived in poverty. He must have made money out of the *Fable*, which was enormously successful, even if it was a success of scandal. He is known to have been an intimate friend of Lord Macclesfield, the Lord Chancellor, as Hawkins himself notes, among others. (It was at Macclesfield's house that Mandeville met Addison and later made the famous remark that he was 'a parson in a tie-wig'.)[11] Benjamin Franklin who, unlike Hawkins or Newman, actually met Mandeville, draws a picture rather different from Hawkins's. Working as a printer in London, Franklin set up the second edition of Wollaston's *Religion of Nature Delineated*, and was

---

[9] *Treatise on the Hypochondriack and Hysterick Passions*, 1711, p. 272.
[10] Ibid., p. 273.
[11] S. Johnson, *Lives of the English Poets. Works*, 1823, vol. 7, p. 114; Hawkins, op. cit., p. 264.

moved to write an answer to it, *A Dissertation on Liberty and Necessity, and on Pleasure and Pain.*

My pamphlet by some means falling into the hands of one Lyons, a surgeon, author of a book entitled *The Infallibility of Human Judgment,* it occasioned an acquaintance between us. He took great notice of me called on me often to converse on those subjects, carried me to the Horns, a pale-alehouse in — Lane, Cheapside, and introduced me to Dr. Mandeville, author of the Fable of the Bees, who had a club there, of which he was the soul, being a most facetious, entertaining companion.[12]

But this must have been in 1725 or 1726, during the nineteen months Franklin spent in London. The undated letter to Sir Hans Sloane, cited by Kaye as evidence of Mandeville's success in his profession, could not have been written, as Kaye himself points out, before 1716, when Sloane was made a baronet. Mandeville's will, which shows him to be in relative affluence, is dated 1729. It is quite possible, therefore, that Mandeville did have to struggle to make a living in his earlier years in London, and he may very well have spent as much time on journalism as on medicine. At least this would seem to be true for the five months between November 1709 and March 1710, during which he wrote thirty-two issues of the *Female Tatler.* If Anderson is right, the other thirty-three issues were written by Mrs. Susanna Centlivre, the playwright. Probably she and Mandeville had taken over the paper between them, which would mean editing and perhaps publishing as well as writing.

The medical treatise in 1711 was at least partly a bid for patients. Mandeville's preface suggests that he is a little on the defensive about this. It may possibly have been used against him by Bluet, who says that Mandeville's 'Vindication' of the *Fable* 'is writ in the true Spirit of a Quack Bill'.[13] Given the controversial manners of the times, however, a doctor with Mandeville's opinions would have been called a quack in any case. It is also possible that the publication of the *Treatise* had something to do with the feud between Mandeville and Dr. John Radcliffe, whose bequest to Oxford is put forward in the *Essay on Charity and Charity-Schools*

[12] B. Franklin, *Autobiography. Works.* ed. J. Bigelow, New York, Putnam's, 1904, vol. 1, p. 92.
[13] [G. Bluet], *Enquiry whether . . . Virtue tends to . . . Wealth or Poverty . .*, 1725, p. 97.

as a prime example of vanity masquerading as philanthropy: 'what must we judge of his Motive, the Principle he acted from, when after his Death we find that he has left a Trifle among his Relations who stood in need of it, and an immense Treasure to an University that did not want it?'[14] Richard Fiddes, who was related to Radcliffe, devotes several pages of his preface on Mandeville to answering this attack. While admitting that the charge about leaving a trifle to his relations is 'not altogether groundless', he denies that Radcliffe's motives were unworthy ones. In reply to another comment of Mandeville's, that Radcliffe was known 'to look down with contempt on the most deserving of his Profession, and never confer with any other Physician but what will pay Homage to his Superior Genius, creep to his Humour, and never approach him but with all the slavish Obsequiousness a Court-Flatterer can treat a Prince with'[15] Fiddes says: 'If the Doctor did really look down with Contempt upon any Persons, it was upon those, and those only, who had Recourse to vile and ignoble Methods, towards opening a Way to Practice. And this might be, and I have Reason to believe was, the true Cause why he, sometimes, refused to confer with others of the same Faculty.'[16]

This may not have been a direct hit at Mandeville, but it may be significant that Mandeville seems to have changed his mind about Radcliffe some time between 1709 and 1714, when Radcliffe died, or at least before 1723, when the *Essay on Charity* first appeared. In the *Female Tatler* for 21-3 November 1709, 'Lucinda' criticizes Steele's *Tatler* for publishing scandal about real people under 'ingenious Nicknames' easily seen through, and refers unmistakably to a piece in which Radcliffe (called Aesculapius) had been ridiculed over a love-affair with a much younger woman. She imagines the delight of Steele's readers: 'Pray, Madam, did you see the Doctor in the *Tatler*; did you mind the Gold Buttons, was not that very Witty? I declare I am glad to see him exposed, because he wou'd not come to my Sister *Patty*, tho' my Father sent twice, and never yet gave him less than three Guineas for a Fee.'[17] In 1709 Mandeville is virtuously protesting

---

[14] *Fable of the Bees*, ed. Kaye, vol. 1, p. 263 (*Essay on Charity and Charity-Schools*).
[15] Ibid., p. 263.
[16] R. Fiddes, *General Treatise of Morality*, 1724, p. cxii.
[17] *Female Tatler*, no. 60, 21-3 Nov. 1709.

against such attacks on 'a Physician famous for the Splendour of his Practice': in 1723 he is himself attacking the same physician much more severely. It is possible that all he objected to in the first place was the trivial ground of the attack: 'In Writing Scandal', he says, 'I wou'd draw the Picture of those upon whom it is design'd, not from Things that are indifferent, and have neither good nor harm in them, but from the Folly and Vices of which they are really guilty.' But he also criticizes the practice of referring to real people who can be readily identified; and in any case the *Tatler*, though mainly making fun of Radcliffe as an ageing lover, also anticipates Mandeville in mentioning his avarice: 'Love has taken place of avarice, or rather is become an avarice of another kind, which still urges him to pursue what he does not want.'[18] One thing that happened between 1709 and 1714 was the publication of Mandeville's *Treatise*: in view of Fiddes's remark, it is at least possible that it was the repercussions from that event that made him less tender of Radcliffe's reputation.

If Mandeville did have difficulty in establishing himself in practice, probably this situation did not last. Whether or not the *Treatise* brought him patients, it is likely that the *Fable*, with the celebrity that followed it, did. If the *Fable* brought him money as well as fame, he may have deliberately kept his practice small, to give himself time for his writing, and for evenings of witty talk at Lord Lansdowne's or the Horns.

Most of this is, of course, conjecture. As Kaye points out, 'there is no authoritative first-hand evidence whatever as to Mandeville's character and habits except what he himself has told us and the brief remark of one single contemporary.'[19] We come back, then, to the ground already surveyed; and to the question at the beginning of this chapter.

It is obvious, I think, that neither of the views outlined in the first chapter is wholly accurate. Mandeville was neither a Savonarola nor Law's missioner come from the kingdom of darkness to do us harm: the *Fable* is not an evangelical tract, but neither is it, as *Chambers' Encyclopedia* was still proclaiming in 1891, 'a pothouse fulminant'.[20] Any brief characterization of Mandeville is inadequate. To take one example: there is some plausibility in

[18] *Tatler*, no. 44, 21 July 1709.
[19] *Fable of the Bees*, ed. Kaye, vol. 1, pp. xxvii–xxviii.
[20] *Chambers' Encyclopedia*, 1888–92, vol. 7, p. 16, under Mandeville, Bernard de.

Wilde's suggestion that he was the mouthpiece of the diehards of the Restoration who were made uneasy by the softening of manners and the higher moral tone of the new age; but it does not survive examination. Consider Wilde's illustrations of the new moral temper: 'Attempts were made to improve and educate the poor, and charity schools were founded. Laws were enacted against gaming and cock-spitting and the more brutal amusements of all kinds were discouraged.'[21] Mandeville, as we know, opposed charity schools, and was contemptuous of the Societies for Promoting a Reformation of Manners, but he also condemned cruelty to animals. I have been unable to find the law against cock-spitting which Wilde refers to, unless he has in mind 4 & 5 William and Mary, c. 23 (1692), which forbids the burning of heath-lands to trap grouse or heath-cock. This, like other Acts for preserving game, was intended to benefit landowners rather than their prey. Another possibility is that he means cock-throwing (the practice of tying a cock to a stake and throwing stones or sharp sticks at it) though I have found no evidence that that was prohibited at this time. But whatever cock-spitting may have been, we may safely assume that the man who wrote so movingly of the death of an ox would have been opposed to it. Mandeville's attack on the cult of Honour hardly fits Wilde's thesis; and, in general, his satire is directed quite as often against rakes of the old as against moralists of the new school.

Again, it is tempting to say that Mandeville's essential characteristic is his hatred of cant and hypocrisy: his refusal to be blinded by comforting conventional fictions, and his insistence on showing men as they really are. 'You, Sir', he tells Berkeley, 'think it for the Good of Society that human Nature should be extoll'd as much as possible: I think, the real Meanness and Deformity of it to be more instructive.'[22] And, indeed, there is a suggestion in *Alciphron* that Berkeley himself regards Mandeville as a reckless and uncompromising utterer of inconvenient truths. Alciphron says in the first dialogue: 'Convenience is one thing, and truth is another. A genuine philosopher, therefore, will overlook all advantages, and consider only truth itself as such.'[23] Euphranor in reply seems to be suggesting that, when it

---

[21] N. Wilde, 'Mandeville's Place in English Thought', *Mind*, 11 (1898), 224.
[22] *A Letter to Dion*, 1732, p. 48.
[23] G. Berkeley, *Alciphron. Works*, ed. Luce and Jessop, vol. 3, p. 60.

comes to the general happiness of mankind, expediency is more important than truth: 'Might it not therefore be inferred, that those men are foolish who go about to unhinge such principles as have a necessary connexion with the general good of mankind?'[24] The same argument is used against Lysicles in the second dialogue:

Euphranor: Virtue then, in your account, is a trick of statesmen?
Lysicles: It is.
Euphranor: Why then do your sagacious sect betray and divulge that trick or secret of State, which wise men have judged necessary for the good government of the world?
Lysicles hesitating, Crito made answer, that he presumed it was because their sect, being wiser than all other wise men, disdained to see the world governed by wrong maxims, and would set all things on a right bottom.[25]

Probably, there is no single characteristic of Mandeville's as prominent as his hatred of hypocrisy and self-deception; yet the moment we try to set him up as the champion of candour and frankness above all, doubts begin to rush in. Why, in that case, is it so hard to take his professions of religious belief seriously? Does he not himself think it necessary to pander to the stubborn belief in an invisible cause, which is a congenital human weakness, hardly less strong than the instinctive tendency to overvalue oneself? Would an apostle of candour be quite as fond of irony as Mandeville? Would he use literary devices like the alleged answer to the *Modest Defence*, purporting to come from the Societies for Promoting a Reformation of Manners? Would he share Lucinda's weakness for treating an argument like a pot of tea, and straining the last drop out of it?

Moreover, it must be admitted that, as a controversialist, Mandeville does not always show an uncompromising devotion to strict honesty. He protests, quite rightly, against Berkeley's unfairness to Shaftesbury in ignoring 'the many admirable Things he has said against Priestcraft, and on the side of Liberty and Human Happiness'. Few of Berkeley's readers, he adds, 'among those that have read, and are not lash'd in the *Characteristicks* . . . will think that My Lord *Shaftsbury* deserves one Tenth Part of the Indignity and Contempt, which you treat

[24] G. Berkeley, *Alciphron. Works*, ed. Luce and Jessop, vol. 3, p. 62.
[25] Ibid., p. 80.

Cratylus with'.[26] Yet elsewhere Mandeville himself makes capital out of the charges levelled against Shaftesbury by those who had been lashed. 'The *Characteristicks*', he makes Cleomenes say, 'have made a Jest of all reveal'd Religion, especially the Christian.'[27] He at least hints that Shaftesbury was remiss because 'he did not follow Arms when his Country was involved in War':[28] a charge one hardly expects from the author of the *Enquiry into Honour*, or the other works in which Mandeville tells us what he thinks of warfare. Similarly, any reader of *Free Thoughts on Religion*, with its plea for religious tolerance, would expect Mandeville to welcome Shaftesbury's humane policy for the treatment of heretics. They should be laughed at, he said, but not persecuted. Ridicule was a test of truth: a solemn opinion that could be punctured by a little raillery could have no substance in it. Ridicule was also a more effective way of discrediting cranks and enthusiasts than making martyrs of them.

The *Jews* were naturally a very cloudy People, and wou'd endure little Raillery in any thing; much less in what belong'd to any Religious Doctrines or Opinions. Religion was look'd upon with a sullen Eye; and Hanging was the only Remedy they cou'd prescribe for any thing which look'd like setting up a new Revelation. The sovereign Argument was, *Crucify, Crucify*. But with all their malice, and Inveteracy to our Saviour, and his Apostles after him, had they but taken the Fancy to act such Puppet-Shows in his Contempt, as at this hour the Papists are acting in his Honour; I am apt to think they might possibly have done our Religion more harm, than by all their other ways of Severity.[29]

This remark naturally scandalized the orthodox; but was it quite sincere of Mandeville to echo them?

Cleo.: . . . Lord *Shaftsbury* takes Joke and Banter to be the best and surest Touchstone to prove the Worth of Things: It is his Opinion, that no Ridicule can be fasten'd upon what is really great and good; his Lordship has made use of that Test to try the Scriptures and the Christian Religion by, and expos'd them because it seems they could not stand it.
Hor.: He has exposed Superstition and the miserable Notions the

---

[26] *A Letter to Dion*, 1732, p. 48.
[27] *Fable of the Bees*, ed. Kaye, vol. 2, p. 47 (First Dialogue).
[28] Ibid., p. 332 (*Search into the Nature of Society*).
[29] Shaftesbury, *Characteristics*, 2nd ed., 1714, vol. 1, pp. 29-30 (*A Letter Concerning Enthusiasm*).

Vulgar were taught to have of God; but no man ever had more Sublime Ideas of the Supreme Being and the Universe than himself.
Cleo.: You are convinc'd that what I charge him with is true.[30]

So no doubt it is; and Cleomenes' remarks (if quoted, say in *The Rationalist Annual* for 1974) might even be taken as commending Shaftesbury. But not in 1729, and in the context of a discussion in which Shaftesbury's views are fairly thoroughly demolished. Mandeville is undoubtedly making a point against Shaftesbury that he knows will tell against him with his readers. And he is probably making it tongue in cheek.

It is true that Horatio makes an able defence of Shaftesbury. This might be taken as proof of Mandeville's fair-mindedness, and his care not to do what he blamed Berkeley for, and make the characters in his dialogues mere men of straw. But Horatio's defence reminds us of another possible piece of deviousness on Mandeville's part. Cleomenes, we are told in the preface, is Mandeville's mouthpiece; yet whenever he and Horatio discuss religion, it seems (at any rate to a careful, perceptive, and sympathetic editor like Kaye) that Mandeville agrees, not with the orthodoxy of Cleomenes, but with Horatio's criticisms of it. This almost certainly applies to this exchange in the *Origin of Honour*:

Hor.: It is better to have no Religion, than to worship the Devil.
Cleo.: In what Respect is it better?
Hor.: It is not so great an Affront to the Deity not to believe his Existence, as it is to believe him to be the most Cruel and the most Malicious Being that can be imagin'd.
Cleo.: That is a subtle Argument, seldom made Use of but by Unbelievers.[31]

It was an argument made use of by Shaftesbury, as Mandeville's readers would probably know. It is also not very far removed from what Cleomenes himself says in Part 2 of the *Fable*: 'I could as soon believe, that he could cease to exist, as that he should be the Author of any real Evil.'[32]

It is hard to escape the impression that Mandeville is decrying Shaftesbury for holding opinions that he secretly shared. If there is any doubt of this, it is because of the difficulty of pinning

---

[30] *Fable of the Bees*, ed. Kaye, vol. 2, p. 53 (First Dialogue).
[31] *Enquiry into the Origin of Honour*, 1732, p. 154.
[32] *Fable of the Bees*, ed. Kaye, vol. 2, p. 252.

Mandeville down; and that is enough in itself to cast doubt on the representation of Mandeville as a fearless upholder of truth and sincerity at all costs.

Shall we, then, go to the opposite extreme with Minto and (in a rather less charitable version) Wilde, and say that Mandeville is primarily a wit, who cares little for consistency as long as he can propound an ingenious paradox or score off an opponent? Mandeville has too many favourite opinions, sustained over too many books, for that to be wholly true. But it is part of the truth. Why, after all, did Mandeville make such a parade of not being a deist or an atheist? Understandable caution, in a man whose books attracted the attention of grand juries? But it did him little good: almost everyone took his godlessness for granted. Caution may have had something to do with it; but less, I think, than his pleasure at turning the believers' arguments against themselves, at gravely reminding contumacious clergymen that they are committed to 'meekness, patience, humility, peace and charity to all men',[33] their worldly parishioners that slander and back-biting are not 'less heinous in the sight of God than murder or adultery',[34] and both of them that, in a matter on which St. Paul himself could only appeal to the impenetrable mysteriousness of God's ways, 'the subtlest logician or most learned theologian . . . can have no more claim or colour to be dogmatical . . . than the simplest shepherd, or the most illiterate plowman.'[35] Mandeville is quite genuinely deploring sectarian bitterness and worldly spitefulness, and he does want to make a point about predestination; but he is also having fun. His is not the simple-minded earnestness of a man with a message. It would not quite be true to say that he prefers the booby-trap to either the rapier or the bludgeon; but it is characteristic that, when he wants Cleomenes to attack Shaftesbury, he begins by making him pretend to have been converted to Shaftesbury's views. He enjoys an ingenious argument or an apt parallel (the parable of small beer, the analogy of the dirt in the streets of London, or the castrati, the likening of society to a bowl of punch) for its own sake. Sometimes I think he lets virtuosity take over, as when (with doubtful taste, but an undoubted gift for parody) he imagines the pious exhortations of the poor wretch being hanged at Tyburn by his

[33] *Free Thoughts on Religion*, 2nd ed., 1729, p. 16.
[34] Ibid., p. 13.   [35] Ibid., p. 124.

improved method, and renders them in the most nauseating of evangelical styles.

Yet, if Mandeville is not earnest, he is usually serious: he does have something he wants to say. If one had to characterize him briefly, one might do worse than take as a text a sentence from *Free Thoughts on Religion*: 'My aim is to make men penetrate into their own consciences and by searching without flattery into the true motives of their actions, learn to know themselves.'[36] So put, this sounds, and is intended to sound, like the earnest preacher again, the enemy of hypocrisy; but it might also do for the psychologist. Mandeville may have been disingenuous at times; but disingenuousness and self-deception are not the same thing. He does take 'Know thyself' seriously; and he sees (and makes Cleomenes point out, with side references to weeding gardens and exterminating moles)[37] that moralizing about the passions can get in the way of understanding them. The botanist is just as interested in weeds as in the prize-winners at the garden show; and Mandeville is not so much exhorting men to repent as to understand themselves. Hutcheson's sneer: 'so dearly does he love making a very *Dispensatory of Passions*'[38] does fasten on to one truth about Mandeville. This love of his was not unrequited: his analysis of the code of Honour, or of the motives underlying politeness and good breeding, his pursuit of 'self-liking' in all its manifold disguises, his speculations on the origin of language, his insistence on the evolutionary principle in explaining human behaviour, all represent genuine achievements. Yet this is clearly not the whole truth about Mandeville either. The satirist, the novelist, and the moralist all intrude upon the dispassionate psychologist. Even after he has substituted the neutral word 'self-liking' for the tendentious 'pride' (which is in any case, he comes to realize, only one manifestation of self-liking), his thesis is still about human weakness and frailty. When he preaches the sermon of 'a crafty divine' rallying the troops before battle or gives us a character sketch of Oliver Cromwell, he is not just grappling with the problem of why men risk their lives in war, or how they maintain themselves in power: he is also writing as an anti-clerical and as a debunker.

[36] *Free Thoughts on Religion*, 2nd ed., 1729, p. 11.
[37] *Enquiry into the Origin of Honour*, 1732, pp. 4–5.
[38] F. Hutcheson, *Reflections upon Laughter and Remarks upon* The Fable of the Bees. *Works*, G. Olms, Hildesheim, 1971, vol. 7, Opera Minora, p. 166.

So far, then, it seems that Mandeville cannot be characterized in a sentence or two, and that he will not fit neatly into any single pigeon-hole. He was a highly complex and sometimes inconsistent man. Like most of us.

Perhaps one should stop there and accept that, once we have looked at the satirist, the wit, the social reformer, the medical man, the theologian, the psychologist, and the moralist, and perhaps one or two others not dealt with here, such as the economist or the politician, there is nothing useful to be said further about Mandeville the whole man. Yet perhaps there is, after all, something that is fairly central to all of these: a vision of the universe and of man's place in it. It is mainly, if not entirely, a comic vision: one might perhaps call it tragicomic.

Visions are notoriously difficult to capture. Let us approach this one obliquely, by considering another vision of the universe which both resembles it and contrasts with it. In his much anthologized and uncharacteristically dithyrambic essay, 'A Free Man's Worship', Bertrand Russell asks how we are to come to terms with the universe revealed to us by modern science, in which 'Man is the product of causes which had no prevision of the end they were achieving' and 'his origin, his growth, his hopes and fears, his loves and his beliefs, are but the outcome of accidental collocations of atoms'. 'Only within the scaffolding of these truths', he tells us, 'only on the firm foundation of unyielding despair, can the soul's habitation henceforth be safely built.'[39]

We are inclined to think of this as a purely twentieth-century problem; but of course it is not. Something like it presented itself to Spinoza, who proceeded to reinterpret the traditional theological formulas so as to accommodate the view that man was a small and insignificant part of nature, and nature essentially indifferent to man. God, he suggested, was just another name for Nature, mind and matter were reverse sides of the same medal, and the Love of God the frame of mind of one who admires the neat way in which every part fits into the whole (the spider's web and the fly's delicate wing, to take Shaftesbury's example) and the laws of nature work themselves out with austere perfection, regardless of the hopes and fears of self-centred individuals who

[39] B. Russell, 'A Free Man's Worship', in *Mysticism and Logic*, New York, Norton, 1929, pp. 47–8.

cannot see past their own noses, especially when they are dropping off with frost-bite. It is the frame of mind in which a biologist might take pleasure in observing the inexorable progress of his own disease and noting how well it exemplified the laws of physiology and biochemistry, themselves exemplifications of those more general physical laws, which, by realizing all their manifold possibilities, produce a varied but unified whole, that perfection which is the sum of all being, and also its ground and sustaining cause.

Russell's solution is different. Instead of consoling himself with the reflection that this pitiless universe has its own austere beauty, man can remind himself that this beauty, like all beauty, is after all a creation of the mind of man. 'Brief and powerless is Man's life, on him and all his race the slow, sure doom falls pitiless and dark. Blind to good and evil, reckless of destruction, omnipotent matter rolls on its relentless way.' Freedom is to be found, not in the consciousness of necessity, or in prostrating oneself before it, but in man's ability to fashion his own ideals even though they are doomed to frustration: 'to worship at the shrine that his own hands have built; undismayed by the empire of chance, to preserve a mind free from the wanton tyranny that rules his outward life; proudly defiant of the irresistible forces that tolerate, for a moment, his knowledge and his condemnation, to sustain alone, a weary but unyielding Atlas, the world that his own ideals have fashioned despite the trampling march of unconscious power.'[40] It is a solution that also seems to have commended itself to the existentialists.

But not to Mandeville. He too is impressed by the cruelty and indifference of nature, and by the extent to which man is the sport of forces outside his control, even when, like his own passions and appetites, they are inside him. He is sure that there is no solution to the problem of evil; in that respect Shaftesbury's optimistic deism is no better than orthodox Christianity. He is just as sure as Russell that man does not live in a cosy little world in which somehow good will be the final goal of ill: no one misinterpreted him more egregiously than Browning. Man is of very little importance in the scheme of things: if the sun's sole purpose was to warm the earth, it would not need to be so large. It must have been made 'to enlighten and cherish other Bodies

---

[40] B. Russell, 'A Free Man's Worship', in *Mysticism and Logic*, p. 57.

besides this Planet of ours'.[41] And even on this planet Providence has 'no greater regard to our species than it has to Flies, and the Spawn of Fish'.[42] But Mandeville does not take up Russell's stance of heroic though hopeless defiance. In some ways he is nearer to Spinoza's scientific quietism: though 'quietist' would be an odd word to apply to Mandeville. But consider this snatch of dialogue:

Cleo.: . . . All Actions in Nature, abstractly consider'd, are equally indifferent; and whatever it may be to individual Creatures, to die is not a greater Evil to this Earth, or the whole Universe, than it is to be born.
Hor.: That is to make the First Cause of Things not an Intelligent Being.
Cleo.: Why so? Can you not conceive an Intelligent, and even a most Wise Being, that is not only exempt from, but likewise incapable of entertaining any Malice or Cruelty?[43]

Cleomenes' retort may be only a debating point: perhaps this is one of the places in which Horatio is meant to get the better of the argument, and Cleomenes to be merely evasive. I think that this is true to the extent that Mandeville meant (though he could not let Cleomenes say) that the First Cause was incapable of malice or cruelty only in the sense that it was also incapable of compassion, or fatherly love, or the other attributes of a personal god. But it is probably not just as a debating point that Mandeville makes Cleomenes deploy the argument from design:

From the little we know of the Sun and Stars, their Magnitudes, Distances, and Motion; and what we are more nearly acquainted with, the gross, visible Parts in the Structure of Animals, and their Oeconomy it is demonstrable that they are the Effects of an intelligent Cause, and the Contrivance of a Being infinite in Wisdom as well as Power.[44]

Mandeville may have been a deist rather than an atheist. Most proponents of the argument from design do not take it seriously enough: they triumphantly produce the conclusion, that the universe is controlled by an intelligent being, and do not go on to ask what attributes such a being, who designed such a universe, must have. It is clear to Mandeville that the First Cause is certainly not benevolent; but he readily concedes its extraordinary

---

[41] *Fable of the Bees*, ed. Kaye, vol. 2, p. 244 (Fifth Dialogue).
[42] Ibid., p. 251 (Fifth Dialogue).   [43] Ibid., p. 252 (Fifth Dialogue).
[44] Ibid., p. 311 (Sixth Dialogue).

ingenuity. Death is an ingenious contrivance for preventing the world from being overpopulated; and how neat the arrangement by which one animal keeps alive by eating another!

Cleo.: ... For the Continuance of every Species, among such an infinite Variety of Creatures, as this Globe yields; it was highly necessary, that the Provision for their Destruction should not be less ample, than that, which was made for the Generation of them; and therefore the Sollicitude of Nature in procuring Death, and the Consumption of Animals, is visibly superiour to the Care she takes to feed and preserve them.

Hor.: Prove that pray.

Cleo.: Millions of her Creatures are starv'd every Year and doom'd to perish for want of Sustenance; but whenever any dye, there is always plenty of Mouths to devour them. But then again, she gives all she has: Nothing is so fine or elaborate, as that she grudges it for Food; nor is any thing more extensive or impartial than her Bounty: She thinks nothing too good for the meanest of her Broods, and all Creatures are equally welcome to every thing they can find to eat. How curious is the Workmanship in the Structure of a common Fly; how inimitable are the Celerity of his Wings, and the Quickness of all his Motions in hot Weather! Should a *Pythagorean*, that was likewise a good Master in Mechanicks, by the help of a Microscope, pry into every minute part of this changeable Creature, and duly consider the Elegancy of its Machinery, would he not think it a great pity, that thousands of Millions of animated Beings, so nicely wrought and admirably finish'd, should every Day be devour'd by little Birds and Spiders, of which we stand in so little need?[45]

This is Shaftesbury's 'Animal-Order or Oeconomy', the Great One of Nature, more sardonically observed; but Mandeville does not deny the skilfulness and the intricacy of the contrivance. Nature's solicitude in procuring death has been responsible for other master-strokes of ingenuity: disease, for example, and war (including 'general Massacres, private Murders, Poyson, Sword, and all hostile Force'):[46] in order to perfect this device it was necessary to endow man with a large stock of innate aggressiveness.

For man is a part of nature: as much a puppet in her hands as the spider or the fly. And this rules out a response like Russell's. It is no use trying to console oneself with thoughts of man's

---

[45] *Fable of the Bees*, ed. Kaye, vol. 2, pp. 249–50 (Fifth Dialogue).
[46] Ibid., p. 254 (Fifth Dialogue).

indomitable spirit and his lofty ideals. Man is nature's tame lapdog like everything else, and his ideals are themselves illusions by which he is tricked into serving nature's purpose: all the swagger about national honour and martial glory, for example, is just a way of getting him to keep the population down.

The system works, of course, by means of the passions and appetites of animals: hunger, for example. And clearly man is no exception. Intent on gratifying his passions, he is constantly contributing to results he does not intend: his lust perpetuates his species, his greed keeps other animals from getting too numerous, his anger and malice perform the same service for his own kind. His fear and his weakness gradually lead him, when enough of his fellows have been eaten by wolves or lions, to stumble into society; his aggressiveness, his urge for dominance, and his unreliability make it necessary for the social bonds to be tightened, and a morality devised; his taste for luxury and display lead to the development of civilization. All this he does without knowing clearly what he is doing, or seeing where he is going: often enough he only does it because he is nursing fictions which tickle his vanity.

That is the universe, and man's place in it, as Mandeville sees it. It is not a spectacle to call forth Russell's defiant glorification of man, or Spinoza's pietistic reverence, or Shaftesbury's beaming optimism. It is on the whole a comic spectacle. It is particularly diverting to notice how everything has the opposite effect to what you might expect: how men's weakness and fear make them eventually the lords of creation, how arrogance and vanity make men invent modesty and politeness and apparent self-effacement, how the poverty and ignorance of the labouring poor create a rich, sophisticated, and luxurious civilization; how fear can make men risk their lives, and vanity lead them to mortify the flesh, and self-seeking make them contribute more to the wellbeing of other men than ever benevolence would: how, in short, good springs up and pullulates from evil as naturally as chickens do from eggs.[47]

In such a universe, what is to be done? Nothing very much, except to lean back and enjoy it, with a wry kind of enjoyment: noting that respectable businessmen behave very much like criminals, and that the professional devotees of humility and

[47] Ibid., vol. 1, p. 91 (Remark G).

charity have a formidable record of rapacity, contentiousness, and readiness to persecute. One may, perhaps, try to stop some of the more obvious silliness, like whipping prostitutes to make them virtuous, when society offers them no alternative means of making a living, or allowing criminals to go to their death in an atmosphere of boozy adulation. And one may make a protest against men's cutting each other's throats in a frenzy of brotherly love. But one need not expect to achieve much:

If you ask me, why I have done all this, *cui bono*? and what Good these Notions will produce? truly, besides the Reader's Diversion, I believe none at all ... Mankind having for so many Ages remain'd still the same, notwithstanding the many instructive and elaborate Writings, by which their Amendment has been endeavour'd, I am not so vain as to hope for better Success from so inconsiderable a Trifle.[48]

One should, of course, try to remain clear-sighted oneself, surrounded though one is by a fog of almost universal self-deception and hypocrisy. But one should not delude oneself that one can blow away the fog or be too earnest in denouncing it: better to write for the diversion of one's readers, and oneself. One might as well, then, pretend to go along with some of the delusions, and have some fun on the way, by pointing out the less comfortable conclusions that might be drawn from them, but seldom are. Besides, human knowledge really is very limited: we know practically nothing even about our own bodies, let alone about First and Last Things. With a little ingenuity, it is possible to make a plausible case for all sorts of unlikely hypotheses. And there really is something to be said for that last resort of the theologian when pushed into a corner (like St. Paul): man can hardly expect to understand fully a universe of which he is a small and insignificant part. No doubt the proper conclusion from that is that one should suspend judgement on ultimate metaphysical questions, not that one should feel free to dogmatize about them, and accept the most unlikely hypotheses without question, on the doubtful evidence of 'revelation'. But it might be amusing to ignore that from time to time and demonstrate to the theologians that theirs is a game that two can play.

Is that 'the real Mandeville'? I think that it at least represents one of his moods, and a fairly constant one; and that it may help

[48] *Fable of the Bees*, ed. Kaye, vol. 1, p. 8 (Preface).

to explain how he can be at once tough-minded and tolerant, visionary and cynical, a denouncer of deception who constantly dissimulates. In his writings, as in the bowl of punch to which he compared society, apparently incompatible ingredients combine to make a stimulating and palatable mixture. Even if it was too potent for many of his contemporaries (though they drank it avidly) the time may now have come to recommend it to connoisseurs.

APPENDIX

Private Vices, Public Benefits in the 1970s

I

A novel published in 1971, *The Buttercup Spell*, by Henry Cecil (His Honour H. C. Leon), is a modern treatment of much the same theme as *The Fable of the Bees*. The central idea is that a small dose of buttercup pollen fills anyone who takes it with brotherly love for all mankind, and the social effects of this discovery are amusingly described. Judges noted for the severity of their sentences administer a mild rebuke instead; politicians make speeches praising their opponents and modestly emphasizing their own deficiencies; trade unions suggest that profits should be increased and wages reduced; employers insist on the opposite policy.

None of this makes much difference to the actual conduct of affairs, except that people change sides, but before long the economy begins to run down. This is apparently because businessmen are reluctant to charge prices high enough to cover their costs, company directors, full of love for their shareholders, make their dividends absurdly high, and so on. Moreover, no employer or government official has the heart to get rid of an incompetent underling.

As a result the taking of buttercup, originally made compulsory by means of introducing pollen into the drinking water, is declared illegal, and the nation waits eagerly for the contagion of brotherly love to pass off. The first signs of returning aggressiveness are hailed with delight, and eventually the normal order is resumed, with policemen and prison warders no longer idle.

This is the sort of novel that frequently prompts reviewers (wistfully, perhaps, in their Grub Street garrets) to talk about *soufflés*. Possibly one thing they mean is that, while it makes a delightful meal if swallowed at once, it begins to collapse if one takes time to inspect it too carefully. It would of course be unfair to blame the author for that: he is not trying to do anything but entertain his readers. But Mandeville, though he was certainly doing that, wanted to do other things as well; and it is worth noticing that Cecil's story is not entirely convincing. Asked if he would let a murderer go, the unexpectedly lenient judge who was the first to take buttercup says: 'No, because he might hurt someone.' He adds that he has no rancour against the murderer. There seems no reason why justice, administered in that spirit, should not be as effective as before. In the story this question hardly arises, since, after buttercup has been given to everyone, no crimes are committed; but the same considerations apply to business and to administration. In the story the citizens all agree to the banning of buttercup because they see that this is necessary. There seems no reason, then, why businessmen should not have seen the necessity of raising prices or even of finding other work for their less efficient employees, especially since we are told that these employees themselves would be ready to step down at the slightest hint.

The Buttercup Spell, indeed, makes one realize how much Mandeville's argument depends on the identification of virtue, not with brotherly love but with asceticism and the avoidance of luxury.

II

Under the heading 'The Irregular Economy' an article in *Time* for 19 February 1973 discusses the effects of crime on the economy of black communities in the United States. Crimes like drug peddling, prostitution, and gambling, it says, are 'major money-making activities of the ghetto', constituting 'a kind of irregular economy that churns over huge sums that never figure in the gross national product', and providing 'jobs and capital that many blacks and others find it difficult to get in the regular economy'. A Cornell University sociologist, Lisle C. Carter, is quoted as saying that 'ghetto crime is a source of investment resources, of both equity and debt capital', since some flourishing criminals lend money to people who want to go into honest business. He warns against 'moving too fast in rooting out crime in the ghetto, lest this capital source dry up, leaving the inhabitants worse off than ever'.

SELECT BIBLIOGRAPHY

I. MANDEVILLE'S ENGLISH WORKS

1. Some fables after the easie and familiar method of Monsieur de la Fontaine. 1703.
2. Aesop dress'd, or A collection of fables writ in familiar verse. 1704. (1 republished, with some additional fables.) Modern edition: ed. J. S. Shea, Los Angeles, Calif., Augustan Reprint Society Publication no. 120, 1966.
3. Typhon: or the wars between the gods and giants: a burlesque poem in imitation of the comical Mons. Scarron. 1704.
4. The grumbling hive; or, Knaves turn'd honest. 1705.
5. The virgin unmask'd: or, Female dialogues betwixt an elderly maiden lady and her niece, on several diverting discourses on love, marriage, memoirs and morals, etc., of the times. 1709. (Republished in 1714 as The mysteries of virginity.)
6. Thirty-one issues of the *Female Tatler* between no. 52 (2 Nov. 1709) and no. 111 (29 Mar. 1710) signed Lucinda and Artesia.
7. A treatise of the hypochrondriack and hysterick passions, vulgarly call'd the hypo in men and vapours in women . . . in three dialogues. 1711. (Enlarged edition, with 'passions' changed to 'diseases' in the title, 1730.)
8. Wishes to a godson, with other miscellany poems. 1712.
9. The fable of the bees: or, Private vices publick benefits. 1714. (4 republished with An enquiry into the origin of moral virtue, and Remarks. The 1723 edition has additions to the Remarks, the Essay on charity and charity schools, and A search into the nature of society. The 1724 edition adds the Vindication.) Modern editions: ed. F. B. Kaye, Oxford, Clarendon Press, 1924 (vol. 1); ed. Irwin Primer, New York, Capricorn Books, 1962; ed. Phillip Harth, Harmondsworth, Penguin Books, 1970.
10. Free thoughts on religion, the church, and national happiness. 1720.
11. A modest defence of publick stews: or, An essay upon whoring as it is now practis'd in these kingdoms. 1724.

Modern edition: ed. R. I. Cook, Los Angeles, Calif. Augustan Reprint Society, Publication No. 162, 1973.

12. An enquiry into the causes of the frequent executions at Tyburn. 1725. (First published as six letters to the *British Journal* in the six weekly issues between 27 Feb. and 3 Apr. 1725. A further letter on the same subject, not republished, appeared in the issues of 24 Apr. and 1 May.) Modern editions: ed. M. R. Zirker, Los Angeles, Calif., Augustan Reprint Society Publication no. 105, 1964; facsimile reprint, Ilkley, Scolar Press, 1971.

13. The fable of the bees, Part II, 1729. Modern edition: ed. Kaye, Oxford, 1924, vol. 2.

14. An enquiry into the origin of honour, and the usefulness of Christianity in war. 1732. Modern edition: ed. M. M. Goldsmith, London, F. Cass, 1971.

15. A letter to Dion, occasion'd by his book call'd Alciphron, or The minute philosopher. 1732. Modern editions: ed. J. S. Viner, Los Angeles, Calif., Augustan Reprint Society Publication no. 41, 1953; ed. B. Dobrée, Liverpool University Press, 1954.

Note: Two dissertations and a matriculation 'oration', all in Latin, survive from Mandeville's student days. Other works have been attributed to him: in the above list I have followed Kaye, with the single addition of the *Female Tatler* papers. See section II below.

II. THE MANDEVILLE CANON

F. B. Kaye. The writings of Bernard Mandeville: a bibliographical survey. *Journal of English and Germanic Philology*, 20 (1921), 419–67.

This is an authoritative review of all the attributions to Mandeville made up to the time Kaye was writing. Except for those listed above under I, Kaye shows most of the attributions to be false, but some he thinks probable: these are listed under 'Doubtful Works' in the bibliography in his edition of the *Fable* (vol. 1, pp. xxxi–xxxii). They have been ignored in this book.

A minor addition to the canon is made in

H. Gordon Ward. An unnoted poem by Bernard Mandeville. *Review of English Studies*, 7 (1931), 73–6.

This refers to a Latin poem prefixed to a medical treatise in Latin by another Dutch physician, Joannes Groeneveldt (or John Greenfield). It was translated by John Marten as *A Treatise on the Safe Internal Use of Cantharides in the Practice of Physick*, 1706. The Latin version was first published in 1698, with a second edition in 1703, and a third in 1706. Mandeville's poem is in the second and third editions: Ward did not have access to the first. Marten's translation contains the poem together with an English translation of it, possibly by Marten and not Mandeville.

Since Kaye, a number of attributions have been made by Paul Bunyan Anderson:

P. B. Anderson. *Times Literary Supplement*, 28 Nov. 1936, p. 996. [Letter]

—— Splendor out of scandal. *Philological Quarterly*, 15 (1936), 286–300. (The *Female Tatler* attribution.)

—— Innocence and artifice; or, Mrs. Centlivre and the *Female Tatler*. *Philological Quarterly*, 16 (1937), 358–75.
(Attributes the other papers in the *Female Tatler* during the period of Mandeville's contributions to a playwright, Mrs. Susanna Centlivre.)

—— Cato's obscure counterpart in *The British Journal*, 1722–1725. *Studies in Philology*, 34 (1937), 412–28.

—— Bernard Mandeville on gin. *PMLA* 54 (1939), 775–84.

Anderson was undoubtedly right about Mandeville's contributions to the *Female Tatler*, a very valuable discovery. A convincing case has, however, been made out against his other attributions to Mandeville in

Gordon S. Vichert. Bernard Mandeville and *A Dissertation upon Drunkenness*. *Notes and Queries*, 209 (Aug. 1964), 288–92.

—— Some recent Mandeville attributions. *Philological Quarterly*, 45 (1966), 459–63.

Shortly before Anderson's attempts to add to the Mandeville canon, another writer tried to subtract from it:

J. H. Harder. The authorship of *A Modest Defence of Publick Stews*. *Neophilologus*, 18 (1933), 200–3.

His arguments, however, are based on inadequate evidence, and there seems no reason to doubt that the *Modest Defence* is by Mandeville.

III. SOME WRITINGS ON MANDEVILLE BEFORE 1924

Note: Kaye's bibliography (vol. 2, pp. 418–53) is admirably comprehensive and helpfully annotated and makes it unnecessary to do anything here except list works that have been referred to in this book.

Fiddes, Richard. A general treatise of morality, form'd upon the principles of natural reason only, with a preface in answer to two essays lately publish'd in *The Fable of the Bees*. And some incidental remarks upon an *Inquiry concerning Virtue* by the Right Honourable Anthony Earl of Shaftesbury. 1724.

Law, William. Remarks upon a late book entitled *The Fable of the Bees*. 1724.

Bluet, George. An enquiry whether a general practice of virtue tends to the wealth or poverty, benefit or disadvantage of a people? In which the pleas offered by the author of *The Fable of the Bees* . . . are considered. With some thoughts concerning a toleration of publick stews. 1725.

Hutcheson, Francis. Reflections upon laughter, and Remarks upon *The Fable of the Bees*. 1750. Originally published in the *Dublin Journal* in 1726.

Berkeley, George. Alciphron, or, The minute philosopher. In seven dialogues, containing an apology for the Christian religion, against those who are called free-thinkers. 1732.

—— A discourse addressed to Magistrates and men in authority. 1736.

Campbell, Archibald. An enquiry into the original of moral virtue wherein it is shown, against the author of *The Fable of the Bees*, that virtue is founded in the nature of things, is unalterable and eternal, and the great means of private and publick happiness. 1733.

Brown, John. Essays on *The Characteristics*. 1751.

Smith, Adam. The theory of moral sentiments. 1759.

Hawkins, Sir John. The life of Samuel Johnson, LL.D. 1787.

Whately, Richard. Introductory lectures on political economy. 1831.

Minto, William. Article on Mandeville in *Encyclopaedia Britannica*, ninth edition, 1875–88, vol. 15 (1883).

Browning, Robert. Parleyings with certain people of importance in their day. 1887.

Robertson, J. M. Essays towards a critical method. 1889.
Selby-Bigge, L. A., ed. British moralists, being selections from writers principally of the eighteenth century. 1897.
Wilde, Norman. Mandeville's place in English thought. *Mind*, 7 (1898), 219-32.
Stephen, Leslie. Essays on freethinking and plainspeaking. 1907.

IV. SOME WRITINGS ON MANDEVILLE SINCE 1924

Rogers, A. K. The ethics of Mandeville. *International Journal of Ethics*, 36 (1925), 1-17.
—— Morals in review. New York, Macmillan, 1927.
   (Mandeville is 'a moral realist' who 'sets out to treat man in a naturalistic and genetic way', though his taste for satire leads him into inconsistency.)
Lamprecht, S. P. *The Fable of the Bees. Journal of Philosophy*, 23 (1926), 561-79.
   (Mandeville 'sets the achievements of civilization in contrast to the crude nature of untrained human beings ... the *taught animal* is the glorious achievement for which the *natural man* is the raw material.' Some interesting comments but overestimates Mandeville's admiration for the Man of Honour.)
Hearn, Lafcadio. Some strange English literary figures of the eighteenth and nineteenth centuries. Tokyo, Hokuseido Press, 1927.
   (Possibly the most thoroughgoing misinterpretation of Mandeville so far. Lectures originally given in Tokyo in 1899. Mandeville 'saw a great truth ... [that] moral evolution is the result of pain produced by vice and cruelty and injustice ... it is through suffering caused by these that humanity strengthens its noble and unselfish side. Vices are useful ... in this sense—they are obstacles to be overcome ... there is his glory as a rude strong thinker of the eighteenth century.')
Burton, Jean. Mandeville, a post-Augustan pessimist. *Dalhousie Review*, 8 (1928), 189-96.
   (Somewhat inaccurate sketch of Mandeville's life and works.)
Bonar, James. The moral sense. London, Allen and Unwin, 1930.
(Discusses Mandeville mainly as a critic of Shaftesbury.)
Dobrée, Bonamy. A variety of ways. Oxford University Press, 1932.

(Contains an appreciative account of Mandeville as a writer and thinker.)

Harder, Johannes Hendrik. Observations on some tendencies of sentiment and ethics, chiefly in minor poetry and essay, in the eighteenth century, until the execution of Dr. W. Dodd in 1777. Amsterdam, M. R. Portielji, 1933.

(Contains a brief chapter, mainly expository, on Mandeville.)

Shorey, Paul. Platonism ancient and modern. Sather classical lectures, vol. 14, University of California Press, 1938.

(Brief comments on Mandeville's references to Plato. 'Mandeville was the eighteenth-century Nietzsche and Bernard Shaw and Westermarck.')

Willey, Basil. The eighteenth century background. London, Chatto and Windus, 1940.

(Treats Mandeville as 'an obstinate amalgam' of conflicting elements in eighteenth-century thought, combined into a new and idiosyncratic pattern.)

Wade, Ira O. Studies on Voltaire, with some unpublished papers of Mme du Chatelet. New York, Russell and Russell, 1947.

(Discusses Mandeville's influence on Voltaire in detail. Mme du Chatelet's papers include a translation of parts of *The Fable*.)

Skarsten, A. Keith. Nature in Mandeville. *Journal of English and Germanic Philology*, 53 (1954), 562–8.

(Stresses Mandeville's 'profound distrust' of human nature.)

Miner, Earl Roy. Dr. Johnson, Mandeville and 'publick benefits'. *Huntington Library Quarterly*, 21 (1958), 159–66.

(Disputes the view that Johnson's views on economics are largely derived from Mandeville.)

Alpers, Paul J. Pope's *To Bathurst* and the Mandevillian state. *ELH* 25 (1958), 23–42.

(Discusses Mandeville's influence on Pope in his *Epistle to Bathurst*. Argues that Pope's 'fundamental opposition to Mandeville' has been overlooked.)

Young, J. D. Mandeville, a popularizer of Hobbes. *Modern Language Notes*, 74 (1959), 10–13.

(Sees Mandeville as 'beset with a popularizer's peculiar difficulties: inconsistency, incompleteness and inaccuracy'.)

Jones, Harry L. Holberg on Mandeville's *Fable of the Bees*. *CLA Journal*, 4 (1960), 16–25.
(Discusses the attack on Mandeville by the Danish dramatist, Baron Ludvig Holberg.)

Lovejoy, Arthur O. Reflections on human nature. Baltimore, Md., Johns Hopkins Press, 1961.
(Lectures given at Swarthmore in 1941. Discusses eighteenth-century theories of human motivation, and especially the place given to pride and self-esteem. Very good on Mandeville's sources and influence.)

Suits, Conrad. The meaning of *The Fable of the Bees*. [Unpublished Ph.D. thesis.] University of Chicago, Dept. of English, 1961.
(Stresses that Mandeville was primarily a satirist. Believes his rigorism to be genuine.)

Smith, Leroy W. Fielding and Mandeville: the 'war against virtue'. *Criticism*, 3 (1961), 7–15.
(Compares and contrasts Fielding's views on man and society with Mandeville's.)

Preu, James A. Private vices—public benefits. *English Journal*, 52 (1963), 635–58.
(Simple exposition of Mandeville for high-school students.)

Price, Martin. To the palace of wisdom: studies in order and energy from Dryden to Blake. New York, Doubleday, 1964.
(Sees Mandeville as stressing the artifice of the amoral politician who creates order out of man's vices—a different order from the one that God would impose if men were virtuous, but the only one possible to fallen man.)

Edwards, Thomas R. Mandeville's moral prose. *ELH* 31 (1964), 195–212.
(Analyses Mandeville's prose style in order to demonstrate his genuine moral indignation at society. 'He stands as one of the first modern divided minds, those men who embody in their own uncertainties the painful split between public practice and traditional imperatives.')

Scott-Taggart, M. J. Mandeville: cynic or fool. *Philosophical Quarterly*, 16 (1966), 221–32.
(Examines Mandeville's thesis about private vices, public benefits in order to show that he was not advocating vice, but was a

serious moralist grappling with the implications of a naturalistic explanation of morality.)

Hayek, F. A. Dr. Bernard Mandeville. *Proceedings of the British Academy*, 52 (1966), 125–41. (Lecture on a mastermind.)

(Mandeville's great achievement is his discovery of the evolutionary principle in human affairs, and his realization that order is often achieved without conscious design.)

Sprague, Elmer. Article on Mandeville in *Encyclopedia of Philosophy*, ed. Paul Edwards, New York, Collier-Macmillan, 1967, vol. 5, pp. 147–9.

Grave, S. A. Eighteenth-century attempts to use the notion of happiness. In Brissenden, R. F., ed., *Studies in the eighteenth century*. Canberra, A.N.U. Press, 1968.

Hind, George. Mandeville's *Fable of the Bees* as Menippean satire. *Genre*, 1, (1968), 307–15.

Harth, Philip. The satiric purpose of *The Fable of the Bees*. *Eighteenth Century Studies*, 2 (1969), 321–40.

('*The Fable of the Bees* . . . is as much an intellectual satire against the rigorism of Christian theory as it is a moral satire, not against the laxity of Christian practice, indeed, but against the hypocrisy to which the discrepancy between theory and practice inevitably leads Christians.' The attack on Shaftesbury, it is suggested, was added later, and represents an independent part of Mandeville's thought.)

Chiasson, Elias J. Bernard Mandeville: a reappraisal. *Philological Quarterly*, 49 (1970), 489–519.

(Argues for the genuineness of Mandeville's professed Christianity. '. . . he must be seen, not in the tradition of Hobbes and Calvin, but, secure and amused, within that "massive but flexible" tradition of Christian humanism.')

Noxon, James. Dr. Mandeville: 'A thinking man'. In Hughes, P. and Williams, D., eds., *The varied pattern: studies in the 18th century*. Toronto, A. M. Hakkert, 1971, pp. 233–52.

(*The Fable of the Bees* 'should be read as an indictment and a plea: an indictment of the hypocrisy of preaching self-denial and practising self-indulgence, and a plea for self-awareness and honest speaking about human nature'.)

Vichert, Gordon. The theory of conspicuous consumption in the 18th century. In Hughes, P. and Williams, D., eds., *The varied pattern: studies in the 18th century.* Toronto, A. M. Hakkert, 1971, pp. 253–65.

(Mandeville's anticipation of Veblen.)

Colman, John. Bernard Mandeville and the reality of virtue. *Philosophy*, 47 (1972), 125–39.

(Argues that Mandeville does not deny the reality of virtue, but merely its innateness.)

V. MANDEVILLE AND ECONOMICS

This book has ignored Mandeville's economic theory. Some recent discussions of his place in the history of economic thought are:

Viner, Jacob. Introduction to his edition of *A Letter to Dion*. Los Angeles, Calif., Augustan Reprint Society Publications no. 41, 1953. Republished in Viner, *The long view and the short: studies in economic theory and practice*. Glencoe, Ill., The Free Press, 1958.

(As well as discussing Mandeville's ethical and religious views, Viner argues that Mandeville was not, as commonly supposed, 'a pioneer expounder of laissez-faire individualism', but an advocate of economic planning by 'skilful politicians'.)

Rosenberg, Nathan. Mandeville and laissez-faire. *Journal of the History of Ideas*, 24 (1963), 183–96.

(Argues against Viner that Mandeville was not an interventionist.)

Chalk, Alfred F. Mandeville's *Fable of the Bees*: a reappraisal. *Southern Economic Journal*, 33 (1966), 1–16.

(Argues that Mandeville's economic thought represents a transition between mercantilism and *laissez-faire*.)

INDEX

Addison J., 43, 251
Aesop Dressed, 26–30, 43
Anderson, P. B., 250
Animal nature, man's, 204–7, 220, 231, 232
Animal spirits, 61–8
Apothecaries, 68–72
Art, realism in, 112–14; taste in, 179, 181–2
Asceticism, and Christianity, 158, 168, 206, 210; and Mandeville, 13–23, 178, 191, 206, 223–37, 242–5
Atheism, 88, 168–72
Atonement, 168
Avarice, see Self-interest

Backer, J. and C., 251
Bacon, F., 63
Beer, small, parable of, 209–10, 226, 259
Belloc, H., 27
Benefits, 208–9, 242
Benevolence, Hutcheson on, 137, 140; Mandeville on, 124–5, 133–4, 137, 140, 181–3, 215–16; Shaftesbury on, 107–14, 137, 140, 181–3
Bentham, J., 239
Berkeley, G., 19, 74, 192–9, 204–5, 206, 207, 217, 219, 246, 255–7
Bible, 12, 154–8, 174, 175, 176, 177, 195
Black puddings, and fornication, 175, 244
Blasters, 194
Bluet, G., 22, 192, 194, 199–200, 203, 208, 212–14, 219, 220, 252
Body, and mind, 61–8, 159
Boswell, J., 83
Bowlby, J., 144
Brain, 61–8, 159
Bredwold, L. I., 2
British Journal, 84
Brothels, 17–18, 75–83, 97, 218
Brown, J., 184
Browning, R., 3, 262
Buckingham, Duke of, 245
Bunyan, J., 17
Burnet, G., 190
Butler, J., 107, 114, 115

Carter, L. C., 269
Castrati, 214, 259
Cause, invisible, see God
Cecil, H., 268–9
Centlivre, S., 252
Chambers' Encylopedia, 254
Character sketches, 39, 43–5, 122
Charity, 134, 142
Charity schools, 18, 20, 93–7, 99, 101, 217
Chastity, 6, 80–2, 130–1, 228
Christianity, crimes of, 17, 20, 152, 177; scarcity of, 15, 132; and duelling, 8, 9, 22; and fornication, 175, 243–4; and happiness, 242–3; and Honour, 8; and luxury, 3, 4, 6, 158; and power, 12, 151–3, 157–8; and war, 8–12, 156
Civilization, 124–8, 187–8, 220–1, 247
Claret, mulled, recipe for, 59
Clergy, crimes of, 17, 20, 23, 152, 177; function of, 174; power-seeking, 151–3, 173; and asceticism, 158, 206, 209, 228–30
Coat, scarlet, 215–16
Compassion, 134–8, 191
Constantine, 152
Courage, 87, 122–3
Courtship, 31–2
Crackenthorpe, Mrs., 41–2
Cromwell, O., 148, 260

Death, an ingenious device, 264; Mandeville's, 249
Deism, 171–2, 263
Dennis, J., 194
Determinism, 160–2
Devil, Mandeville an emissary of, 1, 3, 254; worshipped in Dublin, 194
Dictionary of National Biography, 249–50
Dissection, of criminals, 91
Dissoluteness, Mandeville's alleged, 2, 16, 184
Dobrée, B., 224, 237
Drink, Mandeville on, 250–1
Dublin Weekly Journal, 190
Duelling, 8, 9, 22, 42, 102, 122–3, 141, 211

INDEX

Edwards, T. R., 20
Egoism, 239–41
Emilia, character of, 43–5
Empirics, 52–3
Encyclopaedia Britannica, 2, 21, 25
Enquiry into the Causes of the Frequent Executions at Tyburn, 39–40, 84–93, 98, 101, 215
Essay on Charity, 18, 95, 96, 134, 142, 210, 252–3
Evil, problem of, 161–8, 260
Evils, choice of, 83, 244–5

Fable of the Bees, Part 1, a book of severe morality, 15, 22; an elaborate joke, 46; an election pamphlet, 21–2; lucrative, 251, 254; title-page, 189, 208; quoted (the poem), 4, 5, 6, 10, 208; on asceticism, 229–30; on author's expectations, 266; on brothels, 97; on charity, 142; on charity schools, 95, 96; on conspicuous consumption, 217; on duelling, 22; on good and evil, 220; on good manners, 119–20; on Honour, 7, 8; on impossibility of virtue, 15, 132, 233–4; on incompatibility of virtue and wealth, 20–1, 214; on man's cruelty, 224; on origin of society, 125; on origin of virtue, 127, 128, 143, 178, 233, 234; on parable of small beer, 210; on pity, 135, 136, 137, 191; on the poor, 98–9, 101; on pride, 139–40, 206, 217, 237; on prostitution, 218; on Radcliffe, 203; on relativism, 179, 180, 185; on road to virtue, 19, 25, 209; on salesmanship, 146–147, 219; on a scarlet coat, 215–16; on self-deception, 205; on self-regulation of society, 216–17; on Shaftesbury, 183, 257; on Sparta, 210; on vice (definition), 192, 222, 236; on virtue (definition), 189, 233; on war, 224–5
Fable of the Bees, Part 2, quoted: on atheism, 169; on basic instincts, 118, 188; on belief in invisible cause, 150; on child care, 144–5; on Christianity, 154–5; on Deism, 171, 172, 263; on existence of God, 170–1, 263; on good manners, 119; on Honour, 6, 121, 122, 123; on Mandeville's cynicism, 22, 131–3; on man's insignificance, 263; on mind and body, 159; on origin of society, 125, 126; on problem of evil, 163, 258; on realism in art, 112–13; on self-liking, 115–16, 120; on self-love, 124, 188; on Shaftesbury, 108–11, 215, 257–8; on the state, 198; on virtue, 14, 132, 168, 186; on women, 33
Felton, J., 245–6
Female Tatler, 9, 40–3, 46, 99–100, 144, 145, 252, 253
Feminism, Mandeville's, 33, 99, 145–6, 249
Fiddes, R., 194, 241, 253–4
Fielding, H., 1, 2
Fornication, evils of, 76–80; and black puddings, 175, 244; and Christianity, 242–3; and hypochondria, 62–4
Franklin, B., 250, 251–2
Free Thoughts on Religion, 20, 23, 100, 148–77; quoted: on afterlife, 158; on atheism, 168, 169; on character of Emilia, 44–5, 143; on Christian duty, 176, 259; on church and power, 12, 17, 151–3, 173–4; on Deism, 171; on free will, 160–2; on Mandeville's politics, 21; on Manichaeism, 157; on original sin, 174–76; on reason, 166–7; on religion (definition), 149; on ritual, 174; on Scripture interpretation, 175; on self-knowledge, 260; on sexual restraint, 228; on tolerance, 160, 225; on the Trinity, 167
Free will, 160–2
Freud, S., 47, 68, 202

Gay, J., 84
Gentleman's Magazine, 2, 249
Gibbon, E., 2
Gilbert, W. S., 45, 229
God, arguments for existence of, 170–2; indifference of, 165, 263; ingenuity of, 264; like a Man of Honour, 176; origin of belief in, 149–51; unity of, 154–7, 172; and evil, 161–8
Goldsmith, O., 226
Good manners, 119–21, 127, 196, 260, 265
Gregory, Pope, 152

INDEX

Grumbling Hive, 21, 25, 28, 30, 43, 46, 101, 208

Hadrian VI, Pope, 152
Hawkins, J., 250-1
Hedonism, psychological, 134-8, 141
Hill, J., 58
Hobbes, T., on human nature, 104-5, 110; on morality, 231-4, 238-41; on self-interest, 107, 118, 134, 190; on the social contract, 126-7, 187-188, 221, 232; on sovereign power, 246; on the will, 160
Honour, analysis of, 121-3, 127-30, 141-2; described, 6, 7; discussed in *Female Tatler*, 42, 99-100; God like a Man of, 176; inconsistent with Christianity, 8; less onerous than virtue, 7, 188, 203; Montesquieu on, 142; ridiculed by Mandeville, 22, 227; self-worship involved in, 139; verses on, 99-100
Howard, J., 97
Howson, G., 39, 84, 86, 87
Humanitarianism, 224
Hume, D., 104, 107, 131, 134, 190, 203, 204, 206, 207, 208, 240
Hutcheson, F., on human dispositions, 140; on luxury, 3, 212; on Mandeville, 3, 190, 194, 236, 260; on morality, 190; on pity, 137
Hypotheses, 52-8, 266

Immoralism, 178, 192-223
Immortality, 158-60, 209
Informers, 86, 218, 223
Invisible cause, see God

Julian ('the Apostate'), 152

Kaye, F. B., 143, 148, 156, 224, 227, 230, 231, 237, 238, 249-50, 254, 258
Knox, R., 45
Kuhn, T., 55

Lactantius, 161
La Fontaine, J., 26
Laisser-faire, 216, 219
Language, origin of, 143
La Rochefoucauld, F., 2
Law, W., on human nature, 204, 206, 207, 221; on Mandeville, 1, 3, 74, 184, 192, 194, 199-201, 219, 220, 254; on morality, 190, 221, 233-4; praised by Gibbon, 2
Leon, H. C., 268-9
Letter to Dion, 19, 193, 198, 199, 208, 210, 217, 218, 242, 255-7
Life, Mandeville's, 249-54
Locke, J., 183
London Journal, 190, 250
Luxury, inconsistent with Christianity, 3, 4, 6, 158; Mandeville's attitude to, 211-12, 215, 222, 235, 243-4, 269; and national prosperity, 5-6, 210-12, 216

Macclesfield, 1st Earl, 251
Mackintosh, J., 2
Man, a venomous creature, 14, 45
Man of Honour, see Honour
Manichaeism, 157, 162, 164, 221
Marriage, 32, 64, 75-6, 79-80, 101-2
Maxwell, J. C., 180, 184, 185, 242-4
Medicines, see Physic
Mill, J. S., 239, 241
Mind and body, 61-8, 159
Minto, W., 21, 25, 46, 259
Modest Defence of Public Stews, 16-18 75-83, 92, 99, 174-5, 242, 256
Montesquieu, Baron, 142, 226
Monthly Mirror, 3
Moral relativism, 179-82
Moral scepticism, 178-92
Moses, inspiration of, 154-7, 172
Mothers-in-law, 144

Newgate, 39-40, 86-9
Newman, J. W., 250
Newton, I., 104, 154

Origin of Honour, quoted: on atheism, 169, 258; on Atonement, 168; on belief in invisible cause, 150-1, 172, 188; on Bible, 156, 174; on duelling, 9, 22, 102; on ethical rationalism, 231; on fasting, 89; on God and evil, 164-5; on Honour, 7, 102, 121-2, 123-4, 133, 187, 203; on luxury and Christianity, 3-4, 168, 206, 229; on Mandeville's 'revolution-principles', 197; on the passions, 102, 260; on pride, 190, 222; on search for happiness, 187; on self-liking, 117, 130-1, 138,

Origin of Honour—contd.
     222; on self-worship, 139; on unity of God,156; on vice, 102; on virtue, 130–1, 143, 187
Origin of Moral Virtue, 127, 136, 143, 178, 185–91, 204, 222
Original sin, 174

Painting, 112–14, 179
Passive obedience, 19, 20
Paul, Saint, 162, 266
Physic, 6, 68–72; advertisements for, 41–2
Pitt, R., 69
Pity, 134–8, 191, 247
Politeness, 119–21, 127, 196, 260, 265
Poor, 96–101, 114
Predestination, 160–2
Prefaces, 30
Pride, 116–41, 188–90, 215–23, 227, 233, 237, 260, 265; in animals, 206
Private vices public benefits, 16, 189, 193, 203, 204, 207–23, 246
Prostitution, 17–18, 75–83, 97, 218, 266, 269
Psychological hedonism, 134–8, 141

Radcliffe, J., 252–4
Rationalism, moral, 229–37, 240
Realism in art, 112–14
Reason, and revelation, 166–8
Relativism, moral, 179–82
Revelation, 166–8
Revolution, Mandeville accused of fomenting, 197–8, 200
Rigorism, Mandeville's: 13–23, 178, 223–37, 242–5
Rousseau, J.-J., 125
Russell, B., 165, 261–5

Sabbatarianism, 99, 210
Salesmanship, 146–7, 219
Scarlet coat, 215–16
Scepticism, moral, 178–92
Schools, charity, 18, 20, 93–7, 99, 101
Search into the Nature of Society, 125, 178, 191
Selby-Bigge, L. A., 3, 223, 226, 230
Self-deception, 143, 183, 194, 205, 209–10, 224, 227, 260, 265
Self-denial, 13–15, 132–5, 158, 174, 176, 180, 183, 184, 186, 187, 191, 205, 206, 222, 223–37, 244, 247

Self-esteem, 138–41, 223
Self-interest, Butler on, 115; Hobbes on, 104, 118, 190; Hume on, 107, 131; Mandeville on, 114–41, 142, 183, 188, 190, 215–21, 236; Shaftesbury on, 104–12, 115
Self-liking, 116–41, 188, 189, 215–23, 226, 233, 260, 265
Self-love, see Self-interest
Servants, insolence of, 96
Shaftesbury, 3rd Earl, attacked by Berkeley, 192, 194, 196–7, 256; optimism of, 261, 262, 264–5; a self-deceiver, 183; on beauty, 180–182; on benevolence, 137; on human nature, 105–15, 118, 124, 142, 215, 235, 241; on humour, 46; on virtue, 132, 140, 180–5, 240; mentioned, 148, 259
Shakespeare, W., 63
Shaw, G. B., 219
Shea, J. S., 28
Sheppard, J., 87
Sidgwick. H., 244
Sin, Original, 174
Sloane, H., 73, 252
Small beer, parable of, 209–10, 226, 259
Smith, Adam, economic theory anticipated, 47, 216–17, 220; on Mandeville, 2, 191, 192, 227
Societies for Reformation of Manners, 93, 99, 101, 255, 256
Society for Promoting Christian Knowledge, 94
Society, origin of, 124–8, 187–8, 220–1, 247, 265
Some Fables after ... de la Fontaine 26–30
Soul, 159
Sparta, 210–11
Spectator, 39
Spinoza, B., 104, 261, 265
Steele, R., 9, 41, 43
Stephen, L., 2, 16, 23, 250
Subversion, Mandeville accused of, 197–8, 200
Suicide, 116
Suits, C., 189
Swift, J., 16, 226

Tatler, 9, 39, 40, 41, 253–4
Temple, W., 125
Tenison, T., 94

Tennyson, A., 165
Time, 269
Transportation, 91-2
Treatise of the hypochondriac and hysteric passions, 48-74, 158, 236, 249, 251
Trinity, 167, 177
Tyburn, Enquiry into the Causes of the Frequent Executions at, 39-40, 84-93, 98, 101, 215
Typhon, 26

Utilitarianism, 16, 83, 184, 187, 218-19, 224, 230, 237-48

Vanity, 38, 115-42, 190, 215-23, 226, 227, 230, 233, 265
Veblen, T., 207
Vice, defined, 192, 222, 236, 245-6; in men and horses, 126; moralists on, 102; pride in, 190; really virtue, 16, 21, 191-223, 227; and civilization, 220-3, 247; and wealth, 4-16, 20-1, 208-20
Virgin Unmask'd, 13, 30-9, 45, 68, 99, 249
Virtue, defined, 189; an empty pretence, 22, 131-2, 178-92; impossibility of, 13-15, 23, 132, 133, 189, 191, 233-6; origin of, 127-30, 186-91, 201-2; really vice, 192-223, 227; road to, 19, 25, 209; Shaftesbury on, 105-6; and honour, 6, 7, 225; and self-denial, 13-15, 132, 136, 174, 180, 183, 184, 186; and wealth, 4-6, 16, 20-3, 208-20

War, backed by Old Testament texts, 156, 177; how to get men into, 11, 224-5, 260; inconsistent with Christianity, 8-12, 165; part of divine plan, 165, 264-5
War memorials, 225
Wealth, and virtue, 4-6, 16, 20-3, 208-20
Wesley, J., 1
Whately, R., 15-16
Wild, J., 84-6
Wilde, N., 192, 193, 247, 255, 259
Willis, T., 53, 56-7
Wollaston, W., 251
Women, finer clay of, 33, 46, 67; how to keep chaste, 81-2, 101-2, 130-1; how to seduce, 36-8; hysteria in, 66-8; lust in, 33-5, 68; subjection of, 32, 42, 145; why they hate their daughters-in-law, 144; wiles of salesmen on, 146-7